THE GIFT

POLWENNA PAST

BOOK ONE

RUTH SABERTON

KE5

Published by Millington

CHAPTER 1

THE PRESENT

At half past two on a drizzly December afternoon, Alice made her traditional Christmas Eve visit to St Wenn's. The light was already fading and as she paused at the lych-gate to catch her breath she admired the view over Polwenna Bay; it never failed to lift her spirits no matter what the weather might deliver or what sadness lie upon her heart.

It might still be early, Santa still busy packing his sleigh and the reindeer tucking into their oats before the Big Night, but the windows of the cottages huddled around Polwenna's harbour were already forming a warm tableau filled with rainbow twinkles from Christmas trees. Smoke drifted from the chimneys, filling the damp air with the heartening scent of wood fires, and bringing to mind the comfort of coming into the warmth from the wintry rawness. Coloured lights fashioned from seaside buckets were strung through the streets to cheer the wintry gloom, and the big tree on the end of the quay tossed shimmering diamonds into the breaking waves with the careless ease of a Tudor monarch casting pennies to the masses.

Whether you were eight or eighty, Alice reflected, Christmas was a magical time of year. There was something about the air of anticipation that made her heart lift even as the familiar carols plucked at its strings. There was nothing better than holding loved ones close after time parted, and Alice loved the Midnight Mass because it was still filled with the wonderful promise of reunions yet to happen – as well as all the presents yet to be opened! Once, decades ago – decades that had passed in the blink of an eye – Midnight Mass had been followed by late-night present-assembling, the final prepping of vegetables and the last-minute check that the turkey fitted into the Aga. Back then Alice had been the busy grandmother of seven young children, and would have loved nothing more than a lie-in on Christmas Eve; now she was filled with nostalgia for those long-gone days of early morning wake-ups followed by the sound of ripping paper and cries of excitement. Maybe it was only when you looked back that you realised those really had been wonderful times.

The opening bars of 'Silent Night' never failed to move Alice. The plaintive beauty of the music conjured memories of Christmases and loved ones long gone, and the words echoed with loss as well as the unchanging message of love. However full her table might be for Christmas dinner nowadays, there were empty chairs and many dear faces missing. She supposed that when you were in your ninth decade life was inevitably filled with farewells and changes, which were highlighted by the constancy of the carols and the Christmas story. It was an emotive time of year, and much as it was a season of hope and love it was also a time to reflect and remember all the Christmases that had come before.

This was why Alice always visited St Wenn's on the afternoon of Christmas Eve, and as she leaned against the gate to catch her breath she thought of all the times she'd made this journey over the years. The walk up Church Lane seemed to grow steeper with each passing day, and it had been a very long time since she'd made it up to St Wenn's without several stops to rest. It was worth the effort, though, thought Alice as she pushed the gate open and continued along the path, because the church would look beautiful today, and it was a wonderful place to pause before being swept away by the busyness of Christmas.

The stained-glass windows glowed with jewelled brightness against the grey afternoon, and the garlanded door was ajar, spilling light into the porch. Inside it would be warm, the heating switched on early in anticipation of tonight's service, and the ancient stone walls soothed by candlelight and festooned in greenery and festive flowers. Tired from her walk uphill, Alice was looking forward to stepping out of the biting wind for a sit-down, but before she could do this there was one important task for her to attend to.

She turned away from the main path and walked slowly across the churchyard. In the crook of her arm nestled a simple bouquet of white roses and ivy, hand-tied with a simple red velvet ribbon and with the stems wrapped in brown paper. It was the same style of bouquet Alice always carried to St Wenn's on Christmas Eve, and the mirror image of the one she had carried as a young bride a lifetime ago. On that afternoon the sun had been high and warm, the grass beneath her satin slippers velvet-smooth, and the headstones lining the church path no more than background to the formal portrait that had taken pride of place on her mantelpiece for decades. She'd not paid any thought to the sleepers beneath the grassy mounds or dwelt in the sadness of those left behind

– which was, Alice reflected as she made her slow and cautious way over the uneven ground, exactly as it should have been for a young bride of eighteen. Impossible to think that almost seventy years had passed since her wedding day. As much as she might feel the same inside, Alice knew that the mirror told a very different story. Eighteen-year-old Alice Pendeen certainly hadn't lurched drunkenly over tussocks (the Pollards really needed to mow the churchyard more frequently) or fretted about stumbling and breaking a hip.

That wasn't the Christmas she was hoping for.

"You'd probably say it's time to swallow my pride and succumb to a walking stick," she said to the neat headstone she'd paused beside.

Strange how even all these years later the words engraved on the granite could take her breath away. Alice supposed that nothing in life prepared you for laying your beloved ones to rest, and although grief's serrated edge was dulled by time, absence still made her heart contract. Christmas Eve had been a special date in her personal journey, which was why even though the walk to the church on a cold day made her bones ache and her breath come in harsh gasps, she wouldn't dream of missing her visit. It felt right – and it was circular. In the end, life was circular, for she had started her life journey at St Wenn's dangled over the font; her long marriage had begun here; and her husband's last journey had ended at this quiet spot, looking out over the endless ocean he'd so loved to sail on. One day Alice would rest here too, and she was at peace with that notion.

Her younger self had stormed through this churchyard, had wept and shouted, laughed and celebrated, and wept again. Strange how what mattered so much when you were young seemed unfathomable when viewed through the lens of life. It all felt so distant and as though the events of her life had happened to somebody else – a girl she'd once known well, but was now consigned to an early chapter in a long book.

Alice glanced out to sea. Pewter water had turned to molten gold on the horizon, where a sole ray of sharp sunlight pierced the cloud. It brought to mind the old saying about ships not being gone but only out of sight. As she had grown older Alice had found inside herself a deep agreement with that notion, for the whispers of the past and the dearly loved faces never seemed far away these days. She heard them in the voices of her grandchildren. When she caught sight of her own son – in his sixties now, and with hair as silver and gold as the sea – she could be glimpsing her beloved husband. She supposed nothing was ever truly lost while you remembered it.

Alice lay a hand on the cold stone to steady herself against its solidity, something she'd done so often with the man resting beneath, a man who'd been her ballast in every way and whose quiet steadfastness and love had carried her through some of the hardest times in her life.

Painfully, she knelt down to lean the bouquet against the base of the headstone before struggling to straighten up.

"You'd probably say a walking stick would make my life easier," she said out loud. "You always had such wonderful ideas about what would help me, even when I couldn't see it for myself. Being loved by you was such a gift, my love."

There was no reply of course, only the calling of the gulls and the sigh of the wind through the long grass. Alice smiled; her husband would have laughed and shaken his head at any notion of afterlife communication. A lifelong pragmatist, he hadn't been big on signs or given to flights of imagination, but he had believed in love and always known that the love he'd had for Alice was strong enough to carry them through all adversities and for a lifetime. The family they'd built together was the biggest joy (mostly!) of Alice's life, and her husband's greatest legacy – even if their family was expanding rapidly and Christmas dinner would be manic.

"Tomorrow we're eating at Symon and Ella's," she told him. Although Alice knew she was voicing her own thoughts aloud because her husband – the man who would have drilled the rowdy tribe in the style of Captain von Trapp – was not here, there was comfort in telling him what everyone was up to on Christmas Eve, their special day.

"You'd be amazed how many of us there are now! Even *I'm* losing count. All these people – and from just the two of us. We'd never have believed it, would we? I'm not sure we'll all fit around the table."

This was no understatement; the Christmas table would be crowded. Her son was happily settled once again, his children had their own partners now, and Alice's great-grandchildren were arriving at regular intervals. Then there were the friends who might join them, and all the members of the extended blended family. It was just as well that Symon and Ella ran a restaurant, because there was no way that Harbour Watch, Alice's quaint harbourside dwelling, could have accommodated them all. People would have been eating on the stairs or sitting in the garden.

"I'm glad I'm not cooking, that's for sure. Do you remember how I used to be up before dawn to get the goose into the Aga on time and the veg prepped? And the ham boiled? I was always terrified I'd mess up. I'm an old hand now, love, and it's nice to be cooked for. Besides I'm not sure our old Aga could fit a bird big enough to feed us all. We need an emu, don't we?"

Alice suddenly had a vision of the large blue puppet with evil orange beak and staring eyes running amok and savaging diners in Symon's beautiful restaurant, and she laughed; her husband had loved the slapstick of seventies comedy duo Rod Hull and Emu. Odd quicksilver thoughts like this always made Alice feel that he was still present. Could you tune into the energy of those who had already gone onwards, a little like turning the dial on a radio and coming across snatches of a French broadcast? She wondered what Jules, the vicar of St Wenn and her grandson Danny's wife, would have to say about such an idea. Alice suspected she'd say that Christmas was a time for wonder and miracles and magic – after all, the ancient hymns were full of such things, godheads veiled in flesh, virgin's wombs bearing children and wise men following stars. Love remaining close by seemed a simple thing in comparison.

"*There are more things in heaven and earth, Horatio …*" she said softly. "Seventy years ago now you changed my life, and I'll never, ever forget that day. Or you. Merry Christmas, my love, wherever you are today."

Alice's Christmas Eve tradition was honoured. There was no need to linger in the cold. Kissing the tips of her gloved fingers, she rested them tenderly against the carved name for a moment before turning for the welcoming lights of St Wenn's.

It was time to look forward to the celebrations ahead.

CHAPTER 2

THE PRESENT

How many times had she walked through this church porch? Impossible to count, but by now the tally must be in the thousands. There was a comfort in knowing that she was part of something bigger, her feet just another pair of the many which had played a part in wearing the flagstones into dips, smoothing and eroding them in a constant ebbing and rising tide of worshippers just as the sea below shaped the rocks and sands of the bay.

As she had always done since she was a very small child and first had his presence pointed out to her, Alice glanced up at the owl which was lovingly carved into the highest beam. With his age-darkened wood, intricate feathers and wise eyes the St Wenn's owl had spent many centuries watching the tide of worshippers ebb and flow through the porch. Who had carved him and why was a mystery, since he was hardly biblical, but Alice rather liked the idea that a long-forgotten craftsman had added a little artistic flourish purely for his own enjoyment. The jolly little owl, another constant in her life, had seen her passing through six of Shakespeare's seven ages, just as he had seen her son and his children and *their* children passing beneath. It was such a comfort, and a reminder of how life would always continue – even when there were times when you felt sure the world was ending.

She paused to admire the beautiful wreath on the studded door, marvelling that once upon a time her hands had been dextrous enough to twist evergreen and ribbon together like this. The mantle was well and truly passed on now, but Alice still couldn't help tweaking a strand of ivy and adjusting a ribbon to create the perfect effect that her poised and polished mother-in-law would have insisted upon. Alice, the daughter of fisherfolk, had been in awe of her for years until a shared love of gardening had eventually brought them together. Although her mother-in-law was long gone now, her ability to arrange flowers and design gardens had lived on in Alice. How nice to know that those skills had been passed on to all the people Alice had taught to arrange church flowers. It was another reminder that nothing was ever truly lost and that we carry the past with us like a rolled-up rug.

The church smelt of polish and age. As always, the distilled essence of the old building sent Alice tumbling backwards down the decades. So little had changed here. Even the crib taking pride of place at the front of the nave was the one her young son had once stared at, wide-eyed. As a girl she had helped to embroider the altar cloth and stitch kneelers. If that young girl met the elderly Alice, would she recognise herself? And would she approve of the life she had led and the choices she had made? So much had changed since then. But Alice refused to let melancholy settle upon her like snow. Although Christmas was emotive it was most of all a time for joy and for being thankful. It was a time when miracles happened – and who knew this better than she did? After all, hadn't her life changed beyond all recognition on Christmas Eve?

It was hard to believe there had once been a Christmas Eve when a tearful Alice had sat in St Wenn's and prayed that the boy she loved would love her once more. Without him she'd truly believed her life was over and her poor heart shattered beyond all repair – for there is no pain quite like that of unrequited love. How Alice would love to meet that young self now and have a word with her, to explain that her life was only just beginning and her prayers were about to be granted in ways she couldn't begin to imagine. But the young Alice probably wouldn't listen to the ramblings of an old lady, for young people never believed that elderly folk had once been just like them, had felt the very same breath-snatching joy, goosebump-dusted longings and searing heartache. For youngsters old age was as far away as the moon, and just as unlikely to be a destination they would ever visit.

Alice smiled as she made her slow way down the aisle that had seen her arrive as a bride. That sad seventeen-year-old self would never have believed what life held in store, and maybe that was just as well. Perhaps part of the wonder of life was allowing the path to twist and turn as it bore her in directions she could have never imagined. Some people, Vicar Jules for example, might say this was a divine plan. Others would insist that it was Destiny which mapped out frail mortal lives in the stars. Some, like her great-grandson Morgan, a teenager with very firm opinions, would insist that everything was random. Fact. Alice was old enough now to accept that nobody had the answers, but her heart told her she was loved, and at this special time of year miracles were closer than ever. Maybe mystery was the whole point, and it was best not to know too much.

Well, what existential questions for Christmas Eve! Proof indeed that she had time on her hands these days to enjoy the luxury of such thoughts. Back when she'd been in service at Polwenna House there'd been hardly time to draw breath on Christmas Eve, never mind ponder deep and meaningful questions. She would have risen at half four to walk up the hill to the house in time to make sure the fires were laid and lit. Then there was a huge breakfast to prepare. She recalled steaming porridge ladled into fine china bowls, creamy scrambled eggs, kippers, kedgeree, bacon, piles of golden toast and cold cuts of venison. The breakfasts at the big house would have enough food to feed the Pendeen family for a whole *week*, never mind breakfast.

By the time Alice had cleared away and scrubbed the pans clean, it was time to help Mrs Boggith, the cook, prepare for the next day's Christmas feast. Several sackfuls of potatoes had been plunged into buckets of icy water to be scrubbed with a wire brush, and Alice's hands were red raw before the peeling even began. Then there were carrots to top and tail, mountains of sprouts to peel, and the enormous goose to baste and stuff. Once this was done and the bird was resting in the cool of the pantry like an actor waiting for their cue to take centre stage, there was the cleaning to do, followed by luncheon, more clearing away and yet more pan-scrubbing. Then at four o'clock Alice would leave Polwenna House and race home to prepare the Pendeen family's far less grandiose celebration. By Midnight Mass she could hardly keep her eyes open; once, she had nodded off in the service. Reverend Sharpe, who was as pointy and severe as his name, had made a barbed comment about her lack of interest in the Christmas message, almost reducing her to tears.

Almost.

She would have cried – but she had looked across the

chancel and into the eyes of the tall dark-haired boy who stood with his parents by the door. Suited, and with the wavy fringe trying to fall across his face bullied into place by macassar oil, he was every inch the young gentleman. As their gaze held they shared a secret language nobody else could speak, and knowing this took all the sting from the vicar's words. At the end of the service, as the boy's parents shook hands with the great and good of Polwenna Bay, he took advantage of their lack of attention to wink at Alice before pulling a face at the vicar. It had taken all of her self-control not to burst into peals of laughter, and later on when she passed him at the lych-gate and their gloved fingertips brushed, it had taken even more control not to lean in and kiss him.

Memories of those bygone days sometimes felt more immediate than whatever she had done that morning. Alice's mind was running backwards and forwards across the decades, but that was how it seemed to work these days. Her memory didn't seem to operate in any neat and tidy order but mingled the past and present – not in a confused way, but one that was able to appreciate how what was taking place now made sense of what had occurred years before.

She glanced down at the gold band on her left hand, surprised as always to find the skin bruised and the bones beneath it bird-fragile. It was marvellous the way life wove all the strands together into a pattern which only made sense from the great distance of the years. Alice knew that this insight would have been of little comfort to her younger self, but now the sense of a greater design was comforting to her.

As a wife and mother she had found Christmas Eve as busy as her days in service, for her house was always full of family and the friends who popped in for a drink and to exchange gifts. Alice would bake and baste and peel until the kitchen table groaned under the weight of all the food and there was no space left in the Aga. As the afternoon shifted into evening she would put the finishing touches to the Christmas cake, dust mince pies with icing sugar, and wrap presents late into the night once her excited son had been tucked up in bed. It had been hard to squeeze in the Midnight Mass, but she always managed to make the service. It was a welcome pause for breath before the big day.

This year, though, Alice wouldn't have to lift a finger – at least that was what her grandson Symon was promising – but a part of her ached for those full and busy days, and in the unchanging church it was hard not to feel nostalgia tug at her heart. Christmas did that more and more the older you got. Alice thought Charles Dickens had certainly known what he was doing when he wrote *A Christmas Carol*. Maybe she should revisit her writing and pen a timeless festive bestseller ...

She imagined that if Dickens had passed by Harbour Watch he would have been very surprised to see the Muppets reading his words and singing the story. When she'd left the house Hector and Isla, two of her great-grandchildren, had still been glued to the television, singing along to the much-loved film. Tree lit against the gloom, fairy lights twinkling from the old beams and flames dancing in the woodburner, the cosy scene melted her heart. New family members arrived to fill the gaps left by those who had departed, and this was how life was supposed to be. It was not so much moving on as allowing life to move, or so Alice thought, and as she grew older she felt reassured by this idea. Tides turned, waves thrashed the sand before retreating, and new family members arrived to fill the gaps. It was the way of things, for our own stories are only big and important while we have our eye's blink in time. Now, though, Alice understood this, and she was mostly at peace with it.

She leaned against a pew to catch her breath again. It was time to leave thoughts of Christmas past behind and embrace Christmas present. She'd begin by admiring the beautiful flower arrangements. Dressed in its festive finery, the church was looking stunning. Ivy and evergreens, richly threaded with red ribbon and woven with bright berries, were wound around the pillars. Silver pinecones and white carnations were sprinkled in the dark leaves like stars, and the displays on the pulpit and font boasted white fairy lights. The windowsills were festooned with yet more greenery and ribbons, the old crib had been given a makeover, and the freshly painted nativity figures seemed to glow more brightly as though proud at being restored to their former glory. At the side of the crib scene, as though just nudging a little paganism into the mix, was the St Wenn's Christmas tree. It was lassoed in silver streamers, white lights and little cards tied with red ribbon upon which visitors had written prayers and greetings for the festive season. At the very top of the tree was a lopsided star which a gangly young man, wobbling alarmingly on a spindly ladder, was attempting to straighten.

"Careful, Perry!" cried Alice, finding a sudden spurt of energy to dive forward and steady the ladder.

"Thanks, Alice! Aha! Got it!"

Perry Tregarrick tweaked the star and hopped back down to earth. He pushed his glasses back up his nose and tucked his tee shirt back into the loose waistband of his jeans. The lad needed feeding up, thought Alice. What Perry needed was a nice girl. Or boy. Or whatever. As long as they were kind to dear Perry – one of the sweetest and most generous people she knew – who cared? Alice didn't have any time for elderly folk who moaned on about 'young people nowadays not knowing what they are, not like in our day'. The good old days with all their prejudices weren't always so great. *That* Alice could remember.

"What do you think of the display?" Perry asked, a little anxiously since Alice had been in charge for decades. "I grew most of the blooms, and the friends of St Wenn's have worked really hard to put the display together."

"You've all done a fantastic job. St Wenn's looks absolutely beautiful," said Alice warmly, and she was rewarded by a sweet smile.

"Then my work's done – well, here at least, because I've promised Sy and Ella I'd give them a hand setting up for tomorrow. Are you looking forward to it?"

"Immensely. I still can't get used to being cooked for. I feel very spoilt," said Alice. Then she frowned, as it occurred to her that Perry, who had no immediate family, would be alone for Christmas. "You're coming too, I hope?"

He nodded. "Sy said I could ask Harry along too, and any other waifs and strays. Nobody should be by themselves at Christmas."

Alice's heart went out to Perry, who looked so wistful. Christmas could be such a lonely time for those who didn't have family to share the holiday with. It was typical of her grandson to think of including friends and neighbours who might be alone, like churchwarden Harry and dear Perry. *That* was what Christmas was about.

Leaving Perry to stow the ladder, Alice stopped for a quick chat with Harry, who was refilling the prayer candle stand with tea lights and already looking forward to his Christmas dinner. Once they'd debated the merits of bread sauce versus cranberry (both firmly in favour of bread sauce) and the thorny matter of custard or brandy butter on the Christmas pudding (both deemed unacceptable – only Cornish clotted cream would do) Harry turned his attention back to sorting out the carol sheets while Alice lit a candle in memory of her husband. She smiled a little as she touched the taper to the wick, because he would have raised his eyebrows. You don't need a candle to remember *me,* he would point out. Not when you've got the clan to remind you!

He'd be right. There were flickers of his face in their family, and all the grandchildren, no matter how individual or different, bore echoes of his nature. Jake had his serious steadfastness. Mo his courage. Zak possessed his grandfather's impatience. Danny's career had followed in his footsteps. Symon had the sharp business mind. And Nick and Issie? They shared the reckless side (not that anyone would have ever believed that about such a pillar of the community) and sense of adventure. Her own son looked more like his father the older he grew, and Alice was often quite startled when she caught a glimpse of Jimmy unawares.

So she didn't need a candle to remember her husband. But nonetheless there was something about the gesture that Alice found comforting. The idea of light in the midst of the wintry darkness felt especially appropriate at Christmas, and every time she dared switch on the news or flick through a paper the world seemed ever more precarious and at odds with itself. Alice thought that today hope was needed more than ever, but maybe people had always thought this – St Wenn's must have seen generations of worshippers fretting about the uncertain nature of the world around them – from plagues to the Reformation to the Civil War to the horror of the trenches – and indeed her own parents, who must have sat here and fretted about the threat of Hitler's forces massed only a short few miles across the sea. It was all history now, as everything must become one day, and in knowing this she found peace.

Alice slid into her favourite pew. It could have been any

Christmas Eve out of the many she'd known, for the hard wood was still as unyielding beneath her backside and the smells and sounds unchanged. She'd sat here since she was a young girl, mainly because she liked the carving of the jaunty pelican etched onto the side. Jules had tried to explain the religious symbolism, but Alice preferred to believe that the long-forgotten artist was having fun here too. As a child she'd thought it was a strange seagull. How her brother had teased her for that! Now it reminded her of the pictures that her granddaughter Issie emailed from her home in the Florida Keys of pelicans perched on wooden piers and silhouetted against a peach melba sunset. How amazing to think that her grandchildren had travelled to, and lived in, places she would never see. How incredible that she had been the starting point for all these bifurcating lives and journeys!

Alice was about to haul herself to her feet and begin the journey home when she heard a muffled sob. A sniff followed. Somebody in the row behind her was crying, and doing their very best to do so without drawing attention to themself. Alice had once been an expert in crying in secret, and she recognised the choked sound of damped-down misery.

For a moment she froze. Had time shivered and sent her back down the years to confront her younger self and offer the advice and hope she'd so badly needed back then? Although she knew she was being fanciful, she felt nervous about turning around – for how might the young Alice Pendeen react? Would she even recognise this old woman as the person she would become? She would probably be horrified.

There was another smothered sob and a heart-wrenching gulp. Alice couldn't bear to hear such distress or think of somebody suffering alone. Ghost of Christmas past or not, their heart was breaking, and nobody knew better than Alice just how lonely this was.

She reached into her bag for a handkerchief and turned around. She needed to know who was breaking their heart in St Wenn's on Christmas Eve.

CHAPTER 3

THE PRESENT

Time travel being the stuff of novels and television shows, it wasn't Alice's younger self sitting in the pew behind, but a girl in her late twenties. Dressed in a scarlet puffa coat and woollen pom-pom hat, and with a diamond nose stud twinkling in the soft candlelight, she was definitely not from the nineteen-fifties. Yet although her clothes were different to those Alice used to wear, the swollen eyes and muffled sobs were a bridge between eras. Fashions might change but heartbreak didn't.

Spotting Alice looking at her, the girl attempted to pull herself together. Her chin was wobbling and her green eyes shimmered with unshed tears, but she smiled bravely and blotted her eyes with her sleeve.

"Sorry. I didn't mean to disturb you."

Her nose was almost as red as the coat, and strands of cinnamon-hued hair were plastered to her wet cheeks. She must have been crying for hours, and Alice's heart went out to the young stranger. She was curious, too, but she said nothing. The years after her heartbreak had rolled away like quicksilver, but she recalled nursing her precious misery closely.

Offering her handkerchief over the pew, she smiled kindly at the young woman.

"Here, my dear. It's clean."

The girl accepted it with trembling hand.

"Thanks. My tissue's fallen to pieces."

"Useless things," tutted Alice while the girl blew her nose. "Keep it, dear, I've got hundreds at home because I'm old-fashioned. Anyway, it's impossible to have a proper cry with tissues, isn't it? You end up with paper mâché."

The girl nodded.

"My pockets are full of it."

"Oh dear. It sounds as though you've been doing a lot of crying."

"I can't stop. I thought I'd be okay here because it's so beautiful and far away from everything that reminds me of—"

She looked away, intent suddenly on the candles flickering from the window ledges and sconces.

Another tear slipped down her cheek.

"Sorry," she whispered. "I can't seem to stop crying. I thought it'd be different here."

"We always take ourselves with us," Alice said quietly. She was thinking of how her son had run away from Polwenna Bay to escape his grief, and about Summer, her grandson's partner, who had fled the village when her heart was in pieces. Alice, too, had once planned to start over in a place where nobody knew her. Like Jimmy and Summer, she'd believed you could discard your old self as easily as leaving behind an old set of clothes. But the truth was that you could never run away from yourself. As the girl blew her nose again and visibly pulled her shoulders back, Alice decided that the least she could do was share this knowledge. Maybe it would help?

"I'm Alice," she said.

"I'm Holly," sniffed the girl. "Holly Green. Don't laugh. It's not my fault!"

Alice wasn't laughing; she was thinking that the name suited her new acquaintance. With rosy cheeks, green hat and berry-coloured coat, Holly resembled the jaunty festive evergreen she was named for.

"Let me guess. You were born at Christmas time?"

"Just after lunchtime on Christmas Day," said Holly, dabbing her eyes once more. "Dad says I ruined Christmas dinner that year, because Mum forgot to put the turkey in the oven."

Alice laughed. "*Men!* I think your mother had more on her mind than a turkey that day!"

Although she tried to smile, Holly's lips trembled.

"I'm sure she did. They're still teasing each other about it thirty years on. Thirty *years*. I can't believe it's my thirtieth tomorrow."

Although reaching the age of thirty was a landmark in a woman's life, it was no reason to cry, thought Alice – but there were so many unspoken expectations of what should have been achieved by the start of one's fourth decade. She wondered whether this was what was troubling Holly. Back in Alice's day marriage and babies had been the benchmark of success for a woman, and she suspected that for all that was said these days about careers, that underlying pressure remained.

"I remember being thirty. It's certainly a milestone," she said carefully.

Neither of Alice's brothers had made thirty, and it often shocked her to realise she'd left Sam and Dan behind long ago.

Her cheeky brothers were dragonflies in amber, forever young and always handsome – but the lives they should have led and the families they'd never got to make were forever voids. Few people remained who remembered the handsome Pendeen boys, and it made Alice sad that before too long they would slip from memory and exist only in fading photographs. Nobody would recall Sam's hot temper or Dan's talent for card tricks. Ageing, however tiresome, was a privilege, she decided, and she must do her best to remember that. No more moaning about aching limbs and dimmed vision. She wished she could tell Holly this.

"It's certainly a milestone, but I never thought thirty would feel like *this*." Holly was saying bleakly.

If thirty was a milestone birthday, what was ninety? The thought of all the candles a cake would require made Alice feel quite breathless. Blowing them out would probably finish her off.

"Try adding fifty to that number," she said briskly. "Thirty's a wonderful age. Not old at all, and with everything to look forward to. You shouldn't be sad, my love."

Thirty, which had once felt so ancient, seemed impossibly young nowadays. Oh, to be thirty again with all the possibilities laid before you like a banquet! Wouldn't that be a wonderful Christmas present? Now *there* was a festive story for any aspiring Dickens to pen.

Holly twisted the hanky into a tight knot.

"I was actually really excited about my thirtieth. I'd been looking forward to it for ages. My fiancé had booked Seashell Cottage and planned a romantic Christmas birthday. Walks on deserted beaches. Cosying up under blankets, and reading, and eating. Christmas dinner in the pub. Mulled wine. Sitting by the woodburner. Treatments at the hotel. I've been looking forward to it for ages – but it's not like that at all."

These images would have been plucked straight from the webpages of holiday letting companies. Wintertime in Cornwall, a dark and gale-lashed season when tourists historically stayed away, had been rebranded as the perfect time for romantic getaways. Roaring log fires in low-beamed pubs, windswept Poldark-style beaches and cosy nights in harbourside cottages had become staple clichés of Brand Cornwall in the wintertime, and Polwenna Bay possessed all these in abundance. What the marketing folk conveniently forgot to mention was that in December a small and rain-lashed fishing village could be a hard place to find yourself in. It was no coincidence that many of Polwenna's full-time residents either hibernated or decamped to the pub until March, when the clocks went forward again.

"Well, that sounds lovely …" Alice ventured, sensing a 'but' was coming.

"Jamie broke things off six months ago. It came utterly out of the blue. He said he needed space. Well, he's got that now, because I'm two hundred miles away!"

She tried to laugh, a strangled sound that jarred the stillness. Perry looked up from his tree arranging with a concerned expression.

"Sorry," said Holly, lowering her voice. "I just feel so stupid. I'd thought we were happy. How wrong can you get? Jamie said he felt trapped, and he didn't think he was ready to commit."

"Best to find out he felt that way before marriage," said Alice gently, although she suspected that what this unknown Jamie had actually meant was that he needed space to have fun and meet other women. Alice hadn't got to her age without learning a thing or two about men.

"He said I was *crowding* him. He needed *space*. He needed to *find* himself," Holly said. "What does that even *mean*?"

Thirty was old enough to have found yourself, if you had the luxury to do so. Why, by that age Alice's eldest brother, Dan, had already fought in a war. And died. And her other brother, Sam, had taken on the family fishing boat at seventeen. What was it with some young people nowadays? So many seemed stuck in eternal childhood with their gaming gadgets and apparent inability to knuckle down. Perhaps her husband had been right, and doing away with National Service in 1960 really had been a mistake. Oh dear, she was getting old and grumpy. She must try to be less judgemental.

"Maybe he does need time to think. Marriage is for a lifetime," she offered, doing her very best to be charitable to this unknown fiancé.

"I thought the same at first," said Holly sadly. "I said he could have as long as it took to work things out, but it turns out that what Jamie actually meant was that he wasn't ready for commitment with *me.* He's already moved in with a mutual friend, and since we live in a small town there's no way I can avoid seeing them together. It's so *painful.*"

Alice saw as clearly as though it was only yesterday a triumphant girl holding the arm of a young man with dark hair. A swift slice of pain snatched her breath. In a small village there was no hiding place and no escape from scrutiny; all eyes were upon you, yet somehow her own heartache, at least, had been a secret.

"I decided to come to Polwenna anyway to get away from everything," said Holly, "but somehow I feel even worse here."

"When we're hurting even the most beautiful places feel wrong. Maybe it's because we can't leave ourselves and our troubles behind no matter how much we'd often like to," Alice said gently, thinking of a time when she had once contemplated throwing a few belongings into a holdall and taking the train to London. Losing herself in the city had seemed a tempting proposition, but she would only have wept in a different location.

"That's so true. I'm here, and it's lovely – but I keep thinking of all the things we should be doing together and how wonderful things were meant to be," sighed Holly. She glanced down at her bare left hand and bit her lip. "Mum wanted me to be at home for Christmas – but I couldn't bear the thought of everyone pitying me. Poor Holly. Dumped and thirty."

Alice knew well the fierce flame of protection that must burn brightly in Holly's mother's heart just as she also knew there were some hurts that even the most loving parents couldn't soothe. It had taken her own son a lifetime to find happiness again, and watching him suffer while knowing she couldn't help had been almost unbearable.

"My friends all say I need to get over him and move on – but I miss Jamie so much. I miss the life I was looking forward to. I'm not sure who I am any more, and I can't see a future."

"You have a future, my dear. One far better than you can imagine," said Alice firmly.

But Holly only cried anew at this thought. Her tears fell thick and fast, dripping from her chin and splashing onto the hymn books.

"It doesn't feel that way. It feels like my life's over."

"Is that why you came to the church?" Alice asked. "Because you felt there was nothing left to live for and needed help?" The pew seemed to dip beneath her buttocks because it felt as though time was slipping and sliding until she was the young woman, red-eyed and broken-hearted, who was desperate to bargain with the Almighty.

If you let him love me again I'll never moan about doing the washing. I'll come to church every Sunday. I'll even scrub the pots and pans until my hands are raw – just bring him back to me!

Holly shrugged red-quilted shoulders.

"I don't know really. It's not like I *believe* or anything, but I couldn't bear being alone. I tried sitting in the pub, but I felt like the ghost at the banquet. Everyone else looked so happy."

"Christmas is very hard when your world's falling apart," Alice agreed. "Everyone else seems so happy, and that somehow makes it worse. But things'll get better and you'll feel happy again, my love. It might not feel like it, but … this too shall pass."

Holly didn't look convinced.

"I'm sorry to go on about myself. I'm sure you've got better things to do on Christmas Eve."

"What could be better than listening to someone who's feeling sad? That's surely more in keeping with the true spirit of Christmas."

"I guess so …"

"I *know* so," said Alice. "But let me tell you a story that might help you believe me. It's the story of a seventeen-year-old girl who sat in this very church one Christmas Eve and who prayed with everything she had that her true love would come to her. That girl would have done *anything* to have him back. There was nothing she wouldn't promise, and no feat too great to attempt if she thought it might help. She loved him so much that with his rejection of her she thought her life was over."

"I know that feeling," Holly said. "Does her story have a happy ending?"

"Alice Pendeen couldn't have imagined so back then – but I'll let you be the judge of that."

"Alice Pendeen? Is that you?"

There were many versions of herself folded into one another like Russian dolls. Which one was the real Alice? The girl? The lover? The mother? The respectable grandmother?

Or was she all of them, each one a part of the next, and unable to exist without the rest?

"She was me once, and although I've been many people since then I've never lost her. She's the map to the woman I've become, and I owe her everything. But I'm getting ahead of myself. I need to start at the beginning if I'm to make any sense at all."

Alice touched the old pew to steady herself before she leapt out of the present and tumbled back down the decades. This was the place where her story and Holly's collided. The only thing that divided Alice from that moment was time's curtain. Her memories would pull it back and allow Holly Green to peek into the past. They would allow Alice to pass on a gift that had been given to her one Christmas so long ago …

She took a deep breath and prepared herself to travel back in time.

"In December 1953 it was bitterly cold. Although back in the fifties the winters always seemed to be hard, nothing was colder than the splinter of ice that had shattered my heart …"

CHAPTER 4

1953

In the depths of winter there were fewer places colder than a damp harbourside cottage. Alice Pendeen huddled beneath her candlewick bedspread and did her best to hem a skirt. Her icy fingers were so numb she kept dropping the needle, and she groaned with despair. This dress had to be finished soon, or she'd be attending the Tregarricks' Christmas Eve dance wearing slacks and a sweater.

Alice re-threaded her needle yet again and returned to stitching. At least the light was good up in her low-beamed attic bedroom, and although it was a bitter afternoon it was sunny. Outside folks were scurrying along the fish quay clad in heavy jackets, bent double against the knifing wind. The boats in the harbour strained against their moorings as though desperate to be freed after weeks of being tied up by gales, while the Christmas lights strung between the lamp posts swung back and forth like skipping ropes. The poor harbour tree had already covered the quay in a thick carpet of needles, and as Alice watched yet another blast of the icy north wind shook more of them from its shivering branches.

It was the hardest winter Alice could remember in her seventeen years. Everyone in Polwenna Bay agreed that this December was on a par with that of 1946, and with the storms tying up the boats it felt as though the dark days of rationing had returned. Alice ached from the cold whenever she strayed far from the warmth of the range, and her chilblains throbbed and itched. May Pendeen had warned her daughter time and time again not to thaw her burning-cold hands on the cast-iron radiators at Polwenna House, but the temptation of such toasty warmth after the chilly early morning walk to work always proved irresistible. How Alice wished she'd listened to her mother!

As Alice continued to sew, she wondered what else May was right about. She hoped the prevention of chilblains was the full extent of any superior maternal knowledge. If not, Alice was also wrong in turning down the latest chance of courtship, this time offered by fisherman Barry Penhalligan, the proud owner of Polwenna's newest lugger, and was doomed to spend her life on the shelf.

Alice wasn't sure what life on this 'shelf' would look like, but she was certain it was preferable to a loveless one spent with fisher lad Barry – or indeed any of the other village boys her hopeful parents had dropped anchor-heavy hints about. From Peter Pollard the builder's son to Keith the curate, they'd all come knocking on the door of Cobbles Cottage, only for Alice Pendeen to turn down every hopeful.

As she pushed the needle in and out of the fabric and did her best to ignore the fact that the tip of her nose was near-frozen, her thoughts drifted to the previous evening. She'd been sewing in the kitchen when Barry had arrived clutching a bunch of flowers and asking her mum whether he could have a chat with Alice. It was about the dance, he explained with a blush. He wondered whether she would do him the honour of accompanying him.

May Pendeen had ushered Barry into the front parlour, propelling her daughter in after him and hissing at Alice to be *nice*. The parlour was saved for best, Alice's mother cleaning and dusting it weekly as though the Queen might drop in on the off-chance for tea, so to be allowed in there was an indication of just how important this visit was deemed. Alice had sighed. It wouldn't be just Barry who was disappointed when she sent him packing.

After a rather awkward exchange, Alice had shooed Barry out of the cottage looking as dejected as the wilting bunch of flowers still clamped in his paw. She had shut the door behind him with a mixture of irritation and pity. She'd known Barry all her life, and never shown any romantic interest in him. Whatever had made him think she'd want to accompany him to the Christmas Eve dance? As she'd returned to the warmth of the kitchen, she'd shaken her head. How had he been so deluded?

Reflecting on this as she stitched away in her bedroom out of the irritated May's sight, Alice supposed that owning a new fishing boat and belonging to a well-respected Polwenna family lent a certain degree of confidence to a man. Barry had certainly been taken aback by her refusal, and implied that she ought to have been grateful for his attention. He was a Penhalligan and owned the biggest lugger in the harbour! Didn't she *care?*

Not really. No.

Alice knew that her family, the Pendeens, made church mice look rich. They didn't own a television, and their privy was still outside, as Barry had pointed out pityingly. Alice hadn't repeated these comments to her mother; May and Morley Pendeen were proud people, and she couldn't bear to think of them being hurt by a neighbour's disdain. Better by far that they would just think she was being difficult.

She smoothed the velvet fabric and smiled a secret smile. The boy Alice loved didn't give two hoots about boats and outside privies. He didn't care that she was from a poor fishing family while his folks were wealthy. He never made unkind comments either – because he loved Alice and she loved him. This was all that mattered. Alice only wished that everyone could feel this way about their love affair, because it was becoming harder and harder to keep it a secret.

She bit off the thread and smoothed the hem, still smiling to herself. Their relationship wouldn't be a secret for much longer, because soon the whole world would know how they felt. It was exciting and terrifying all at once. There would be no going back then – no matter what his family or hers might say. Her mother might even be pleased, since the family of the boy Alice loved had a lot more to their name than indoors plumbing and a fishing boat.

May Pendeen certainly hadn't been pleased the previous evening, that was for sure.

"Well?" she'd said, peeping around the kitchen door hopefully. "Did he ask you to the dance?"

"Yes – but I'm not going with him, Ma."

May's eyes were green dinner plates.

"Whyever not? *Everyone* wants to go to the Tregarricks' dance, Alice!"

The Christmas Eve dance was always held in the old barn

at Polwenna Manor. A traditional yuletide thank you gesture from the landowner to the villagers who worked for or contributed to the estate. Key figures from Polwenna Bay, such as the vicar and Dr Jago, were always invited, and although the Manor was practically falling down around the impoverished Tregarrick family's ears, an invitation was always highly sought after. After the dancing, a buffet supper and more than a few sherries, everyone practically floated to Midnight Mass.

"I don't want to go to the dance with Barry, Ma."

May placed her hands on her hips.

"So who *do* you want to go with, my girl? Prince Philip? Errol Flynn? The Lord of the Manor?"

Although May was being sarcastic she wasn't as far from the truth as she might think, and Alice flushed guiltily.

"Of course not. Anyway, Elsie's got her heart set on Hugo."

Alice's best friend fancied herself in love with the heir to Polwenna Manor, and both girls had read enough romantic novels to be convinced that Elsie stood a fighting chance of winning his heart. In fairness, Elsie, with her big brown eyes, ample curves and long blonde curls, did stand a chance of catching Hugo's eye at the dance, although Alice privately thought that allowing the adoring Peter Pollard to escort her so she could put her plan into action wasn't very fair.

May tutted. "That girl has ideas above her station. Her parents run the bakery."

"If Hugo loves her that won't matter," said Alice.

She knew she was right. In *Pride and Prejudice* Darcy had loved Lizzy Bennet in spite of the family being impoverished. In *Jane Eyre*, Rochester had married the poor governess, Jane. In real life, even the Duke of Windsor had given up his throne for love when he had chosen Mrs Simpson. There was enough evidence if you looked around that love could overcome all. Alice knew that her mum didn't know what she was talking about, because she obviously didn't remember what it felt like to be young and in love. When you loved somebody with all your heart and soul nothing could keep you apart.

Nothing.

May raised her eyes to the ceiling.

"Give me strength. Do you really think that's how the world works? Queen Elizabeth married a prince, not her gardener! Stop reading all those daft books, Alice. Love doesn't make the world go round or conquer all. Elsie's not for the likes of Hugo. Boys of that class have their fun with village girls, but they don't *marry* them."

"They do if they love them," said Alice. Her hands, buried in the pockets of her slacks, balled into fists.

"No, Alice. They *don't.* Hugo's type toss village girls away when somebody suitable comes along, especially if the girl in question's been silly enough to give away what she shouldn't. You mark my words. Many a silly girl's been ruined by a sweet-talking lad wanting some fun."

Alice's bones turned to iced water. She dug her nails into her palms while her top teeth bit down hard on her bottom lip …

"Maybe I need to have a word with Mary Rowe if that's what her daughter's up to," May was saying thoughtfully. She reached for her pinny and tied it around her waist before turning to the range, where a stew was bubbling. "She'll need to put that silly Elsie straight before she gets herself into trouble."

"You don't need to do that," said Alice quickly. Elsie would never forgive her for betraying her secret plan. "It's only a daydream, Ma. Elsie's going to the dance with Pete Pollard."

May stirred the stew. Although her back was to Alice, her

expression would, Alice knew, be one of approval, for Peter Pollard's father was the local builder.

"Peter's a nice boy. You can't go wrong with a trade like building. It's honest work and a good living."

Alice glanced around the tiny kitchen. Even though it was heated solely by the range, it was the warmest room in the house, and the family tended to spend all their time there – especially during a hard winter, when the weather was bleak and the fishing poor. Cobbles backed onto sheer rock, and the building was so damp you could have wrung it out like a sponge. At this time of year ice stabbed the insides of windows in the mornings, and getting up for work felt like torture. Alice struggled each day, and couldn't bear to imagine what it must be like for her father with his bad knee and hacking cough. The old cottage needed work and better heating, but their landlord was not inclined to spend money on it, and the Pendeens had little to spare, even less during this stormy winter, when the sea was too rough for small boats like theirs to venture out of the harbour. Fishing was a precarious living. Alice saw how hard her father worked to put food on the table, and understood that a fisherman's wife lived a life of perpetual worry. Every time Morley and Sam Pendeen set sail there was an unspoken fear it might be the last time.

This wasn't a life that Alice wanted for herself.

"Fishing's so hard, Ma. Look how it is for us."

May span around, brandishing a wooden spoon. Alice, who'd been walloped by that very spoon on many occasions, stepped back hastily as her mother's sea-witch eyes flashed with anger.

"*Girl May* isn't big enough to stand big seas. Do you want your father and Sam to risk their lives?"

"That wasn't what I *meant!*" cried Alice. She slammed her

hand against her breastbone. "I don't want to settle for a man just because he has a good trade. I want love and passion."

And I already have that! she added silently. May could scoff and say she read too many books, but Alice knew her mother was wrong. Alice knew what it was to long for somebody, to live for one glimpse of a dark head, to yearn for a look from sage green eyes and to feel your bones melting into his. That her love was forbidden only made it stronger. Would Juliet have given up on Romeo because a suitor with a fishing boat had come knocking? Of course not!

May Pendeen lowered the spoon.

"Oh Ally, you're so young. Love is about more than passion. Look at all those silly girls who got married in haste during the war, or those who had their heads turned by GIs and got into trouble. There's a lot who thought like you do and have regrets now."

Alice said nothing. She hated these lectures, especially when she knew in her heart they contained more than a grain of truth.

"Love grows with time," May said gently, "and it's often found where you least expect it. You need to give these lads a chance. Barry's a good boy, and the Penhalligans are an honest, hard-working family. You could do a lot worse than to marry him. Don't be so picky that you end up an old maid on the shelf."

It was an old-fashioned attitude, but Polwenna Bay was an old-fashioned place. Although it was the nineteen-fifties now, and a beautiful young woman was on the throne, attitudes had hardly changed in the village for hundreds of years. Daughters of fishermen married sons of fishermen. They made homes and raised children, and were content with their lot. It was the way things had always been in the village.

Alice appreciated that her parents only wanted what they

thought was best for her, and were thinking of her future. Life was hard for the Pendeens, and ever since her older brother had died at Dunkirk her dad, Morley, had struggled to run the fishing boat. His knee, shattered in the first war, was slowing him down and increasingly painful. Even with the help of his younger son, Sammy, the boat was struggling to make an income, for Sam wasn't a natural sailor. Alice knew he would far rather have carried on with his education, but there was a path already set out for him too. He would be a fisherman because his parents needed him to put food on the table – just as they needed Alice to find a good husband and release them from the burden of her keep. Although she already gave May most of the money she earned at Polwenna House it wasn't nearly enough. Alice appreciated why Barry Penhalligan coming to court their daughter would have made the Pendeens think Christmas had come early. But she didn't love Barry. Boats, respectable families and happy parents made no difference, for Alice was already in love.

Gloriously, totally, utterly head over heels in love.

"I just don't *want* to go to the dance with Barry," she said, sitting down at the kitchen table, where her sewing machine was set up.

May watched as Alice lifted the presser foot to turn the fabric before lowering it and sinking the needle into soft velvet.

"You won't be going at *all* now, my girl – and nobody will see that lovely frock."

Alice said nothing. She *was* going to the dance, and when she arrived hand in hand with her partner the truth would be out for good. There would be no going back. And she wasn't sure if she was excited or terrified. Maybe a little of both?

May was still lecturing her daughter, setting off on a new

tangent as she lifted the heavy velvet skirt and weighed it in her work-roughened hands.

"Maybe you should leave the big house and get a place as a tailoress? Nancy Truscott might have a position. Her shop in Bodmin is lovely."

"Maybe," said Alice, turning the handle slowly to avoid fraying the material – velvet was perfect for a Christmas Eve dance, but it was an utter pig to sew. She didn't say anything else, because she had no intention of spending the next forty years cutting fabric or hemming garments at the back of Nancy's workshop. Her life was on the brink of taking a very different direction.

If this hadn't been the case, or if there had been a way that the Pendeens could have afforded to forgo her wage, Alice would have been tempted to study dress design at technical college. Although she loved dressmaking and sewing, design was her passion. But instead she would spend hours at the kitchen table hunched over her mother's Singer, her arm aching from turning the handle as she stitched outfit after outfit. From a young age she had been in demand helping friends and family with alterations or new clothes. Until fabric rationing had ended in 1949 she had been a dab hand at creating garments from old curtains, parachute silk and scraps of fabric from old clothes. The walls of her bedroom were papered with designs for beautiful ballgowns and day dresses fit for the new queen, all fashioned from the ideas she'd gleaned over the years.

In her most cherished daydreams Alice didn't live in a tiny fishing village or work at Polwenna House alongside her housekeeper mother, but inhabited a chic apartment in Paris and was inundated by people clamouring to be dressed by the House of Pendeen. Sadly for Alice, though, the closest she ever came to Parisian fashion was sneaking peeks at the copies of

Vogue which Mrs St Milton, her employer, sometimes left splayed open on the arm of a chair or carelessly used as coasters. Alice, who was supposed to be laying fires or cleaning, would glance around to check the coast was clear before quickly flicking through the pages to swoon over Dior and Chanel and Givenchy.

The St Miltons were wealthy. Factory owner Michael St Milton had made his money during the war by manufacturing gun racking for army vehicles, and his wife Diana possessed a wardrobe of clothes that made Alice pea-green with envy. Sometimes when she was doing the laundry or putting clothes away she would hold a dress up against her body and imagine what it might be like to wear such gorgeous clothes. Her utter favourites were the dresses in the New Look style, and Mrs Milton's long mink coat, so soft and warm, and very Greta Garbo.

Alice adored the New Look. The nipped-in waists and full skirts were so opulent and feminine, a wonderful contrast to the austere styles she'd grown up with during and after the war. The style complemented her own hourglass figure, and she knew that the dress she'd been making especially for the Christmas Eve dance, would suit her perfectly. Elsie had said she'd look just like Elizabeth Taylor. Although Alice couldn't see any similarities beyond her dark hair and blue eyes, she did feel like a film star when she wore the green velvet creation. The fabric had cost all her savings, and every time her fingertips brushed it she shivered with anticipation. This was the dress she would wear when the boy she loved took her hand and declared his feelings for her in front of everyone. This dress would snatch his breath away and make his head spin. It would announce to everyone that although Alice Pendeen might be the daughter of a fisherman, in this situation it was *she* who was the catch.

Now up in her room, as she stitched the hem of her beautiful dress and watched the wintry dusk fall, she knew that although her employer's only son might be as far away from her in birth as the stars peppering the sky were from Polwenna Bay, this didn't matter to the heart. She loved Jonny St Milton and he loved her.

And tomorrow, at the Christmas Eve dance, the whole world would know how they felt.

CHAPTER 5

1953

Alice didn't want to continue working at Polwenna House any more than she wanted to be a fisherman's wife. She'd grown up watching her exhausted mother, May, rise when seagulls still had their heads tucked under their wings simply because, heaven forbid, any of the St Miltons might have to sort some breakfast out for themselves. Alice had promised herself long ago that this would never be her lot.

As the St Miltons' housekeeper, May worked long hours and was expected to be ready to put in even more when Diana and Michael decided to throw a dinner party or invite their friends for the weekend. Sometimes May worked fifteen-hour days, coming home hollow-eyed and falling asleep on the couch before Alice could even fetch her some supper. May always insisted she was fortunate to have such a good position and a steady wage – but Alice privately thought it was drudgery, and her heart hardened towards the privileged family.

Excelling at art and with her passion for dress design, Alice had been quietly hoping to go to technical college and later on find work in couture. Maybe she would travel to Paris and Milan? Become a name herself? But she only shared her dreams with Elsie who, fully intending to be the next Lady Tregarrick, was encouraging. Why not dream big? There was a *woman* on the throne now, after all, and during the war the land girls had run farms just as well as the men had done. Some women had even flown aeroplanes – and some had been spies!

"When I'm Hugo's fiancée I'll order my trousseau from you," Elsie promised. "And you can design my wedding dress, too. You'll be as famous as Norman Hartnell!"

It was a lovely dream, and the girls had great fun sketching designs and planning Elsie's entire wardrobe – but Alice's dream of being a fashion designer was one that she came to be grateful she had never voiced to her parents. She knew her father was already racked with guilt for asking Sam to leave school to crew the boat, and when she overheard her parents worrying about paying the rent Alice understood she had no choice but to find work. It was her duty, and the right thing to do.

So, when a housemaid's position arose at Polwenna House in the spring of 1952 Alice was hired without much more than a cursory nod from Mrs St Milton. It wasn't much fun, but Alice was surprised to find there was something satisfying about making a room beautiful or coaxing a reluctant fire into life on a frosty morning.

She loved the beauty of the old house. Whenever she was in the master bedroom she would pause by the long window to admire the manicured lawns striped by the long shadows cast by the majestic Monterey pines and the oblique rays of sunshine. Beyond the lawns were terraces and fountains, ornate beds filled with lavender and roses and fragrant rosemary, and in the box hedge of the parterre mossy statues played hide and seek. On the edge of the garden was a pretty folly where Mrs St Milton liked to take afternoon tea or read, even though just a sugar lump's roll away the land vanished with heart-stopping abruptness. Below were snarling rocks and foaming waves, and all pretence of taming Cornwall's coastline was abandoned as nature fought to erode the cultivated grounds above.

It was a glorious spot, and Alice enjoyed spending time at the house even if the work was physically demanding and far from glamorous. Her duties varied from scrubbing floors to carrying heavy baskets of logs up to the bedrooms to peeling mounds of vegetables. On one occasion, when the odd-job man was off, Alice even ventured into the cobwebby cellar to coax the ancient boiler into life and feed it coke, piece by piece, as though it was a nervous pony. Mrs Boggith frequently lamented the golden days before the war, when there had been far more staff and the household had run like clockwork. According to her everyone had known their place back then, and the world had been a better place for it. Nowadays it was all going to hell in a handcart, mostly because lowly housemaids were laying fires one minute and pressing fine dresses the next. Who did Alice think she was?

Alice wasn't sure how to answer. She had always thought of herself as just Alice. Social class wasn't a topic she had considered before taking up her position at Polwenna House. Although there was a pecking order in the village it was one that had worked on several levels, the most important being how long a family had lived in the village and how Cornish they were. It could take generations for incomers to be accepted, and even then they would never be Cornish. Since there had been Pendeens in Polwenna Bay for generations Alice's family name carried status, for even if they were only fisherfolk they were Cornish through and through. Her great-grandmother had spoken the language, and May still recalled a smattering of words: *dyth da, darzona. splann ...*

Beyond these Polwenna idiosyncrasies, the wider social hierarchy of 1950s England was reflected within the community. Although everyone knew that the Tregarricks didn't have a pot to piss in (as Morley Pendeen had once so eloquently put it) as landed gentry they were at the top of the heap. After them came the reclusive Lady Yelland from Polwenna Priory, followed by the Tremaines of Seaspray House. Although this family was Cornish and rumoured to be related to the illustrious St Aubyns from St Michael's Mount, they were relatively new to Polwenna Bay, as James Tremaine had built a holiday house there just after the Great War. Elizabeth Tremaine had taken up full-time residence during the war while her husband and their sons were fighting overseas. After the war had ended the house had been closed up once more, and since then the Tremaines had acquired a rather mythical status. David St Milton was probably wealthier than all of those families put together – but he was new money, which explained his obsession with making sure that everything at Polwenna House was just so. Dr Jago, retired early from his lucrative Harley Street practice, and the vicar were next, followed by the schoolteacher, the businessmen, the village doctor and the shopkeepers, with the fishermen right at the bottom.

These distinctions had blurred, though, since the war, for bombs and bullets didn't distinguish between masters and servants. Alice's brother Daniel had died on the beaches of Dunkirk fighting beside Hugo's brothers, who also fell. The sense that everyone was in it together had changed things a great deal. Lady Yelland had given her house up for it to become a hospital; Lady Tregarrick had rolled up her sleeves and toiled in the fields; and Elizabeth Tremaine had filled Seaspray with evacuees who swore like navvies, fought anyone who looked at them askance, and frightened the village children far more than Hitler. With their men gone to fight, the women of the village had proved they were more than capable of taking on challenging work, and Alice, growing up knowing nothing but life at war, always believed she could be anything she chose.

A few weeks at Polwenna House soon disabused her of such notions.

There, a hierarchy existed which was practically feudal. A whole list of unspoken rules existed, all of which made it very clear to Alice where her place was in the general scheme of things. She was only allowed to use the back door; she shouldn't speak to the family unless spoken to; and she must never, *ever* set foot on the grand staircase. She had only discovered this rule when taking a short cut with Mrs St Milton's breakfast tray and was roared at so loudly by Mr St Milton that she dropped the lot.

She had cried bitterly after this incident, shaken by the ferocity of the telling-off, and even more frightened by Michael's threat to sack her for such impudence. Since Morley was unwell and Sam had been forbidden to go fishing single-handed, the boat was tied up. Her family needed every penny. It was hard enough that she would have to replace the tea service from her wages, which would take months. She simply couldn't afford to lose her job.

From that day onwards Alice understood that she had to remember, and accept, her place. Her dreams were just that – dreams – and that was always what they would remain. But it was so hard when she had such big and beautiful dreams. It didn't seem fair. But, as her mum often reminded her, it was just as well that Alice should learn early on that life was essentially very unfair indeed. That way she wouldn't be disappointed.

Sometimes when she was hanging up Mrs St Milton's beautiful clothes, Alice furtively held a dress against herself. She would glance over her shoulder into the full-length looking glass and for a moment there she would be, the glittering Alice from the future she'd hoped for rather than the exhausted skivvy who dragged herself to work when the sun was a red fingernail scraping the horizon and the chimneys were etched inky blue against the pink sky. Whenever she cleaned Mrs St Milton's marble bathroom Alice imagined how wonderful it must be to soak in the rolltop tub, neck-deep in scented bubbles and sipping champagne cocktails while watching the moon rise over the sea. It was a far cry from taking her turn in the tin bath by the range, followed by half a cider in the pub!

The St Miltons spent a great deal of time in London, and as their only son, Jonathan, was at boarding school, Polwenna House was often empty. These were Alice's favourite times. Mrs St Milton's discarded copies of *Vogue* and *Tatler* were put out for the rubbish every now and then, and Alice would pore over these, imagining how it would feel to wear such wonderful clothes or, better still, design them. She could still plan outfits, and she could still dream. Nobody could take her dreams away.

Alice had been working at Polwenna House for several months when the St Miltons decided to host a house party. It was early June and the weather had been perfect for weeks. The hedgerows frothed with cow parsley and splashed with campion and buttercups. The sun sparkled through the trees and tap-danced across the sea. For the lucky guests it would be a weekend filled with tennis and boating and beach picnics, because the St Miltons were generous hosts and keen to lavish the best entertainment and food on their visitors, as they showed off their beautiful home.

Always keen to earn more money to support her parents, Alice had offered to work longer on the Friday to serve after drinks and help clear away. All afternoon she'd watched as Aston Martins, Bentleys and Daimlers rolled up the drive, and the beautiful people spilled out amid much air-kissing and back-slapping. Alice carried their luggage to the bedrooms, then unpacked the suitcases and ironed the clothing for any guests who required her help, before diving into the scullery to change. Her dress was last year's and a little on the short side now, but it was brown and plain and, teamed with a white pinny, would look smart. She smoothed her stockings down and skewered several more bobby pins into her curls to secure her bun, before slipping her feet into the black heels Elsie had loaned her.

She peered into the cracked mirror above the Belfast sink and narrowed her eyes at the reflection. The girl gazing out from the smeary glass was every bit as neat and tidy as Mrs St Milton might expect, and she would definitely fade into the background in her sludge-coloured frock. This girl couldn't be farther away from the guests in their pastel-hued dresses who fluttered across the lawn like butterflies. She was colourless and invisible.

A cold wash swept over Alice's skin. Was this *it* for the rest of her life? Was working for Mrs St Milton all she could hope for? She turned away, telling herself she was lucky to have secure employment and the chance to earn some extra money this evening. She was also fortunate to work in such a glorious setting. She could enjoy the same views of the glittering sea as the guests, even if she was serving the cocktails rather than sipping them. Dan would never see that view again, nor would all the others from Polwenna who'd given their lives so that she could enjoy it. She really must buck up and stop feeling so sorry for herself.

The kitchen was a hive of activity, and the extra staff hired from the village scuttled about as Mrs Boggith and May Pendeen issued their directions. Alice collected her first tray of glasses, taking a sharp breath at the weight. Her heart crunching with the terror of tripping, she made her way along the narrow service passage, through the drawing room and out onto the terrace where the guests were gathered. Flurries of laughter rose into the warm evening air, and witty conversation sparkled like the champagne bubbles. Alice thought wistfully how beautiful the women looked in their evening gowns. She bet none of these pampered creatures had ever as felt as drab as she did at this very moment.

Alice wove through the guests with her tray, offering drinks and making sure nobody was missed out. As manicured hands reached for glasses without either a pause in their chatter or any acknowledgement, she knew what it was to feel invisible. Only Hugo looked up and mouthed *thank you,* but even he was rendered a stranger in his smart dinner jacket and disinclined to chat to a maid.

Oh well, thought Alice as she turned to go back to the kitchen to replenish her tray. It was just as well to know where she stood in the general scheme of things. What was it Mum always said? *Better not to have ideas above your station.* That was one of her maxims. It had always driven Alice spare, for what on earth was wrong with aspiring to higher things? But as she reached the kitchen she realised that her mother hadn't been trying to clip her wings but had been wanting to protect her from the choking unfairness of it all. Her mother knew all too well the disappointment of realising that you counted for nothing.

She *did* count, Alice decided furiously as she restocked her tray with more brimming glasses. Something big lay ahead for her; she was certain of it. There was more to life than this!

"Careful with those champagne flutes, Ally," warned May, glancing up from plating the starters. "That's Mrs St Milton's best crystal."

"Drop that and you're in more hot water than these lobsters," said Mrs Boggith, who was plunging unfortunate crustaceans into a pan of boiling water. Alice looked away. Something about their bound claws and lack of escape route felt horribly familiar.

"Be quick," said May, shooing her out. "I need you to serve the canapés."

Alice picked up the tray. Her arms, tired from the first load, trembled under the weight. Or maybe this was down to knowing that the glasses were worth a fortune. Either way, she needed to focus twice as hard now. Pigeon-stepping must look ridiculous, but it was the safest way to make the distance and keep the glasses intact. She inched her way over the uneven flagstones of the service passageway, and once clear heaved a sigh of relief. This part of the journey safely negotiated, she continued across the hall before turning into the drawing room. Only the Persian rugs and the three steps down to the terrace remained to be navigated.

Outside, Hugo had been joined by another young man. The two had their backs to the rest of the group as they shared a cigarette, plumes of blue rising with their laughter into the soft evening and the tips glowing in the gathering dusk. Tall and dark-haired, the new arrival had a coltish look about him, reinforced by the way he flicked his fringe out of his eyes like a pony plagued by flies. He had long gangly limbs, sharp elbows which flapped as he spoke, and almost knocked Hugo's drink flying, and the flash of pale wrists protruding several inches below the cuffs of his dinner jacket suggested that a sudden growth spurt had taken him by surprise. He had high cheekbones, a smiley mouth and a good-humoured air which must have been contagious, for even the perpetually downcast Hugo was laughing. The man looked vaguely familiar, and couldn't have been much older than her, but Alice couldn't place him.

Sensing her watching him, he looked up. His eyes met hers over the top of Hugo's gingery head and widened as though in recognition. He smiled warmly, and without even thinking about it Alice smiled back, something tightening in her chest and making her heart thump. She dropped her gaze hastily. Mrs St Milton would think it terrifically bad form for a maid to be gawking at her guests, no matter how handsome.

Jolted, Alice continued on her way to the terrace. Focus on a distant point, she told herself. Not at *him*! Look through the French windows and out to the horizon. Pin your gaze on that small boat heading towards adventure and new places ...

Afterwards, Alice was never certain what happened. One moment she was crossing the drawing room with her eyes fixed on the rolling blue, the next she was sprawled amid the wreckage of Mrs St Milton's best glasses, watching as champagne soaked into a priceless Turkish rug. Her head, which had hit the edge of the tray, was throbbing, and she felt the warmth of blood trickle into her hair. She must get up quickly before it stained the rug—

The world whirled. Oh Lord. She wasn't going to be sick, was she? Alice closed her eyes and groaned. Mrs St Milton was going to go *spare*.

"Steady on, there. Don't sit up too quickly. That was some tumble."

Cool hands on her shoulders were pushing her back. She smelt sandalwood and cigarette smoke, and opening her eyes she saw the dark-haired man was kneeling at her side.

"Take a deep breath. Don't move for a moment," he was saying.

"The glasses," Alice gasped, struggling against the weight of his palms to rise to her feet and clear the mess. "I'm so sorry."

"Bugger the glasses," he said cheerfully. "Ma loves them, but I've always loathed them. Hideous things!"

Alice's eyes widened. *Now* she knew why she had recognised him. The St Miltons' only son had changed a great deal from the boy she'd glimpsed over the years in church.

"You're Jonny St Milton," she said.

"I am," he agreed. "And you're Alice Pendeen."

"You know my name?" Alice was taken aback.

"Everyone knows the Pendeens. Your brother Danny was a hero, and we all owe men like him a massive debt. I wish I'd been old enough to do my bit."

Alice nodded, although she didn't really remember much about her eldest brother.

"But the truth is that I had a huge crush on you when I was nine," Jonny continued, his cheeks colouring. "I tried so hard to catch your eye across the church whenever I was home from prep school. I used to leave you little gifts in your family's pew because I thought you were the most beautiful girl in the whole village."

Alice too thought that Jonny St Milton, with his velvet-soft eyes, blackbird glossy hair and gentle smile, was the most beautiful boy she had ever seen. He was porcelain-delicate, yet strong. No longer a boy, but not yet a man. He was confident, yet sweetly shy. She could hardly take her eyes off him, and she shivered at the touch of his hands through the cheap fabric of her dress.

"A marble with a spiral in it," she recalled wonderingly as memories flickered into remembrance like the bright flashes of fish hauled up in nets. The little treasures had appeared sporadically behind her hymn book, and she'd often wondered where they'd come from. "And a pheasant feather."

Jonny's smiled down at her, his eyes shining with delight and his mouth curling. Even though she was in the depths of misery this smile had an extraordinary effect, and Alice found she was smiling back at him through her tears.

"And a huge conker," he reminded her. "Don't forget that!"

She laughed. "I gave it to Sam, and he thrashed everyone at school with it. He was the champion."

Jonny placed a hand on his heart. "I'm thrilled to hear it – and now you've repaid that victory by ensuring I won't have to inherit so many of those dreadful glasses."

He was right. The glasses *were* hideous.

And expensive.

Alice gulped.

"I know they were Mrs St Milton's wedding present. I'll pay for them."

Cool fingers touched her forehead with surprising tenderness.

"Never mind that. How's your head feeling? That's going to be some lump. Are you seeing double? Feeling sleepy?"

The only thing Alice was seeing was Mrs St Milton sacking her because of the mess she'd made. And, up since dawn, she wasn't so much sleepy as asleep on her feet.

"I need to clear this up," she said, trying again to haul herself up.

"You bloody well won't. You need to take it easy after a bash on the noggin like that."

"I'm fine," Alice fibbed. It felt as though the Pollards were attacking her skull with a sledge hammer.

"I don't believe you for one moment. Come and sit down."

Jonny helped Alice to her feet and into a wing-backed armchair, arranging cushions around her and fussing like a mother hen. The feathers were heaven to her aching limbs, and she could have fallen asleep right there and then.

"Can I offer you a brandy? For the shock?"

"No. Thank you."

He passed her a handkerchief.

"Take this, to stanch the blood. It's clean, and – before you protest – I don't care if you ruin it,. Least I can do. It was bloody clumsy of me to knock you flying like that."

Alice stared at him, confused.

"But you didn't. I tripped on the rug."

Jonny's eyes widened. "Golly, you *did* hit your head hard! You were carrying the drinks when I cannoned straight into you. Crash! Down you went like a deck of cards. I can't apologise enough. Everyone knows I'm a clumsy clot. Now, you just have a rest and let me clear this lot up."

The green eyes were twinkling and Alice understood what Jonny St Milton was trying to do. He was like an angel swooping down from heaven. A dark-haired, dinner-suited, clumsy angel.

"I can't let you take the blame," she said.

"Of *course* you can," said Jonny breezily. "Ma'll be angry for a bit, but she'll calm down soon enough. She can hardly sack *me,* can she? Whereas, if she thinks it was a member of staff she'll go spare. She'll probably sack you *and* your mother. Ma has a dreadful temper."

Alice swallowed miserably. He was right. And her family wouldn't survive without those wages. Jonny was offering her a lifeline, and she would be crazy not to grab it. But what might he want in return?

"Why would you do that for me?" she asked.

Jonny St Milton looked at her with such longing that it made everything else fade away, and Alice realised she already knew the answer.

He took her hand and brushed it with his mouth.

"I might not be nine any more, but there's still nothing I wouldn't do for you, Alice Pendeen," he whispered. "Nothing at all."

Jonny was right about the glasses. His mother was furious with him and berated Alice too, but since the accident was clearly her son's fault (Hugo Tregarrick insisting he'd witnessed the whole incident) the glasses were swept up by May, the rug was sent away for specialist cleaning, and the village doctor was summoned. Alice Pendeen was put to bed in a small room under the eaves until the next morning, then given the rest of the week off.

That might have been the end of the matter – except that Alice and Jonny soon realised that the chance encounter in the drawing room marked the moment when they had fallen in love. He was Alice's knight in shining armour, and she had always been the girl he adored. It was Fate. It was written in the stars. It was destiny. Alice spent her week off with Jonny, who had solicitously called at Cobbles Cottage to ask after her and deliver flowers from the hothouse. He'd offered to walk along the beach with her so she could enjoy some fresh air, but as soon as they had rounded the headland, hidden away from prying eyes. he took her hand and told her he was in love with her. By the time she returned home Alice had known she was in love with him too.

They might have only been young, but they understood that this was more than a passing fancy and that they would never feel this way again or love someone else. Like Romeo and Juliet, their love would meet barriers and opposition and even anger, but Alice and Jonny were determined to be together come what may. A year and a half of keeping their feelings a secret had been hard, but Jonny had been away at school and when he was at home his parents were so busy that it had been easy for him to give them the slip. The couple planned to marry in 1954, and they could hardly wait.

And now that time had finally arrived. Jonny had celebrated his birthday at the start of the month and at the Christmas Eve Dance 1953 he and Alice would announce their engagement to the world. Alice knew her parents would be hurt and worried in equal measure, while Jonny knew his parents would be furious because Alice was below him – yet they agreed that none of these things mattered a jot. They loved one another. They were in love. They were soulmates.

What could possibly matter more than this?

CHAPTER 6

St Wenn's was the only place colder than her bedroom, decided Alice, burrowing into her duffel coat. Each time the door opened an icy draught sliced through the church, lifting tattered banners and gusting flurries of newsletters down the nave. After two hours of helping to decorate the church Alice could no longer feel her toes. Even her cheeks were numb. As she did her best to wind red ribbons around a pillar, it seemed to her that even the effigies on the old tombs were shivering. She and Elsie definitely were.

"I'm so cold I can hardly think straight," puffed Elsie, trying to loop ivy around the pulpit. Swaddled in several coats, she was so unbalanced that she was in danger of plummeting over the edge.

"It's all right for Sharpy in the vestry with his fan heater going full pelt," Alice said bitterly.

Her nose was running and she kept having to blow it which was very tiresome, because the last thing she wanted was a red nose for the Christmas Eve dance. Reverend Sharpe could have chosen to turn the heating on for the village women gathered to arrange the festive greenery, but being of the mind that physical suffering was good for the soul, and that pennies saved on the heating were even better for church coffers, he made sure that the old radiators remained, like the parishioners, stone cold.

"Stingy old hypocrite," Elsie said, still dangling precariously. "I bet he's even poured himself a glass of communion wine."

"Ssh!"

Half-laughing, half-scandalised, Alice looked over her shoulder in case the vicar had materialised. He had a nasty habit of appearing where you least expected to find him. Only last week she and Jonny had met on the farthest part of the beach to snatch a few moments alone, only to be forced to dart behind the rocks when they had spotted the vicar striding along the tideline. Frantically trying to button her coat, Alice was a few seconds slower than Jonny, and she felt her stomach drop when the Reverend's sun-caught spectacles glinted straight at her.

She froze. Was their secret love affair discovered? If so, they couldn't have been found out by a worse person, for as well as being the moral guardian of the village snooper *extraordinaire* Reverend Sharpe was also a crashing snob. He wouldn't think twice about revealing to the St Miltons that he'd seen their only son with a *most* unsuitable girl. What a golden opportunity to ingratiate himself while expressing pastoral concern!

Every drop of Alice's blood drained from her limbs. Her terror was not for herself but for her family. If Mrs St Milton discovered that her only son was seeing the housekeeper's daughter she would be incensed. Mum would lose her job –

and then what would become of the family? Jonny was not in a position to help them yet.

"He didn't see us," Jonny promised once the Reverend had vanished around the headland. Dusting sand from Alice's dress, he held her against his heart. "And even if he did, who cares? I love you and I want everyone to know it. I'm not ashamed."

Alice pushed him away, her palms against his chest. She knew he meant every word. But Alice also knew that the boy she loved didn't understand the world as she did. How could he?

"I know *you're* not – but your parents won't like it."

He shrugged. "They'll be angry I've deceived them, but they'll come around when they realise I'm not going to give you up. Anyway, once they know you properly they'll adore you."

Alice wasn't convinced. Jonny was sweetly naïve when it came to his parents – and, never having experienced the constraints of class and rank, was carelessly flippant about defying them.

"They might not," she warned.

"Then they'll have to deal with it," he shot back, his chin jutting out in the way Alice had come to recognise meant he would not be argued with, and which was disconcertingly similar to his mother's expression when demanding jobs were to be redone to her satisfaction.

"I love you, Ally," he declared. "They won't change that, and they can't change how we feel."

"No – but they can make life difficult if they choose. They can keep us apart."

Seeing Alice's worried expression, Jonny softened. He ruffled her curls and then kissed the tip of her nose.

"This isn't the Middle Ages, silly goose! Besides, a decade ago men my age were fighting Hitler."

Alice said nothing. Daniel might have been eighteen when he'd enlisted, but he had been weathered and strong from years at sea, as different to the gentle and academic Jonny as it was possible to be.

"Don't worry about the practicalities," he said when she didn't reply.

But Alice always worried about the practicalities. She supposed it was in her nature. Where would they live? Would Jonny still go up to Oxford in the autumn? Would she go with him or stay in Polwenna? Would the St Miltons forgive her mother? – Or would she be sacked? And then, how would Alice be able to help her parents if she was married to Jonny? The questions went on and on, and Jonny could never fully answer them.

Alice sometimes feared that their dreams would dissolve in the bright light of reality, but Jonny never seemed worried. He wrote her endless poems and beautiful love letters, made grand plans for their future and was always taking photos of her with his Box Brownie. Alice knew he loved her, and she definitely loved him, and she knew he wished she didn't worry so much. Jonny often teased her, saying she was bourgeois, and Alice supposed he was right; but it was easier for him. It wasn't his family's income at stake. Jonny had never gone hungry or seen his father cry because he couldn't pay the rent. Alice, who had witnessed Morley's muffled weeping, had felt a little piece of her heart break at witnessing her father's helplessness. One day she would take all their worries away, she had told herself fiercely. She would make sure that May and Morley Pendeen never struggled again.

"We'll really tell everyone at the dance?" she'd asked Jonny as they strolled hand in hand along the tideline. High above, seagulls were tumbling in the sky and their plaintive cries sounded like warnings. Alice shivered. She had a horrible feeling that everything was poised to fall apart at the seams, their plans as loosely tacked together as her unfinished velvet dress.

"Of course we shall," Jonny said, stopping to cup her face in his hands. "Only a week to wait, Ally! Imagine it! We can tell everyone how we feel. No more hiding. I can't wait to see their faces when we walk into the Christmas Eve dance together! I'll be the envy of every man there!"

He kissed her, a kiss that was soft and tender and full of promises. Alice decided that she loved Jonny even more for being so positive. She had kissed him back and allowed the gentle pressure of his lips to chase away any doubts.

The sun must have dazzled Reverend Sharpe and the rocks must have done a sterling job of providing a hiding place, because since that day nothing had happened to suggest that Alice and Jonny had been discovered. Tonight at the dance they would announce the truth. Jonny had promised to get his father's permission – his father was nothing like so snobby as his mother – so they could make some practical plans and buy an engagement ring. He was right; there was nothing to worry about. This was going to be the most wonderful Christmas of her life!

The pulpit finished, Alice and Elsie moved on to decorate the crib. They were in the middle of a debate as to whether or not Baby Jesus should be left out until Christmas Day, when a blast of cold air followed by the tap of heels on flagstones announced a new arrival. Looking across the church, Alice's heart rose to see Jonny's tall frame silhouetted against the bright light of the bitter December day, only to sink into the crypt when she realised that his mother was accompanying him.

"Hullo! The church is looking terrific," he called to the girls.

Elsie nudged Alice and giggled. "He's got a crush on you! Shall I make myself scarce?"

"Don't be silly," snapped Alice. She reached into the crib and put the baby in place: "Jesus was born on Christmas Eve."

"Don't change the subject. Be nice, Ally. He's not bad for a posh boy, which is more than I can say for his ma. That old boot's got a face on her that could curdle milk."

Diana's gunmetal eyes settled on Alice briefly before flicking to her beaming son.

"I'm not sticking around to be a gooseberry," Elsie said, taking advantage of Alice's lack of attention to whip Baby Jesus from the manger. "Maybe he'll take you to the dance?"

Her friend was teasing, but Alice was on edge. She had a bad feeling about this.

Jonny crossed the church on the pretext of admiring the crib. His face bright with happiness, he beamed at Alice and said,

"I'm glad I accompanied Mother now."

Alice smiled back. It was impossible to keep her features neutral when being close to Jonny made her insides fizz like sherbet lemons.

"Your mother's watching us," she warned, pretending to be engrossed with arranging the crib.

"Oh, don't worry about, Ma. She's off bothering Sharpy about something," said Jonny airily. "Look, she's going into the vestry. We're safe."

Sure enough, Mrs St Milton had vanished into the cosy depths of the Reverend's lair. Alice's legs felt wobbly and she took a deep breath. Goodness, she'd be relieved when all the subterfuge was over.

"Relax," said Jonny, taking her hand and squeezing it.

"We're nearly there. Nothing will go wrong now. I promise. I'll meet you by the manor gate at seven. After tonight there's no more hiding."

Alice returned the pressure of his fingers and did her very best to smile, but she could still feel the chill of his mother's gaze on her skin, and it seeped into her heart like ice. The sooner she and Jonny walked into the dance together the happier she would be.

CHAPTER 7

1953

In the 1950s it wasn't easy for a seventeen-year-old girl to get ready for a dance that her parents didn't know she was attending, and even harder to find a place where she could get dressed and style her hair without arousing their suspicions. Alice, pretending to be going to the Rowe's cottage to help Elsie dress, hated telling half-truths. She consoled herself with the knowledge that after this evening there would be no more deception.

"It's such a shame you turned Barry down," sighed her mum yet again, as Alice let herself out of the cottage. "You would have looked beautiful in that dress."

"Yes – what a waste of a lovely frock," said her brother.

Alice knew that Sam suspected she was planning to go with somebody her parents didn't approve of. He wasn't so far from the truth, although the irony was that it was *she* who was the unsuitable party who would cause a set of parents to have a blue fit – not some bad boy from Bodmin on a motorbike!

Elsie had been getting ready for the dance all day, and her preparations were on a par with the rehearsals for the Normandy landings. First, a shampoo and set at the hairdressers in town, then a bath by the fire, nails painted and makeup fixed. Normally Alice would have loved to have helped, especially since Elsie was determined that this would be the night she'd win Hugo's heart, and Alice, knowing that Elsie was disappointed that she'd made an excuse, hoped that when Elsie knew the truth she'd understand.

Alice could hardly wait to tell Elsie all about Jonny. She hated keeping such a huge secret from her best friend, but Elsie, although she had a heart of gold, couldn't keep a secret to save her life. Alice hoped she would understand why she'd had no choice but to keep her love affair so close to her chest. She hated keeping secrets anyway, and so admired all those who could never speak about their war work – and when it was about something as wonderful as being in love it seemed twice as hard. But by this evening she would be able to shout her feelings from the rooftops, and she could hardly wait. What a wonderful Christmas present that would be!

It would have been lovely to be openly going to the dance with Jonny. Then, thought Alice wistfully as she walked along the harbour with her head bowed against the wind, she too could have soaked in a tub before taking a seat at a dressing table to fix her hair and makeup properly. She would have loved to have copied one of the looks from *Vogue* and arrived at the Manor with glossy curls all pinned up and wearing a dress which had been gently steamed as she bathed, to fall in perfect folds.

But tonight Alice Pendeen would be getting ready by torchlight in her father's fishing store, and her lovely dress would be creased from making the journey stuffed into her duffel bag. Even her satin ballet pumps would soon be dirty from walking up the lane to the manor, and the pins would soon slip from her hair. A Hollywood starlet she was not!

Yet Alice wouldn't let this ruin her night. Darling Jonny wouldn't care if she turned up in slacks and a duffel coat! Still, it might have been nice not to have to walk all the way up to the Manor. By the time she arrived she would smell of woodsmoke and salt, and her little slippers would be ruined. Perhaps she should stomp up in her boots and change them by the gatehouse? She could always tuck them and her duffel bag into the hedge. But these were the least of her problems this evening.

In Morley's store it was arctic, and Alice was shivering before she closed the door. It was inky dark, too, and even with her torch lighting the way shadows swarmed in the corners. She stubbed her toe on a crab pot and pitched into a pile of nets. She brushed herself down and groaned. She really didn't want to arrive at the dance smelling of fish and old fuel. She didn't usually care what people said about her and her family, but tonight she would be raising her head well above the parapet. Girls like Millicent Jago, the retired Harley Street doctor's pretty daughter, always sneered at Alice in her home-made dresses, and made catty comments. Tonight was a special night and Alice wanted to look like a princess. She didn't want to let Jonny down.

Not wanting to catch her death of cold, Alice changed as swiftly as she could, and dived back into her duffel coat with her teeth chattering. Abandoning any idea of styling her hair, she loosed her long curls so they tumbled over her bare shoulders. She dabbed her cheeks and lips with rouge borrowed from May's makeup bag, and swept mascara onto her lashes. Her dress would have to do all the heavy lifting, because this was as far as her preparations could go. Anyhow, Jonny always said she looked beautiful even in her pinny, and his opinion was the only one that mattered.

Polwenna Manor was situated on the outskirts of the village and the walk up was along a back lane which was dark and steep. The journey wasn't easy in long skirts and ballet slippers, but Alice was so excited that she practically floated uphill. Every now and then a car swept past and she pressed herself into the hedge, not wanting to be discovered. Jonny, whose father was driving him over to the Manor, was going to meet her by the gatehouse at seven, and they would walk into the dance hand in hand, leaving no room for any doubt that they were a couple. Alice's stomach swooped like the bats above. This was the moment her life began. Like Cinderella, her handsome prince would whisk her away to her happy ever after.

Finally, and just when her slippers were starting to rub, Alice spotted twinkling lights and the glow of a bonfire burning in the darkness. The drive to the Manor was illuminated with swaying lanterns, while laughter floated on the wind and a band was playing a waltz. Soon she would be whirling round in Jonny's arms and smiling into his eyes.

This was as far as Alice's daydream had progressed. She had played this scenario over and over again until it was reassuringly familiar, but now that the moment had arrived she felt nervous. What if their arrival met with anger and the Tregarricks threw her out? Alice didn't think this would happen, since everyone said Hugo's parents were *bohemian* – but folks could be strange, and the St Miltons were very influential in Polwenna Bay. And what about her mum and dad? She had never paused to consider how they might feel about Jonny becoming part of their family. They might be horrified.

By the time she reached the gatehouse Alice's stomach was

a seesaw of excitement and terror. She glanced around, hoping to spot Jonny waiting for her in the shadows, the white gleam of his smile lighting the night more brightly than any lantern – but there was only emptiness. Alice shivered inside her thick coat and longed for the comforting warmth of his arms.

Where was he?

Guests were arriving in a constant stream, some walking and some in cars. Not wanting to be spotted, Alice retreated into the darkness. She watched as Elsie and Peter Pollard glided past in his father's Ford Anglia, her friend looking like a film star in the front seat with her blonde curls piled high and her lips painted scarlet. More couples and villagers followed – but not Jonny St Milton. Alice began to worry, for Jonny never let her down. They had been planning this evening for months, and she knew that he was as excited as she was to announce their relationship. Had his father or mother been taken ill? Maybe their car had a puncture?

She waited for what felt like an age, but was probably no more than quarter of an hour, when the St Miltons' Jaguar drew up alongside the gatehouse. Alice waited for Jonny to leap out, but there was no movement. Slipping through the shadows, she realised with a shock that Mrs St Milton was at the wheel rather than her husband. Jonny sat beside her, ashen-faced and slumped in his seat. He looked dreadful, and Alice was flooded with panic. What had happened? Was he sick? But if so, why was he here with his mother? Surely she hadn't deigned to attend. She had never before condescended to attend a party thrown for humble villagers.

The driver's window lowered. Diana glared into the darkness with her shark's eyes narrowed.

"Do stop skulking in the shadows, Alice Pendeen," she snapped.

Mrs St Milton knew.

There was a rushing sound in Alice's ears. Her mind shuttled back and forth over the past few days like her father's hands mending nets. Had she and Jonny been careless? Had Reverend Sharpe seen them together? Or had Mrs St Milton become suspicious in the church?

"Did you *really* think we wouldn't find out?"

Alice's thoughts whirled.

"I suppose you thought you were so clever," snarled Mrs St Milton, "by setting out to seduce my son and steal his inheritance, you shameless little hussy. You can forget all that, and anything else you might have hoped to gain. Jonny's now very well aware that if he pursues this foolish infatuation, he won't see a penny."

Her words were like slaps. Alice waited for Jonny to speak, but his head was bowed.

Ice trickled down her spine.

"We don't care about any of that. We love each other," she said quietly.

Mrs St Milton snorted. "Love! *Pah!* You love the money you think he'll be getting from my father, you mean. It's under our control until he's twenty-five. If Jonathan's foolish enough to pursue a liaison with you he'll not see a penny. Not now and not *ever*. We've made it plain to him he'd be on his own because we would cut him off. He can forget Oxford, his grandfather's estate and everything else he thought would be coming to him. He'd be penniless. I wonder how much you'd love him then?"

"I don't care if he's rich or poor. We just want to be together. Don't we, Jonny?"

Alice turned to her beloved –

– but Jonny said nothing. He remained slumped, and didn't meet her imploring gaze. She felt the earth buck beneath her feet. Why didn't he acknowledge her, or come to her defence?

"Don't be a *fool,*" said Mrs St Milton scathingly. "That's not how the world works. Love walks out the door when money goes out the window – and, believe me, my son isn't used to going without. He'd be back in a week begging us to forgive him. You're just his latest fad, you silly girl."

Why didn't Jonny interrupt this flow of vitriol? Why didn't he tell his mother that he loved Alice and was going to marry her? It was awful that they'd been pre-empted, but the truth was about to come into the open anyway, and at least this way they would face the music together.

"Jonny, tell her we're going to get married," she said, hating the begging note in her voice.

He looked up at last. His eyes were red-rimmed and a bruise was flowering on his left cheek.

"His father gave him some discipline," said Mrs St Milton, following her gaze. "Far too late. The Reverend Sharpe was right; sparing the rod has done us no favours."

Alice's heart hardened against the vicar. She was certain this was not what had been meant by *suffer the children*.

"Come back to Cobbles with me," she begged Jonny, ignoring his mother. "Don't let them bully you a minute longer. We'll sort something out."

He swallowed miserably. "I can't, Ally. You know it's impossible."

"*Nothing's* impossible," said Alice, fighting rising panic. She'd never seen Jonny so crushed. So lacking his usual joy and bounce. He was a shell of the boy she loved, and this frightened her far more than his mother's vitriol.

"Ally, I—"

"Be *quiet*." Her words were like the crack of a whip, and Jonny shrank into himself.

To Alice, she added, "My son's not throwing himself away on you. He's going to go to Italy and Paris as planned, and then up to Oxford in the autumn. You're not to see each other again. Do I make myself clear?"

"I don't think that decision's up to you," she replied raising her chin. It was trembling, and Alice felt as though she would pass out with dread – but she wouldn't allow Mrs St Milton to bully her too. She knew that Jonny was afraid of his mother, but with Alice beside him surely he could take her on.

Mrs St Milton smiled her shark's smile.

"I totally agree, my dear. It's down to Jonny, as his father has already explained to him and at some length. He understands why any notion of a relationship between the two of you is out of the question, but as you say – it's his choice. I'll let him explain. Maybe you'll listen to him."

Jonny looked at Alice. His expression was tortured.

"Five minutes," Diana ordered. "Say your goodbyes, Jonathan."

She wound her window up and stared resolutely ahead, towards the merry lights of the barn. Jonny's long frame uncoiled itself into the night with a reluctance that was agonising. Other couples and villagers walked past, glancing over in surprise. Already there would be gossip and speculation.

"Not here," he said hoarsely.

Alice nodded. She had no wish to be anywhere near Mrs St Milton.

Jonny drew her away from prying eyes. Once alone, he wrapped his arms around her and buried his face in her hair. Sobs racked his slight frame. Alice held him and soothed him with soft murmurs. Eventually, he drew a shaking breath before lifting his head to stare down at her as though trying to sear every detail of her face into his mind.

"You're scaring me," she said.

"Oh Christ, Ally. I'm scaring myself. I thought my father was going to kill me."

She touched his bruised cheek. Never normally violent, Alice could have killed Mr St Milton herself for what he'd done to Jonny.

"How did they find out?"

"When Mother saw us together at the church she realised there was something going on, and then old Sharpy told her he'd spotted us on the beach that time. Once we were back at home she confronted me about it. I told her everything, of course. I wasn't going to deny it. As you can imagine she was incandescent. Father was worse, and said he was disappointed in me and that if I pursued the matter I wasn't his son. They're determined to break us up, Alice. We'd have nothing to live on and nowhere to go."

His voiced cracked, and Alice's heart broke. Jonny was gentle and kind, and unused to the harsh realities of life most people faced on a daily basis. His parents were tough people; beneath her silks and makeup Mrs St Milton was a hard woman, and her husband's wartime success was testament to an iron nature.

"I love you," she said, stroking his damp cheek. "We'll work it out."

He turned his face and kissed her palm.

"How?"

"I don't know – but my family won't abandon us. Maybe you could fish with Dad and Sam."

He stared at her. "Me? Go *fishing*? I get seasick in the bath."

Alice struggled for another option. "We'll find something. A trade. The Pollards always need help."

"I haven't been raised for trade. I'm meant to go to Oxford. Then I can do my stint in the National Service before going into the family business. Maybe it's time to face up to the truth and my father's right. Love's not enough."

Alice was shocked.

"Of *course* it is! You *said* it was!"

Jonny swallowed miserably. "I thought I was right. I truly did, Ally, and I told my parents everything. I explained our plans and said that we were going to be married, with or without their blessing. I told them I wanted to be with you. That we had already made promises and it doesn't matter a jot to me that you're the housekeeper's daughter. When they made threats to cut me off I said it was their choice, and I'd make out somehow. That was when my father told me he controls every penny until I'm twenty-five. *Twenty-five,* Ally! That's seven years away."

"So we support ourselves. I'll sew and clean."

He shook his head. "I told Mother all that. I said I didn't care and we'd be together anyway. She laughed in my face. Shall I tell you what she said? 'You won't have a penny from us, and I promise you that if you go through with this foolishness I'll make sure May Pendeen never works again in Polwenna. And as for that miserable hovel, the family calls a home – maybe their landlord needs to put the rent up or evict them. A quiet word with the Trevellyns is all it will take to put them out. They'll all be on the streets. Your beloved Alice and her family can beg for all I care – but is that what you want? Do you want to ruin them? That's what you mean by love, is it?' "

Alice's blood seemed to freeze in her veins. The St Miltons were good friends with the wealthy Trevellyns, Polwenna's main landlords, and one word to them from Mr St Milton would be all it took to push the Pendeens' finances over the precipice. Alice knew that without a reference from Mrs St Milton her mum would never get work again in the area. Her dad was already struggling, and the boat was not making a decent living. Jonny was right; he was no fisherman and would be an extra mouth to feed. With Alice tainted by scandal and sacked, the family would be ruined.

"She'd destroy my whole family because of us?" Alice whispered.

"She would – and I can't let that happen. I *won't* let that happen. I love you too much."

"And I love you," she choked, unsure whose tears wet her cheeks.

"I can't be with you," Jonny said bleakly. "Not at that cost. It'd poison what we have, and we'd end up hating each other."

Alice clutched the lapels of his winter coat in desperation.

"We'll find a way, Jonny. We can find ways to support my family. I can get work as a seamstress. You can find work toc. Maybe a clerk? Or a teacher?"

"I don't think I'd be much use at anything apart from running our family business. It's what I've been raised to do. It's all I know."

"You'd want to do that more than you want to be with me?"

He hesitated.

"Jonny?" Alice pressed, alarmed. "Do you want that more?"

"Of *course* not – but it's complicated."

"It isn't. As long as we're together we can sort out the rest!"

"Don't be so naïve, Alice. That isn't how the world works. Love won't pay the bills or your family's rent. My father has made it clear he'll cut me off. Don't you understand? We'd have nothing."

"We don't need anything from them when we have each other," said Alice desperately. "Maybe we could go to Australia?"

"Oh, Ally! What would we do in Australia?"

"Make a new life."

Jonny nodded slowly.

"Yes … maybe *we* could – but what about your family? While we were busy making our new life, what would happen to them? My parents wouldn't drop the matter just because we'd left. They'd want to punish somebody."

Alice was thinking hard, but no answers came to mind. What would happen to May and Morley without Cobbles Cottage and May's income? Would her brother Sam have to take a job on a deep-sea trawler? Or even join the navy? He had given up so much already, and Alice hated to think of him being burdened further because of her.

"They'd lose everything," Jonny said into the silence. "I'd lose my all my future prospects and my family. We're asking too much of each other, Ally, and it'll destroy us. We have to do what my parents want."

Alice's head was swimming. How could her world change so fast?

"You're giving up on us?"

"I'm making the biggest sacrifice of my life," he corrected. "I can't be responsible for destroying your family. You'd come to resent me, Ally. And I couldn't live with that."

"I could *never* resent you," Alice said quietly. She thought of the magical evening last summer when, in the long grass by St Wenn's Well, she had first given him everything – and she already knew that even this was not something she could ever resent, not when she loved Jonny St Milton so totally and utterly. She had been the one with more to lose – but perhaps it was always this way for a woman.

"I'll always treasure you," he whispered. "Even when I'm old and grey it'll be you I think of. It'll always be you I love."

But as he brushed the tears from her cheeks Alice didn't feel like treasure. She felt like something tossed in the dustbin for the seagulls to squabble over.

"So this is it?" she whispered. "You're not going to fight them for me?"

"It's a fight I can't win. You know that too."

Alice bloody well didn't; she'd have fought until there was nothing left in her.

"You're leaving me?"

Jonny nodded. His dark fringe fell over his eyes. Alice didn't brush it away. There was already a barrier between them. They no longer belonged to one another.

"Not by choice. I'm walking away because it's the right thing to do. But it'll always be you, Alice Pendeen. I'll love you until the day I die."

He kissed her once more, but Alice was too shocked to respond. She reached out her hand and caught his, but his fingers slipped away, just as he was slipping from her life.

"Jonny, please! Don't do this."

"It's already done. I've given Father my word that our relationship is over – and that's the only reason your mother's still got a job and your dad's name has stayed on the rent book. I've made a deal with the devil, Ally. But I *won't* go back on my word."

"You have to *me*," she said bitterly, thinking of all the broken promises.

"And I'll have to live with that forever," he replied. "Which is what I deserve."

Mrs St Milton blared the car horn. Their time was up.

"Be happy, Ally," Jonny said.

Alice's tears fell thick and fast. She had never known such pain. How could she be happy without him?

Once the St Miltons' car had swept away, she stumbled down the lane weeping into the darkness and little caring if she fell under an oncoming car, for Jonny was gone and with him her heart. What was there left to live for now? Her life was over. Her future in ashes. She would never love another. She wished she could close her eyes and never open them again.

It was worse, Alice thought with a sob, that it wasn't lack of love that had made him walk away, but the exact opposite. The St Miltons had placed Jonny in an impossible position, and the threats they'd made against her family had been too much for him to bear. Jonny hadn't ended their relationship because he didn't love her, but because he loved her too much to hurt her family. If there was love there was still hope. There *had* to be a way to win Jonny back.

And Alice was determined to find it.

CHAPTER 8

THE PRESENT

Holly leaned forward, her elbows resting on the back of the pew and her eyes wide. She was clearly caught up in Alice's story, and Alice wondered if it might have been a comfort to her seventeen-year-old self to have known that decades in the future her own heartbreak would be such a distraction.

Probably not. It might have been a lifetime ago, but nothing compared to the intensity of first heartbreak. It was a tessellation of loss, love, joy and sorrow, and Alice still felt the echo of that despair.

"Seriously? He dumped you outside the dance while his mum was waiting in the car?" Holly breathed.

Alice had been granted almost seventy years to put a new spin on this part of the story, but she had never succeeded. Whichever way you looked at it, Jonny hadn't come out of the situation well. She sighed.

"I suppose you could put it that way."

"What a *bas*—"

"Yes indeed – but ssh! We're in church!"

Holly clapped her hand over her mouth. Luckily Jules was too busy persuading Harry not to place a Transformer in the crib to be listening in – unlike the long-departed Reverend Sharpe who had ears on elastic. But anyway, Alice thought, Jules would agree with the sentiment. Elsie certainly had when Alice had eventually confided in her.

"You'd spent *ages* sewing that beautiful dress," Holly said, her outrage penetrating Alice's drift in time. "You were all dressed up and he'd promised to acknowledge your relationship that night after how long ... a year?"

"A year and a half. I was just sixteen when I first met him."

It had been the most exciting year and a half of her life, though! At least up until that point! There was nothing like secrecy and danger to add a *frisson* to a romance, so the forbidden moments they had snatched had been all the more intense and delicious. Was there anything more exciting than making love in old haybarns or deserted coves? She sifted through the memories and shivered. Newness had been intoxicating, each caress a wonder, and the smoothness of young skin and taut muscle delicious. She thought of lips and tongues and the duelling kisses that trailed fire through her belly, all utterly addictive. Jonny had been her first lover, and even now Alice felt a little hot under the collar at these X-rated memories. The two of them had been so young and so in love.

"A year and a half! And he chickened out after all that. What a ... git!"

Alice laughed at Holly's expression.

"Yes, what a git! Especially as I thought we'd be married that spring."

"Men will say anything to get what they want," said Holly bitterly. "Nothing's changed, has it?"

Alice cast her mind back to how it had been in those days. People had talked in hushed tones about 'fallen women'. There had been unmarried mothers' homes. No contraception. Shame. Secrets kept for decades. And clever women like Diana St Milton forced to play second fiddle to their husbands.

"Oh, I don't think that's wholly true. Lots of things have changed since the fifties, and most of them for the better, my love. Besides, Jonny didn't need to sweet-talk me into bed. I was quite willing!"

Holly looked a little bit shocked and Alice felt bad for embarrassing her. Caught up in the past, she'd forgotten that even now sweet old ladies shouldn't even mention sex, let alone admit they'd once been up for it – and enjoyed it.

"What I'm saying, my love, is that not all men are *gits*. That's far too simplistic. Jonny wasn't a bad person. He really did love me."

"Really? You can say that after what he did?"

Holly regarded Alice with the disbelieving expression Alice usually wore when her grandchildren were telling her fibs.

Alice could see that the poor girl was determined to be cynical, a dreadful joy-sucking trap, so if she was to save Holly from such a fate she would need to do, she felt, a better job of telling this story. Holly needed to know just how bad things had been on that dismal Christmas Eve. It really had been the lowest point of Alice's life – or so she'd believed at the time.

"Really," Alice said firmly. "It was a very different time, my love. Parents were like gods to their children in those days, and we had a very healthy respect for them – and we felt obligated, too. They had expectations of us, and there were rules that had to be followed in the home as well as jobs that needed doing. Times were hard for my family, and us children had to help out financially too. Remember how I told you that my brother had to give up his education and go fishing? And that I gave up my dream of being a fashion designer to work up at the big house with my mother?"

"I can't believe your parents laid all that on their kids."

"It was an unspoken understanding that we did our duty and helped them."

"Even if you didn't want to?"

"Especially then. The point was they were our parents, and it was our duty to support them and do our bit for the family."

Alice searched for a comparison that Holly might understand. Spotting the Roll of Honour on the wall, decorated with names still found in the village and which still brought tears to her eyes all this time later, she continued, "Take the war. I'm sure my brother Daniel didn't want to leave Polwenna and fight. None of the boys probably did, but it was their duty to defend this country just as it'd been my father's in the First World War."

Holly nodded. "That makes sense. I've never really thought about it like that, because my parents only ever want me to do what makes me happy. That's sometimes a problem in itself, , though, because I never want to mess up and let them down. Is that duty?"

Duty was an old-fashioned notion. Alice supposed that somewhere along the winding road from the nineteen-fifties to the present day it had slipped from the daily norm along with whalebone corsets and hats, replaced by individualism and me-centric ideologies. The late Queen had certainly understood the meaning of the word, living her life according to her duty until her very last minutes, and Alice thought that when she had died the old world of expectations and standards had passed away as well. Was that a good thing? Would that determined young princess who had worked as a mechanic, hosted state banquets for world leaders (some must have put her off eating, surely?) and never once been known to complain have been happier if she'd written tell-all memoirs, had an Insta page and jetted off on me-time holidays? Alice felt she must be old-fashioned too, because she really didn't think so. Something special had been lost. Something unselfish and good.

She smiled at Holly, knowing she could never articulate this. It was a world as lost to time as horse-drawn carts, milk churns at the side of the road and sunburned children helping gather in the harvest.

"That's duty in a way. I certainly didn't want to let my folks down, and you can see that was especially true for Jonny. The St Miltons had very high expectations of him. He was their only son, and after Oxford and National Service he would be going into the family business and taking over. Marrying the daughter of a local fisherman at the age of eighteen was most definitely not on his parents' wish list. So *he* didn't have a choice, either."

"Bollocks! I mean, rubbish! Of course he did! If he'd loved you he would have fought for you. He wouldn't have let his parents get in the way." Holly paused and then brightened. "Except he *did*, didn't he? Jonny defied them and took you to the dance. You lived happily ever after."

"I'm afraid not," said Alice. "Jonny did what his parents wanted. He left me at the gatehouse, and I never went to the dance."

Holly crossed her arms. "What a cowardly pathetic, mummy's boy."

Alice shook her head. "In fairness, he was right to have

been worried about my family. I was the one living in a dream world."

"You loved him and you were loyal. Jonny should have told his parents to stick it. You would have made it work, and your parents would have been fine. They were adults!"

"It was a different time, my love. Social class was a much bigger deal, and it mattered hugely that I was just a fisherman's daughter. That really upset the St Miltons – and my parents too! It really was a Romeo and Juliet situation. I can't really blame Jonny for choosing to walk away."

"I still think he was a coward."

Life was so black and white at Holly's age, thought Alice. She'd thought the same back then. Or rather, she had swung between loving Jonny and hating him, which was really the same emotion in disguise. Age brought understanding and compassion. Now Alice felt nothing but tenderness for the people she and Jonny had been. They had not been much older than her beloved great-grandson Morgan was now, and they had known nothing of the world. Their emotions had driven them, and extremes of passion (exhausting to even contemplate nowadays) were what they had lived for. Alice recalled how as a schoolgirl she had been smitten by the tragic love story of *Romeo and Juliet.* The grand passion was to die for (literally!) and the young lovers had filled her heart with such pity that she always longed for a happy ending even though she knew it was impossible. As an adult, Alice thought Romeo and Juliet needed their heads knocking together. As if you could be properly in love after five minutes! Real love wasn't all about passion and excitement and wild sex on deserted beaches. True love was listening. It was patience. It was holding a bruised hand during life's last moments. It was being a calm harbour in life's storms.

It was about wanting the best for someone even if it meant breaking your own heart in the process.

That was, Alice knew now, what Jonny had done for her when he had walked away. Had there been some self-interest too? If so, she couldn't blame him. That was only human.

"He was very young," she said gently. "Just a boy, really. He'd thought he was doing the right thing at the time, and that's all any of us can ever do – even if it hurts."

Holly folded her arms.

"Even my ex, Jamie? Has *he* just done his best?"

Alice thought about this.

"Maybe in an unexpected way – if he's the unfaithful type, it's better for you to find out now rather than years down the line."

"That's what my mum said. It doesn't feel like that, though."

"It doesn't, but time's precious and we only have a finite amount allotted, so don't waste a second on a man who isn't worthy of you. One day you'll be old like me, God willing, and you'll look back and think that Jamie did you a favour. Maybe you'll even sit in this church and tell another young woman exactly the same thing."

"Maybe. It doesn't feel like that, though. If he walked in now and said sorry to me, I'm scared I'd take him back, pathetic idiot that I am."

"*Human being* that you are," said Alice firmly. "I'd have forgiven Jonny everything too if he'd turned around that night and taken me to the dance. I would have let him hurt me a thousand times more too, because back then I thought love meant sacrificing yourself and letting somebody break your heart over and over again if that was what it took."

"That's *exactly* it! You can see why I came away. If I'd stayed at home I'd have ended up stalking Jamie. He'd be writing a Netflix drama about me by the New Year."

"I certainly stalked Jonny! Not that we called it stalking back then. I nursed a silly hope I could change his mind."

"And did you?"

Alice laughed. "Not exactly! Let me tell you what happened next, once I'd stopped crying enough to turn around and head home ..."

CHAPTER 9

1953

Once she was far enough away from Polwenna Manor, Alice paused in the shadows. Sadness vibrated in the air like the final quiver of a violin concerto. The finality of the parting with Jonny had punched all the air from her lungs. She hardly knew what to do. Her whole world had fallen apart in minutes, and now there was no meaning in anything.

She brushed at her cheeks with her gloved fingers, but the tears wouldn't stop, and her insides were folding over and over with the pain. This would be her only time for tears. Here, alone and hidden by the friendly darkness, she was free to weep without having to muffle her sobs into a pillow or smother misery beneath smiles. Once back at home she would have to throw herself into the excitement of Christmas no matter how shredded her poor heart might be. And at Midnight Mass tonight she would have to face Jonny knowing that this year there would be no secret looks and stolen midnight kisses. Knowing that he was no longer hers.

But nobody can cry for ever. Eventually Alice's tears ebbed and the racking sobs subsided into small gasps, like the last waves of a violent winter storm. Utterly exhausted, Alice wanted nothing more than to crumple to the ground and let everything stop, but she knew she had to walk home to change and wash her face before her mother spotted her all dressed up and asked awkward questions. There would also be final gifts to wrap, their own goose to prepare, and a table to set before the Pendeen family set off to St Wenn's for Midnight Mass. Christmas was relentless.

Alice dabbed her eyes one final time and took a steadying breath. The walk back would give her time to compose herself, and she could blame her red nose and watery eyes on the cold. Hopefully Mum would be too busy to pay much attention to her, and Dad and Sam far too merry from an evening in the pub. The last thing Alice needed was an interrogation, or for Sam to lose his famous temper and storm off to avenge his sister's honour.

Huddled into her coat, Alice pressed onwards. The narrow back lane, once a haunt of smugglers, was very dark now the stars had been switched off, and Alice wished she hadn't left her torch in her dad's store. When it was pitch black and you were all alone in a sunken lane it was hard to dismiss the stories of headless horsemen and ghost brides as inventions to keep nosey villagers away from the activities of the 'gentlemen'. Now that the lights of the manor house had vanished the face of darkness shifted; it was no longer a kindly friend concealing lovers from prying eyes but something threatening and malevolent.

Alice raised her chin and reminded herself how Daniel and his comrades had been braver in circumstances far, far worse than these. They'd faced bullets as the Germans advanced, and fought on even when it was hopeless. She was pathetic to make such a fuss about a dark lane, no matter how spooky. Shadows swarmed in the hedges, but Alice pulled her shoulders back and thought about Daniel. She was the sister and the daughter of brave men. She was not afraid. How could she be when the worst had already happened?

As Alice passed the path to St Wenn's Well an owl swooped through the tunnel of trees, so close that she felt the breeze from its wings on her cheeks. Surprise made her start, and she stumbled on a rut, pitching forwards and slamming her knees into the lane. One slipper was ripped from her foot and she scrabbled for it, frustrated to discover that the sole had been torn away. Now she would have to walk home with one stockinged foot, in a torn dress and with a bleeding knee.

Hot tears filled her eyes anew, and misery overwhelmed her. How she longed for Jonny to hold her and make everything all right. It was near here, in the secret dappled glade where the spring bubbled up and where people said the old saint granted wishes, that she and Jonny had made love for the very first time and voiced the promises that Alice had believed they'd keep until the very end of their days. Even now she still believed his promises – and she still meant every word of hers. She felt certain she'd love Jonny even when they were old and frail.

"Help me Saint Wenn," she wailed into the darkness. "Please send my love to me."

But St Wenn said nothing, and the only reply was an owl's mocking shriek. Wearily, Alice hauled herself to her feet. She was trying to find a way of re-attaching the sole of the slipper with a hair ribbon when the glare of headlights announced the approach of a car. For a few giddy, seconds Alice thought her wish had been granted and Jonny was at the wheel, ready to apologise and sweep her away, but as the car drew alongside she saw a sporty Austin-Healey that she didn't recognise. A chum of Hugo's, then, down for Christmas.

Hopes dashed, Alice returned her attention to the slipper. Standing on one leg, she was so engrossed in the attempt to tie the sole into place without toppling over that she only realised the car had stopped when a clipped voice rang out through the dark.

"I say, are you all right back there?"

Although she couldn't see the speaker, Alice could tell from the deep tone that this was an older man rather than one of Hugo's daft school friends. The voice resonated with quiet confidence and possessed such imperiousness that she felt compelled to reply.

"I'm fine, thank you."

The man laughed.

"If you don't mind me saying so, you don't look as though that's quite the case. It looks very much to me as though your shoe has broken. Unless you're perfecting a stork impression? If that's so, I'm afraid you need a little more practice. You're rather wobbly."

In spite of her misery, and the embarrassment of being caught in such an ungainly pose, Alice felt her mouth quirk upwards.

"You were right the first time. The sole's come off my slipper and I'm trying to mend it."

The sole fell off again and Alice admitted defeat. It was going to be a long walk back in stockinged feet.

"Allow me to drive you," said the stranger. "You can't possibly walk without shoes – and as for dancing? You'll not manage a step with sore feet."

The car door swung open and a broad-shouldered frame uncoiled from the low-slung interior. The driver was wearing an army officer's uniform and in the headlamps the braiding of his epaulets gleamed almost as brightly as his short golden hair. The khaki suited him as it did a certain type of man, accentuating long legs, narrow hips and strong torso. In the shadows cast by the headlamps, she saw sculpted cheekbones and hollows, a sprinkling of golden stubble and a pair of intense sea-blue eyes. As these swept over Alice, she knew he had instantly assessed the situation.

"You've had quite a tumble. That knee needs dressing. You need to see a doctor."

Alice's knee was throbbing and she feared the velvet was ruined, for it would be hard to get the bloodstains out of the soft pile. Not that she'd ever want to wear this dress again. She should have listened to Sam when he'd reminded her that green was unlucky for seafarers. That must apply to their womenfolk too.

"It's just a cut. I'll dress it when I'm home."

He arched an eyebrow.

"I wish my men were half as stoic. Very well, at least allow me to drive you there."

"Thank you, I'm fine to walk."

"Nonsense. You're hurt, you're cold and you're practically barefoot. I can't possibly leave a young woman stranded in the middle of nowhere. I won't *hear* of it."

His authority was clearly born of a lifetime of privilege and giving orders.

Alice bristled. She was done with men who wanted to be knights in shining armour.

"As much as I appreciate the offer, I'm not interested in what you will or will not hear of."

He stared at her in disbelief. "I'm offering to *rescue* you!"

Alice could see that nobody ever told this man what to do or refused him. He probably had women queuing up to ride around in his elegant sports car. Elsie would have dived into the front seat like a shot. This man looked so shocked that Alice felt a little sorry for him. Good Samaritans weren't usually told to push off.

"I haven't asked to be rescued."

"Good God! I didn't need to be *asked*. Look at the state of you! Your dress is torn and you're bleeding. It's bloody cold, too, and you'll catch your death wandering around in a ball-gown. Now stop arguing and get in."

He was right about the cold. Alice's teeth were chattering like starlings.

"And you can't possibly walk far with that knee," he added.

The cut was throbbing now, and very painful. The idea of being driven home was tempting, but this man was far too sure of himself and Alice was determined not to give in.

"I don't like being ordered about. I'm not one of your soldiers."

His lips twitched. "No, you're most certainly not. Apologies. I've clearly spent far too much time on the parade ground. Let me start again if I may. Would you please allow me to drive you home? You'll be doing me a favour. Otherwise, as I can't leave you here I'd have no choice but to walk with you. I might even have to carry you."

"You can't carry me all the way to the village!"

"I assure you I can. They make us train hard in the army, you know, and you can't possibly weigh as much as my rucksack. I'm not saying it'd be easy, but if you left me no choice I'd do it."

Alice was horrified. The mere idea of this man, this *stranger*, sweeping her into his arms and carrying her through Polwenna was appalling. The villagers would be talking about it for the next decade. She suspected, too, that he was more than capable of carrying out this threat. (*Threat?* Alice could practically hear

Elsie screech in outrage. *Are you insane? Gone Bodmin? He's an officer and he's handsome. Get in the bloody car!)* Besides, this handsome man was right; her knee was growing more painful by the second. She realised she'd have to accept his offer or be lugged down to the village. She had very little choice.

"And," added the officer with a heavy sigh, "walking you back and then returning for the car will make me dreadfully late. My mother's expecting me for dinner, but that can't be helped. Besides, she'd never forgive me if I left a lady alone and in a state of distress. I'll just lock the car, shall I?"

He moved towards his car and Alice knew she was outmanoeuvred. This determined Good Samaritan wouldn't accept no for an answer, and since she appeared stuck with him no matter what she said she decided that five minutes sitting in a car with him was better than thirty being carried like a sack of spuds …

"Don't doom me to eat chops that have sat the Aga for hours," he said beseechingly. "An army marches on its stomach after all, Miss Pendeen."

"How do you know my name?" Alice was startled and alarmed. "We've never met, have we?"

She was certain they hadn't, for he was the kind of man everyone noticed.

"I was wounded. You don't remember?" he grinned. "Then again, you were a tiny thing, probably no more than five or six. You'd have been more interested in playing with the other children at my parents' house than talking to the old fogeys."

Although there was something vaguely familiar about this man, Alice was still at a loss.

"I'm not surprised you were reluctant to clamber into my car if you thought I was a random stranger," he continued. "I recognised you at once, but then everyone in the village knows the Pendeens. Morley supplies us with fish when my family are up at the house, and your mother helped mine with her vegetable garden during the war. I'm Henry Tremaine, Elizabeth's son. From Seaspray."

Now Alice knew why he seemed familiar. Although the Tremaines weren't full-time residents in the village, Henry's mother had spent the war years there with a house full of evacuees, so she been a familiar figure in Polwenna. She had clearly shared her blonde good looks, spare angular frame and sharp blue eyes with her son, along with that air of command. Alice recalled that during the war, as the Tremaines were a military family Elizabeth's husband and their three sons had been away fighting. Danny, who had been a gardener at Seaspray for a while, had been desperately impressed by the dashing Tremaine boys.

"Of course. I remember you now. My brother Danny joined your father's regiment. Mostly, I think, because he wanted to be like you and your brothers."

Henry Tremaine fell silent. Too late, Alice remembered that the Tremaines had lost their two eldest sons in the war. Henry, the youngest, was the last of their boys.

"The Duke of Cornwall's 2nd Battalion. Good men. They fought like tigers," he said quietly. "Please give Danny my regards."

Alice swallowed. "We lost him at Dunkirk."

Henry Tremaine bowed his cropped head. "I'm truly sorry. Dunkirk was bloody."

"You were there too?"

The searing blue gaze drifted away to focus on a spot over her shoulder, and Alice knew he was no longer in a dark Cornish lane, but far away on a French beach watching his friends fall and their blood flow. She would sometimes see the very same look in her dad's eyes, a look always followed by screams and sobs in the depths of the night.

"Yes. I was there."

There was another silence, one filled for both of them with long-lost faces and sadness. Alice knew enough of Dunkirk to understand that Henry Tremaine must have seen, and done, the unspeakable in the name of defending his country. Like her father, he would carry the knowledge of those deeds to his grave. Henry Tremaine might be a stranger to her, but Alice knew enough of his glowing reputation and his heavy burden to be certain that he was a man of honour.

"I'd really hate to keep you from your dinner," she said. "Since you're heading to Polwenna and it isn't out of your way, I'd be grateful for a ride to the village."

And that easily, with no more than a chance meeting, Fortune's wheel turned one more click as Henry Tremaine helped Alice into his car and changed the course of her life.

CHAPTER 10

1953

December 1953 was a memorable month in many ways for the Pendeen family – not least because the front room was used twice.

"You can let me out now," she'd told Henry as the sports car rounded the tight corner by the forge, gently nudging a cluster of carol singers out of the way. She pointed towards the old bridge which divided the village. "Here will do."

Henry whistled. "You live under a bridge? You don't look like a troll."

With eyes red-rimmed from crying, her hair a mop of wild curls and dirty feet, Alice imagined a troll was exactly what she looked like even if Henry Tremaine was too much of a gentleman to say so. Back where they'd met in the lane he had quietly cleaned her knee as best he could with his handkerchief, then draped his jacket over her shoulders and wound a cashmere scarf around her neck. The soft fabric carried the warmth from the nape of his neck and the scent of his skin, which felt strangely intimate – and somehow a betrayal of Jonny. Telling herself she was being ridiculous, Alice accepted it and Henry's gloved hand as he helped her into the low-slung car.

They talked a little on the short journey to the village, but short of telling her that he had resigned his commission and had been visiting a friend of his father's near Fowey, Henry Tremaine gave little away of himself. His voice was assured but curiously unaccented, containing none of the rolling richness of his Cornish heritage or the polished vowels of his mother. Alice found he was easy to listen to and she liked the way his words curled and fell around her like autumn leaves. She also appreciated not being pressed to explain her tears. She hoped that Henry assumed she was crying because her knee hurt and she'd missed the dance.

If only. Knees would scab over and there would always be more dances – but how could she live without Jonny? What was there without him? Alice's eyes prickled and she dug her nails into her palms.

"Our cottage is on the quayside. You can't get a car to it," she explained.

"I wasn't going to sail across, Alice. I'll leave the car here and carry you. If you walk the knee will bleed. I know enough of such injuries to tell you that much. Please don't argue."

Henry Tremaine wasn't a man who would be concerned what the neighbours might say. Not when there was a matter of honour to be attended to.

"You've already done enough," she protested.

His eyes met hers. The pain in them startled her, for it was raw and bleak and spoke of a grief so deep it couldn't be articulated.

"Not as much as men like your brother."

His words prodded the past with a fingertip, but this was enough to help Alice understand him. The guilt of coming home when so many had been lost had gnawed at her father for decades, just as the guilt of having been too young to fight still filled Sam with a bubbling inadequacy. Like Henry's brothers, Danny Pendeen had given everything, and his absence was always with them. His had been the first empty chair at the dinner table, his the first face missing at Christmas, and he had been the first member of their close family to say farewell. There were too many missing faces now in Polwenna, as there were across the whole country. Far too many men gone who should have been the same age as Danny or Henry Tremaine.

"Then, thank you," she said softly. "That's very kind."

Alice was rewarded with a smile of such brilliance she blinked, unable to believe how utterly it transformed his stern features into something quite breathtaking. It reminded her of how sunlight cut through storm clouds and lit the grey seascape into a dazzling display, kicking diamonds from the waves and filling the sky with unexpected golds and silvers. Henry Tremaine should smile more often, thought Alice. He looked like a different man.

There was a problem, though. Although not as socially exalted as the Tregarricks, or as rich as the St Miltons, the Tremaine family owned the impressive Seaspray House as well as the old sardine works down by the harbour, and several acres at the top of the village. New arrivals to Polwenna in the early nineteen-twenties, they were relatively wealthy, and very well-connected through Elizabeth Tremaine. So, because nobody in the village knew how to pigeonhole them, they inhabited a strange social hinterland. Being part-time residents they also possessed an air of mystery and, although generally approved of for playing their part in the war and being Cornish, they were still regarded with an air of suspicion for being *incomers.*

And now, when she'd agreed to Henry Tremaine carrying her from the car all the way along Quay Street to her parents' front door she knew that curtains would be twitching and the village gossip machine would be cranked up into overdrive – but since her knee was swelling like a loaf in the bread oven she resigned herself to being the subject of gossip for the next decade. Besides, Jonny was bound to hear how the enigmatic Captain Tremaine had carried her home like a Jane Austen heroine, and would hopefully be so jealous he'd defy his parents and tear down the hill to declare his love for Alice. She'd make him grovel, but she'd forgive him eventually. Of course she would. Alice could forgive Jonny anything. A torn dress. A cut knee. Even a broken heart.

When May Pendeen opened the front door to discover an army officer on the doorstep with her daughter in his arms, Alice knew what a great joy it was for her to usher him into a spick and span best room while she called for her husband and did her best not to flap. It was an even greater joy, though tempered with caution, when May realised this caller was none other than the only son of the Tremaine family and a war hero to boot! Thank goodness she had washed the net curtains and beaten the carpets only the week before! Imagine if Henry Tremaine were to leave Cobbles Cottage under the impression that May Pendeen didn't know how to treat a guest. That would have been the biggest shame imaginable.

The best china was being fetched and rich fruit cake sliced almost before Henry had deposited Alice on the sofa and arranged a footstool. While May fussed over him all Alice could do was hope she didn't dirty the armchair or make marks on the carpet. She hoped her rescuer would stay for as long as possible because there was no way her mother would begin an interrogation with a guest present, even though she could see question marks practically floating above her head. Morley Pendeen did his best to overcome his bewilderment and make small talk about Henry's plans for a boat yard and marina. He didn't show any signs of noticing that his daughter was tearstained and wearing a party frock – but Sam's gaze flickered between Alice and their guest, and he frowned. Sam would want to know what she'd been up to, and if he ever discovered the truth he'd be furious. Sam was her big brother – her only big brother now – and he was very protective.

Jonny had been quite scared of him.

"He'll punch my lights out if he thinks I've laid so much as a finger on you," he'd said once, and Alice hadn't argued. Sam's temper matched his red hair.

So Sam *mustn't* find out what had happened today. There would be the mother of all scenes, and Alice wasn't ready for that. She ignored her brother and watched her rescuer try to refuse a third slice of cake without causing offence. If her mum had her way he would roll out of the door.

Finally Henry departed after insisting that his detour was no trouble and wishing them all a merry Christmas. Morley closed the front door and the family retreated into the kitchen. As May brewed more tea, this time in the chipped everyday pot, Alice braced herself for an interrogation.

"Henry *Tremaine* in our cottage," said her dad slowly. The furrows between his eyes deepened and he raked a hand through his silver hair. "Whatever next?"

"I'm sorry, Pa," said Alice, hanging her head.

But Morley wasn't upset. He was recalling the conversation he'd just enjoyed.

"The Captain wants to turn the old sardine factory into a boatyard and even create a marina. A marina in a fishing village? Whoever heard of such a thing?"

"He's a wealthy man," said May, who was rinsing out the hanky even though Henry had insisted he didn't need it returned. "He's probably got all sorts planned for Polwenna."

"He asked my opinion," Morley continued wonderingly. "Thought I might have some thoughts as to what might work. Imagine!"

"Why *wouldn't* he ask you, Pa? Nobody knows the harbour like you do. He's only been here five minutes," said Sam, glowering at Alice.

"He liked my fruit cake. Said it was the best he'd ever had." May was still smiling at the compliment. Henry Tremaine was certainly good at charming people. You could use May's cakes as chain anchors.

Sam leaned against the range and regarded Alice through narrowed eyes.

"Strange he came here. His sort usually prefers the jolly old sailing club in Fowey."

"He insisted on taking me to the door," Alice said.

"That's because he's a gentleman," sighed May.

Sam snorted. "He liked the look of Alice, Ma! It was written all over his face. Poor sod could hardly take his eyes off her."

"Hardly surprising, the state she's in. What must he have thought?" tutted May.

"Do you really want to know?" Sam asked.

Alice glared at him. The last thing she needed was her brother planting daft ideas in her mother's head. Besides, Sam was talking utter nonsense. Henry Tremaine was years older than her. He was practically ancient.

"He felt sorry for me," she said. "He was being kind."

"You'll feel sorry for yourself if there's any blood on my best furniture. I'll have you scrubbing it until next Christmas," warned May. "And you've got some explaining to do, my girl.

What were you doing out in that dress? You said you *weren't* going to the dance."

Alice crossed her fingers beneath the velvet pleats.

"I thought Hugo might let me in since he's Sam's friend. I didn't want to miss it."

This sounded plausible. Hugo and Sam might come from different backgrounds, but they had fished and swum and wrestled for years, and they shared an eye for the local girls.

"Did you fight Hugo to get in? Is he bloodied too?" Sam asked.

"Don't be silly," said Alice. "I tripped walking up the back lane and cut my knee. That's how Captain Tremaine came across me.

"You should have gone with Barry," sighed May. "Buttering Hugo up was one of Elsie's daft ideas, I suppose?"

"Hmm," mumbled Alice. She sent her best friend a silent apology, although in fairness this was just the kind of thing Elsie might have suggested. And then, at the thought of the dance and Jonny, her throat tightened. What was he doing right now? Was he all right?

"I'm going back to the pub," said Morley, reaching for his coat. "I want to have a word with some of the others about this boatyard business. See what they say to the idea of a marina! I'll catch you at Midnight Mass, love."

Sam abandoned his perch by the range and tugged his gaberdine from the drying rack above it.

"I'll come too."

"You've had too much Pol Brew already. I won't have you falling over at Midnight Mass," May said.

Sam hugged his mother.

"Not so much that I can't see what's going on right under my nose, and I'm not just talking about Captain Tremaine. He's not the problem. Is he, Ally?"

His blue eyes met Alice's over their mother's head and anxiety clawed her heart.

Sam knew about Jonny.

"What's that supposed to mean?" May demanded

Sam shrugged. "Just that all the boys are sweet on my sister. Why should a distinguished army captain be any different?"

"She's a pretty girl, when she isn't falling over in lanes and getting into scrapes with that flibbertigibbet Elsie Rowe," May agreed. She gave her son a push. "Now, off with you Sam Pendeen – and woe betide you if you're not up at the church later on."

Sam promised with his hand on his heart and busied himself lacing his boots. And then, once May was out of earshot and Morley was striding off towards the lights of the pub, Sam turned to Alice with a scowl.

"Did *he* do that to you?"

"Who?"

"Jonny St Milton, that's who. If he's hurt you I swear to God I'll bloody kill him."

"Jonny?"

She tried hard to look confused, and Sam curled his top lip in disgust.

"I know, Ally. You don't need to lie"

"How? Who told you?" Her mind shuttled back and forth. "Was it Reverend Sharpe?"

Sam laughed. "Like that old fart would bother talking to the likes of me! No, I worked it out for myself. It wasn't hard. I've seen you slipping away to talk to him after church enough times and moping about like a wet weekend when he goes back to that posh school of his. What *were* you thinking?"

"We're in love, Sam. We want to get married."

Even her brother's freckles looked taken aback.

"Ally, you can't seriously think he'll marry you! His parents would be horrified – and ours too, I wouldn't wonder. Mrs St Milton will go spare. Christ! What about Ma's job?"

This was such an echo of Alice's earlier conversation with Jonny that she began to cry.

"I don't want to talk about it, Sam!"

"Why not? Did he try it on? Is *that* why you're bleeding? He tried it on and you had to run? The bastard! I'll bloody *kill* him!"

There was a darkness in her brother's eyes Alice had never seen before.

"Of course he didn't! I really did trip."

"You've hurt yourself before," said Sam slowly. "You broke your arm that time when I dared you to jump off the beach steps, but you never cried. Not once. But now you've dressed up for the dance, slipped out and then come home bleeding, with your dress ripped and red-eyed. It doesn't take a genius to know you've been crying." He grabbed Alice's hands. "Tell me the truth, Ally! What *really* happened this evening?"

She dashed her tears away.

"Jonny told me it's over. He doesn't want to see me again."

The statement was so final that she began to sob, no longer caring whether anyone knew her secret, for what did anything matter without Jonny? While she cried, Sam held her, and his wiry frame grew taut with anger as she choked out her story.

"I really thought he loved me, but it wasn't enough. Jonny doesn't want anything to do with me, because his family thinks I'm not good enough. *We're* not good enough. If he wants to have the future he's always been raised to expect, he's found he has to let me go."

Sam's face was mottled.

"You bloody idiot, Alice. He's had what he wanted and

thrown you aside. What did you *think* would happen? That you'd get married and live happily ever after?"

Alice wept even harder. "Yes! *Yes!* We were going to get engaged. We were to be married. He promised."

"I bet he did," grated Sam. He dropped her hands and rose to his feet, his mouth set in a grim line. "Well, it's high time Jonny St Milton learned what happens to people who break promises to the Pendeens."

Alice looked up, suddenly afraid.

"What does that mean?"

"It means I'm going to kill him for what he's done to you."

Sam was strong and well-muscled from hauling crab pots and lifting fish boxes. Jonny would be no match for him.

Alice was horrified.

"Don't hurt him, Sammy. I love him."

"*You* might," said Sam. "But *I* bloody well don't."

He turned on his heel and stalked out of the kitchen. Moments later cold night-soaked air swirled through the cottage and the front door slammed.

Alice buried her face in her hands. Christmas or not, if her brother ran into Jonny St Milton the season of goodwill would be utterly forgotten.

CHAPTER 11

1953

Alice really couldn't face Midnight Mass. She would have preferred to hide away in her bedroom nursing her sore knee and even sorer heart, but May Pendeen wouldn't hear of it. If Alice was capable of skulking about the place to get dressed in secret and falling into the arms of army captains, then she was more than capable of going to church. Alice couldn't, of course, explain how even the smallest glimpse of Jonny would break her heart all over again, and she tried to plead her swollen knee, but her mum wasn't having it.

"It's Christmas Eve, Alice. We always go to Midnight Mass. Everybody we know is there."

Yes, thought Alice despairingly, that was the problem. Mrs St Milton would be there in the family pew glowering at her, whereas Jonny's head would be bowed and he'd avoid looking at her. Elsie would be agog, especially if Henry Tremaine made an appearance and came to say hello. *That* would set tongues wagging. Worst of all, what if Sam caught up with Jonny at St Wenn's and the red mist came down? If the two young men came to blows in such a public place her secret would well and truly be out, and her mother's job would be history.

Alice gnawed her nails. She'd never known such a miserable Christmas. Jonny had promised that this would be one she'd remember for the rest of her life, and he hadn't been wrong. No matter how hard Alice tried to forget it, this festive season was forever etched on her memory.

Once Morley had returned from the pub, full of beer and ideas for marinas, Alice limped up to St Wenn's with her parents. Her knee throbbed and she was glad when Barry's father kindly gave the family a lift up in his pony cart. Somehow she managed to hobble up the aisle, and she sat down with great relief, an emotion intensified a thousandfold when she didn't spot Jonny's dark head between his parents. This relief, though, was quickly swamped by bitter disappointment, because any glimpse, no matter how brief, was surely better than nothing.

The church was packed with worshippers and the atmosphere flickered with anticipation just as the dripping beeswax candles with their red ribbons and green foliage flickered from the window sills and the altar. Spirits were already high with Christmas excitement, and as the revellers from the dance arrived in a floodtide their loud voices and laughter created a party atmosphere. Alice glimpsed Elsie looking dishevelled but beautiful in her midnight-blue dress. Of Peter Pollard there was no sign, and Elsie was escorted to a pew by none other than Hugo Tregarrick, which must mean that her hard work hadn't been in vain. They were looking a little flustered, and Elsie was pointing towards the Pendeens and whispering. A knot of unease tightened in Alice's chest.

"Where's Sam?" her dad asked, craning his neck. "He'd better not be in a heap somewhere."

As if on cue, Alice's brother emerged from the porch. His red hair was standing on end and his face was flushed. When he slid into the Pendeens' pew his breathing was laboured and the cuffs of his coat were splattered with mud. This was a look Alice recognised from the school playground, and it didn't bode well. She looked around the church with rising anxiety. Where was Jonny?

"The *state* of you," tutted his mother, trying to smooth his hair down. "What have you been doing?"

Sam didn't meet her eye. "Just a bit of unfinished business."

Alice's anxiety knot tugged tighter. She was on the verge of challenging her brother when the organ swelled into life, Aubrey Keverne launching into 'Hark the Herald Angels Sing' as Reverend Sharpe swished along the aisle. As the congregation rose to their feet and began to sing the familiar magical words, Alice finally caught sight of Jonny's dark head as, unusually late, he slipped into the St Milton pew. Only Aubrey's determination to literally pull all the stops out and make St Wenn's shake with his enthusiastic playing prevented everyone hearing her gasp when she saw Jonny holding a blood-drenched hanky to his nose.

The rest of the service passed in a blur. Although Alice stood up and sat down and recited all the familiar responses, the whole time her thoughts were flying across the church, and she longed for nothing more than to tear over to Jonny's side. She prayed that he would come back to her. She prayed for this as hard, if not even harder, than she'd once petitioned the Almighty to make sure the Germans wouldn't invade. To a small child, though, the red skies above Plymouth and the small planes dogfighting above had seemed so far away; the Germans had been a vague lurking menace, no more tangible than monsters which hid under the bed after the lamp was extinguished. But this pain was real and immediate, and just as likely to destroy her as any bomb.

She tried to catch Jonny's gaze, but just as she'd foreseen he pointedly looked ahead. She spent the rest of the service in a daze of misery as she tried hard to strike a bargain with the Almighty.

"Change his heart," she implored the stained-glass figures which glowed in the candlelight. "Don't let me lose Jonny. I'll wait for him. Please, please bring him back to me."

Of course, there was no reply. Christ hung on the cross and at his feet the disciples remained intent on His suffering, as was biblically sound and right. Only St Wenn, floating on her millstone and refusing to sink beneath the weight of her halo (which always seemed like a second miracle) twinkled at Alice as though saying all was not lost.

When the service was finally over and the church rang with cries of 'Merry Christmas!' Alice was trapped in the pew behind her parents and unable to reach Jonny. In the past they'd managed to slip into the dark churchyard to steal a Christmas kiss beneath the sharp stars while their parents were distracted. But tonight, and to Alice's searing disappointment, Jonny remained with his parents. He was still dabbing at his nose and refusing to look her way. She wasn't sure whether this was because he wanted to ignore her or because Sam was nearby with a scowl etched onto his freckled face.

"Take that look off your face before the wind changes," said May to her son. To Alice she added, "Look, love! There's Barry. Doesn't he look smart?"

"Everyone looks smart, Ma," Alice said wearily. "It's Midnight Mass."

"But he looks especially nice, all dressed up," May insisted, giving her daughter a poke in the ribs. "Go and say hello, Ally.

It's not too late to change your mind. He keeps looking your way. I'm sure he'd give you a second chance."

Alice gave her mother full marks for persistence, if not for factual accuracy. Barry was born to wear a smock and oilskins, and haul nets. Legs planted apart as though the stone floor might crest a wave at any moment, he was squeezed into a tight suit and looking uncomfortable as he ran a finger around his collar. It was true, though, that he was looking her way, and Alice, fearing that her mother was about to begin matchmaking once again, made her excuses and squeezed out of the pew to join Elsie.

Her friend had been waving at her from the moment the final amen had been uttered, and was looking fit to burst.

"At last!" she said, grabbing Alice's arm and spinning her around to face the back of the church. "Who's *that?*"

"Who?"

"Him!" Elsie hissed, pointing to where Reverend Sharpe was shaking hands with the better-connected members of his flock. "The fair-haired man? There, behind the Kevernes! Looks a bit like James Stewart."

Alice craned her neck to better see through the throng and glimpsed a familiar golden head, tilted back as its owner stood apart from the crowd to study the roll of honour. As though sensing her attention was resting on him, Henry turned and his piercing cobalt gaze flashed above the crowd to meet hers. Alice looked away hastily, jolted by a strange tug of recognition.

I know you.

I see you.

She turned back to Elsie.

"That's Henry Tremaine. From Seaspray House."

"So *that's* the hero son! I love the uniform and that aloof thing he's got going on," sighed Elsie. "What an utter dish!"

"I think he's probably shy," said Alice.

Elsie gave her an arch look.

"So he's caught your attention. He was looking at you all the way through the service."

Alice flushed. "Don't be ridiculous."

"I'm not! If I wasn't head over heels in love with Hugo I'd be making eyes at him, no word of a lie. Anyway, apart from being to die for, he stopped your brother half-killing Jonny St Milton just before the service.

There was a rushing in Alice's ears.

"Whaaaaat?"

"I don't know what's happened tonight, but whatever it was really upset Sam," said Elsie, eyes bright with vicarious excitement. "Hugo and Jonny were chatting in the lane, and I was doing my best to earwig in case they were talking about me, when Sam stormed over. Honestly, Ally, he was in some rage. He was all hunched up and his face was puce. He told Jonny he was a bas—"

"Elsie! Shush!" Alice looked across at Reverend Sharpe, but fortunately he had exchanged eavesdropping for social climbing.

Elsie lowered her voice. "He called Jonny a bastard and said he was going to kill him for what he'd done. Then he punched him. Jonny went down like a felled oak."

Alice could imagine. Jonny was no match for her brother.

"Sam didn't stop," Elsie continued. "Even when Jonny was down Sam carried on swinging at him and calling him all sorts of things I can't repeat in here. Jonny didn't put up much of a fight, to be fair. Each time he staggered to his feet he just let Sam hit him again."

Alice's hand flew to her mouth. Sam was defending her honour, however uninvited that defence was, and Jonny had chosen to take his punishment, probably believing he deserved it. Perhaps he'd even welcomed the distraction of physical pain rather than the knife-slice of heartbreak? She knew which she'd prefer.

"Hugo was trying to pull Sam off, but he was like a madman. I thought he'd kill Jonny." Elsie paused and nodded towards Henry Tremaine. "Luckily *he* appeared from nowhere and lifted Sam off Jonny as though he was made of feathers. It was seriously impressive, Ally. He told your brother he needed to calm down, and said it in such a way nobody dared argue. Then he gave Jonny a hanky and told him to clean himself up. He said this was not the time and place for fighting, and they ought to be ashamed of themselves."

Alice recalled Sam's glowering face as he'd joined his family, and Jonny's bright blood flowering into his white handkerchief. Henry Tremaine was down by two of those now, thanks to her.

Elsie was chattering on about the dance and Hugo, but her words washed over Alice. She was barely listening. All she could think about was Jonny. How badly had Sam hurt him? And what would the St Miltons do if they found out that Sam had hurt their only son? Mother would lose her job for certain and so would she – there was no way Mrs St Milton would wish to set eyes on either Pendeen woman ever again. The ancient floor surged beneath Alice's feet and she was awash with guilt that her actions had led to this. Why had she believed for a second that she and Jonny could ever be together?

She stole a look towards the St Miltons and was relieved to see them deep in conversation with the Tregarricks. Jonny stood beside his parents and, catching sight of her, finally smiled. Alice inclined her head towards the door.

And to Elsie she said, "I'm going outside for some fresh

air," interrupting her halfway through a description of Millicent Jago's expensive pink ball dress.

Alice scurried out of the church, ignoring Elsie's surprise and the tuts and huffs of her neighbours. Her knee was swollen and painful and she hobbled like a lame gull, but because she'd made this journey so many times she instinctively avoided the uneven ground and tussocks in the oldest and most neglected part of the graveyard. Here the ancient tombstones huddled under gnarled trees – no more than saplings when the sleepers beneath had been laid to rest – and ivy made slow and stealthy progress over the earth. At the farthest end a large monument to a long-forgotten resident of Polwenna Manor shielded anyone who wished to be concealed from view. Alice and Jonny had met here on many Sundays. It was their special place.

Tonight it was bitterly cold, and Alice wished she could travel back in time to the long summer days when the grasses rippled in imitation of the sea and unseen birds trilled songs which had been sung long before St Wenn's had been built. She had been so happy then as she lay in the long grass, drowsing to the thrum of the bees. Life was full of sunlight and hope and Jonny. When he pulled her into his arms and promised to love her for ever she had believed him – but what if for ever had proven to be too long? What if he only loved her for a season of his life?

"Ally?"

Jonny emerged from the shadows. Even in the darkness Alice could see that his nose was bloodied and that more bruises were blooming on his pale skin.

"Oh my God! What has he done?"

She flew towards him, but Jonny held his hands up and stepped back.

"What any brother would have done in his position. I totally deserved it. Even Mother said so."

Alice's stomach dropped. Her mum's job was as good as lost.

"Mrs St Milton knows?"

"Don't panic, Ally. She won't sack your mum. Mother said what did I expect from a fisherman's family, and that she hopes I've learned my lesson." His hand rose to his nose. "Trust me, I won't forget in a hurry."

"Sam had no right to hit you."

"He did, Ally. He was defending your honour."

"I didn't ask him to!" Alice flared. "How *dare* Sam wade into my business?"

Jonny gave her a defeated look.

"Face it, your family would have hated us being together as much as mine do. It's time to be honest. There's no future for us. We can't walk away from our families or who we're born to be. If I had any doubts earlier that breaking up was the wrong thing, I certainly don't now. It's never going to work, Ally. No matter how we feel. We have to accept that."

Gone were the words of love. Gone was the warm smile she loved. Gone too were the promises that they would do whatever it took to be together.

Alice felt winded.

"You love me. I know you do."

Jonny nodded. "That's why it ends here, while we still care about each other and while it's perfect. It's over not because I *don't* love you – but because I *do*. Goodbye, Alice."

He turned into the darkness, leaving Alice alone. This time she didn't call to him. She had heard the note of finality ringing through his words like the iron chill through the midnight air.

But she had also heard him say that he still loved her. That was the small raft Alice would cling to in a storm-stirred ocean of misery. Jonny still loved her. He'd said he would always love her. He didn't want to lose her any more than she wanted to be apart from him. All Alice had to do was find a way of persuading him that they could make it work.

On Christmas Eve, a magical night when miracles happened, animals knelt down in their stalls and wishes were granted, Alice's Christmas prayer was for love to return to her life. As she walked down to the village and saw the flickering squares of lamplit windows reflected in the dancing water of the harbour, the world brimmed with beauty and she was filled with an utter certainty that her wish would be granted. One day she would walk down this lane as a very old lady and look back at this evening and laugh. Maybe she would even tease Jonny about it. Alice would win Jonny back and they would live happily ever after. All she had to do first was make him realise that he'd made a terrible mistake.

It was time to tell Elsie the truth. If anyone was good at devising plans and winning hearts against all the odds, it was Alice's best friend. This would not be the end for Alice Pendeen and Jonny St Milton.

CHAPTER 12

THE PRESENT

Alice had been so deep in the past that when she paused to gather her thoughts it was a jolt to find herself inside St Wenn's rather than going home to Cobbles. How powerful the pull of the past was!

"That was it? He walked away *again*?"

Holly was riveted.

"Yes," Alice said. "That was it. Jonny had made his mind up and he could be stubborn. He had told himself it was for the best, and that he was making a noble sacrifice on my behalf."

"But he still loved you."

"Yes, I knew that – but it didn't help much."

Holly crossed her arms. "Sorry, Alice, but I still think he was a right chicken."

Alice was touched by the young woman's outrage. She had forgiven Jonny a long time ago, but it was nice to hear her younger self championed. Still, she supposed she ought to stick up for Jonny a little.

"That Christmas Eve my brother had sent him a strong message. Jonny was probably really scared, because Sam was a big lad! Jonny had also had his parents to contend with, and they were tough. And, don't forget, we were very young too."

Holly's eyes were bright with hope. "Did he change his mind? I know! You faced both your families together. You're telling me I should fight for love."

Alice felt impossibly ancient. Young people were so beautifully romantic.

"Not at all, my dear. My advice to you is quite the opposite. That Christmas Eve our love affair was over, and my heart was utterly broken – or so I thought back then."

Holly looked crestfallen and, realising her young companion had been hoping for a happy ever after, Alice felt a little uncomfortable. Although there would be a happy ever after – and life was full of these even if they never seemed obvious at the time and often came in disguise – Alice suspected hers wouldn't be quite what Holly was hoping for. Life wasn't a rom-com.

"So you decided to win him back," said Holly. "What did you do? Did you make sure he knew the Captain fancied you? That would work! Maybe I should try and make Jamie jealous?"

Alice was debating how best to reply when a nervous throat-clearing announced the presence of Perry Tregarrick.

"Sorry to interrupt, but Jen Wheeler's made hot chocolate for all the helpers, and I thought you two might like some to warm up. Harry's cranked the heating up, but it's still a bit nippy in here."

He was bearing two steaming mugs and smiling the

slightly lopsided smile Alice had once known so very well and which she still missed.

"Bless you, Perry. I'd love one," she said, reaching for a mug and sighing with bliss at the warmth of the ceramic against her cold hands. Simple pleasures were the best.

Perry offered the second mug to Holly, who accepted gratefully.

"I didn't realise how cold I was," she admitted, blowing at the steam before taking a sip.

"I don't think they designed St Wenn's with its heating properties in mind. A bit like my place," sighed Perry, who was bundled up in a battered wax jacket, old school scarf and rainbow-hued Peruvian hat with tassels. "Our heating system probably dates from the same era."

Holly laughed, and Alice was pleased to see her new friend looking a little happier. She really was a very pretty girl. If only Holly could realise that this dark time was just a season and, like a cold winter's afternoon, would pass. This understanding was a gift that Alice wished somebody had given her all those years ago.

"Holly, meet Perry Tregarrick, our resident organic market gardener, a talented painter and St Wenn's unofficial barista. Holly's staying in the village for Christmas, Perry."

"Welcome to Polwenna Bay," he said warmly.

Holly's cup paused halfway to her lips. "Tregarrick? As in *Hugo* Tregarrick?"

Perry looked surprised. "Hugo was my great-grandfather."

"I've been telling stories about my misspent youth," Alice explained.

"Ah, I see ... Great-grandpa was one of the most colourful members of my family, which is saying something! I never met him, but they say he was mad as cheese towards the end. He turned the parterre into a football pitch for sixty-six, he bred parrots that flew around the house, and painted over the sixteenth-century frescoes with magnolia. British Heritage went crackers, and the fine they imposed is probably the reason why I'm so skint."

Holly was wide-eyed. "I feel like I've bumped into an old friend."

"Holly's been indulging my meander down memory lane. I was telling her all about my friend Elsie's crush on Hugo, and how she made poor Pete Pollard take her to the Christmas dance," said Alice.

"Hugo didn't stand a chance once Great-granny had decided on him, that's for sure. It's practically a family legend," Perry told Holly.

"Hugo *married* Elsie?"

"I don't think he had much choice. She was a very determined lady," Perry said.

"I was chief bridesmaid and chief dressmaker," Alice recalled. "Elsie insisted on peach chiffon even though I pleaded with her to choose again, because that fabric's a devil to sew. I had to make seven dresses and her wedding dress. I nearly went cross-eyed!"

"But wasn't Hugo ... posh?" Holly asked. Her jade gaze flickered over the dishevelled Perry, who looked like a fight in a jumble sale. "Wasn't he going to be a duke or something?"

"Viscount," mumbled Perry, looking down awkwardly at his scuffed chainsaw boots. He hated drawing attention to his title, always pointing out that without land and money (mostly lost by Hugo) it seemed like empty showing-off. He kicked at the edge of a flagstone. "A viscount's nowhere near such a big deal as a duke."

"Sounds very Bridgerton to me."

"There you go, Lord Tregarrick, you're a Regency hero." Alice patted Perry's arm.

He flushed. "I haven't seen Bridgerton, but Ella says it's racy."

"Just a bit," said Alice, who had stopped watching on account of her heart.

"I've never met a viscount before," said Holly.

"We're nothing special," said Perry, blushing even more. "Bit boring really. Utterly obsessed with repairing leaky roofs and paying inheritance tax."

"Wasn't marrying a village girl a big deal for Hugo's family like it was for Jonny's parents? If they were aristocracy?" Holly asked.

Perry shuffled his feet.

"My family don't care about stuff like that. They're quite an eccentric bunch. Or mad. Depends on your point of view. I think one of them married a ploughboy in the seventeenth century. Or was it the eighteenth? Another famously ran off to Barbados and married a slave. Anyway, once Hugo's parents knew he was set on Elsie they were happy enough by all accounts. I think his father was just glad that Hugo wasn't six feet under and could press on with continuing the line."

"Hugo's elder brothers died in the war," Alice explained. "Like my brother and Henry Tremaine's."

"So much tragedy," Holly sighed.

"Archie was a Spitfire pilot and went down over the Channel during the Battle of Britain. Tristan was lost on Omaha Beach. Rafe caught typhoid while out in India," said Perry. "Can you imagine? Three sons gone and only one left. No wonder Hugo's parents felt they couldn't upset him, the only direct heir. Without him the estate would have gone to some distant relly in the Caribbean."

"Those were tough times," said Alice. "We never got over losing Danny."

"Their names are all on the memorial, along with the three

lost in the first war." Perry pointed to the big brass plaque on the far side of the nave. "Hugo could have painted himself blue and married pretty much anyone, and his folks wouldn't have batted an eyelid."

"And socially his family didn't need to prove a thing either – unlike the St Miltons, who were new money and socially ambitious," added Alice. "Everyone looked up to the Tregarricks because of who they were."

Perry pulled a face. "It's weird. My dad was a seventies hippy, and I spent most of my childhood travelling to festivals watching him and Ma skin up. Or I was running barefoot about the estate – the bits my grandpa hadn't sold off anyway! Great-grandma Elsie seemed far grander than all of them. She always spoke like Margaret Thatcher."

"Once Elsie had been married she took elocution lessons and became very proper," Alice recalled fondly. She'd teased her old friend a lot about this, gently reminding Elsie of her roots whenever she grew a little too pompous or bullied the WI.

"I still miss her. She made a great pasty," said Perry.

Alice patted his hand. Although her old friend had passed away a long, long time ago there was nothing like a deep friendship with someone who'd known you from childhood to sustain you through hard times and nourish your life throughout all its seasons. Elsie in her turn had kept Alice grounded – especially when Alice's son had got married at eighteen after a whirlwind romance. Elsie pointed out that he wasn't the first in the family to defy his parents over love!

"I miss her too," said Alice quietly. *May the earth rest lightly on you, Elsie.*

They sipped their hot chocolate quietly until Jen Wheeler bustled over to collect cups and chivvy Perry back to work. With a promise to crank up the heating another degree or two, he retreated to the vestry, where a loud debate over carol choices was taking place.

Holly regarded Alice with a worried expression.

"Elsie had her happy ending – but what happened to you?"

Holly's attention, Alice could see, was no longer trained on her own broken heart. That was a good sign.

She pulled her scarf a little tighter.

"I limped home, tore a strip off Sam, cried my eyes out and spent Christmas nursing a broken heart and a sore knee. Captain Tremaine was kind enough to call to enquire after my injury, and he brought me some beautiful flowers from his mother's hothouse. But apart from that it was a gloomy time."

"I think the dashing Captain was into you!"

Alice shrugged. "I was so in love with Jonny that poor Henry hardly registered. When he returned to his regiment I didn't even notice. I was far too busy trying to think of ways to win Jonny back that I couldn't think of anything else. He was at home now, planning his Grand Tour of France and Italy, and might as well have been on the moon, but that didn't stop me plotting ways of bumping into him. I couldn't believe it was really over." She shook head ruefully. "Oh dear. Looking back I realise I must have been quite obsessed. Practically a stalker, as you say!"

Holly sighed. "I get that. It's hard to think about anything else."

Her young friend was right, but even so life has a habit of marching onwards regardless of emotions, and Alice had soon discovered that even with a broken heart it was possible to function. After Christmas had passed in a blur of misery she had gone about her daily tasks even though she'd felt like an empty husk of the person she had been. Elsie, wrapped up in the excitement of her new romance with Hugo, had chattered away nineteen to the dozen to Alice and hadn't required much more than a yes or no response, and Sam had tried his best to cheer her up. He was sorry, he'd said, for over-reacting at Christmas. He'd only wanted to stand up for her. Maybe she could go to the pictures with one of his friends? Denzel Charles was keen. And there was always the faithful Barry. Alice had appreciated the apology, but she'd had no desire to start a new romance. She had been quite certain that if she couldn't be with Jonny she would never love again.

Now, with Holly in the chill of the church, she drew a deep breath and continued her story.

"I carried on working at Polwenna House. Diana St Milton never spoke of the matter again. Presumably she was confident that Jonny would toe the line, and there was doubtless a degree of self-interest, too, since good domestic staff were hard to come by in the fifties. After the war women wanted more than drudgery. We'd been pilots, farmers, and even mechanics."

"Mmm, yes. The Queen used to fix lorries," Holly agreed.

Alice felt a warm glow at the memory of Princess Elizabeth, clad in overalls and servicing engines with the same intent dedication later applied to her reign. Alice always had a suspicion the monarch was at her happiest during those times. Funny how the war days, so dark in many ways and always bookended by huge losses, stood out in her memory as forever sun-filled and oddly carefree. Perhaps childhood recollections were always such? The sun was brighter, the sky a deeper blue, summers stretched out forever, and whatever was happening beyond home, no matter how ominous, felt far away …

"So, what happened next?" Holly prompted as Alice's mind drifted back to the forties. "Did you bump into Jonny when he came home from Italy? Did he tell Diana to stick it? Please tell me he dragged you into the laundry cupboard, kissed you and begged to be forgiven!"

In a way that was what *had* happened – but it hadn't been quite as Holly was imagining. Alice knew that if she leapfrogged to that part, the whole purpose of her story would be lost.

"I'm afraid not, love. Life isn't like that. I was desperate to catch a glimpse of Jonny, so I lived for the time he'd come back on leave. Winter ebbed into spring, then summer, and he did come back to Polwenna Bay, but he brought some of his new friends with him and was never alone. He also tried not to be about when I was working. In the end I hardly saw him. He made sure of that."

"That must have been awful."

"It hurt," Alice admitted. This was an understatement; it had felt as though her chest had been flayed open. "Jonny knew exactly where I could be found, and in the past he would always meet me to steal a kiss or to chat. So I knew that now he was actively avoiding me. When we did meet he was polite but distant, and I think that hurt more than anything when we had been so close."

"You'd been ... you'd ..."

Holly, searching for words she thought Alice might find suitable, coloured.

Alice smiled. The young were so coy, assuming they had the exclusive right to have, talk about and enjoy sex. She took pity on Holly.

"We were lovers. Jonny was my first, and I truly thought he'd be my only. I loved him desperately."

"Gosh," said Holly, turning even pinker. "Back then it was a really big deal, wasn't it? Not to be married, I mean. Especially if unmarried girls got pregnant, like in *Tess of the D'Urbervilles*."

Alice nodded. Those times had been very different from the present, which often left her feeling like a dazed shipwrecked visitor from a distant land. Squashed between the *carpe diem* of the war years and the liberation of the sixties, she'd been trapped in a narrow world of rules, beliefs and gendered expectations – most of them, thankfully, now consigned to history books.

"The consequences were harsh for any girl who 'got into trouble'," said Alice, finger-quoting. "But people were still people, my love, with all the same emotions and passions. There were quite a few shotgun marriages as I recall, Hugo and Elsie being a case in point, and I had to sew like crazy because the heir to the Tregarrick title had to be born in wedlock. But I'm digressing. Going back to Jonny, he'd made it plain to me that things were over. But I couldn't understand how he could change his feelings when mine were as strong as ever. I knew I *never* would have given him up."

"I get that," said Holly and her eyes glistened. "How can things change so fast?"

"Hearts and friendships have a time and a season," Alice said. "Feelings can change too – that's something you learn by the time you're my age, and it's not always a bad thing. They can also appear from nowhere and be the most wonderful surprise. Trust me, love can ambush you in the most unlikely places."

She stopped herself before she vaulted ahead. This part of the story would come later.

"That spring of 1954 I still believed we could make it work. I went back to St Wenn's Well and wished for love, and I prayed every night to God that He would change Jonny's heart."

"Hmmph," said Holly. "I know we're in a church, but I'm not so sure about *that* working."

Alice glanced down at her wedding ring. The hand it rested upon was a little more liver-spotted and wrinkled these days but, as her granddaughter-in-law Reverend Jules might say, the Lord worked in mysterious ways. What was time to Him when it came to answering prayers? Alice had come to understand that life's tapestry was often woven with a greater and far more complex design than possible to comprehend when you were young and caught up in a maelstrom of emotion.

"I carried on hoping and praying. Then I heard a rumour that Jonny was walking out with Dr Jago's daughter. *That* was when everything changed."

Elsie had broken the news, but Alice had refused to believe a word of it. Apart from being certain that Jonny still loved her, she knew that pretty Millicent Jago was as cold and empty as one of Mrs St Milton's antique vases. There was no way Jonny, who was intelligent and sensitive and kind-hearted, would be able to bear her company for more than five minutes. Although Milly looked like a delicate china doll with her white-blonde hair and pale eyes, a core of steel ran beneath the fragile surface. She looked down her perfect nose at the village girls, sneered at those who didn't attend a smart private school, and had her indulgent father wrapped around her manicured finger. Elsie, Alice and all the other girls loathed her with a passion – unlike the boys, who all turned into utter ninnies whenever Milly was about, tripping over themselves to help her into her sailing boat and competing to carry her bags.

Men were often so easily fooled, Alice thought pityingly. Beneath Milly's beauty was something very ugly, since she possessed a spiteful streak. According to Hugo she had been sent off the hunting field in disgrace last season for thrashing her pony when it had refused to jump a gate, and it had been sold shortly afterwards. Alice, who'd been mocked by Milly on several occasions for her patched clothes and tangled hair, knew that Dr Jago's daughter's possessed a tongue which could slice granite. Jonny wouldn't fall for her superficial charms!

But Jonny wasn't the first boy to be dazzled by a pretty face, and he certainly wouldn't be the last. Now, looking back, Alice could understand how Milly's beauty combined with the approval of his parents must have been a heady mix – but this insight had only come with age, and back then she had blamed herself, feeling that she'd not been good enough. It truly had felt as though her life was over.

Alice had been changing the bed linen in Mrs St Milton's suite when she'd glimpsed Jonny and Milly strolling through the garden. The sheets had slipped from her fingers to pool on the carpet. She'd blinked, but the couple had remained in full focus, Milly a vision in white broderie anglaise with her perfect ringlets shining in the spring sunshine as she'd simpered up at Jonny. Alice's hand had stolen to her own unruly mass of curls, pinned as always into a collapsing bun, and she'd glanced down at her dowdy dress and grubby apron with a hot wash of shame. The visual reminder of her own station in life had been stark.

When Jonny had tilted Milly's chin up with his forefinger and brushed her mouth with his, Alice had sunk to her knees. She'd stuffed her fist into her mouth and smothered the howls of pain. There was no way she could have competed with a girl like Millicent Jago.

And if Jonny had truly loved her there would have been no need.

"*Was* he seeing another girl?" gasped Holly.

Alice pulled herself back from the tableau of a young couple kissing and a housemaid weeping alone. She pressed her hand to her chest; beneath the thin skin and fragile bones, her heart was pounding so hard it was as if she had just witnessed the embrace for the very first time.

"I'm afraid so. As it turned out, Jonny was courting Millicent Jago. His parents were satisfied."

"Men. They're all the same," said Holly bitterly.

"Ah," said Alice slowly, "but that's where you're wrong. If you're not in too much of a hurry, my love, let me tell you what happened next ..."

CHAPTER 13

1954

There was no way she could continue folding laundry as though her whole world hadn't just been upended. How could she calmly hang up Mrs St Milton's clothes or dust the dressing table when the ground had just bucked and heaved beneath her feet? When everything she had believed was false? It was not a lie to say she was feeling sick and needed to go home. She truly felt she might throw up, and wanted nothing more than to crawl into her little boxroom and pull the bedclothes over her head.

Jonny had kissed Millicent. He had forsaken Alice and broken every promise he had ever made. All the words he had whispered when, hearts as one, they had lain together by the well had been nothing but lies. Every touch, every caress, every kiss had been paid in false coin. Sam had been right all along, as had her mum and even Mrs St Milton; Jonny had only been having fun with Alice until a more suitable girl came along. He had never wanted to marry her.

And he had never loved her.

Alice fled the house and tore down the drive. She stood in the lane and tried to pull herself together for just long enough to make the walk back to Cobbles Cottage, but she simply couldn't, and now tears were falling down her cheeks and her shoulders heaved with sobs.

How could she carry on now she knew her love affair was truly over? How could she ever return to work at Polwenna House? There was no hope to cling to. No fleeting joy of catching a smile or brushing fingertips in a passageway. Jonny obviously didn't care whether she was there or not – and it was his indifference to her that really broke Alice. She couldn't bear to see him with Millicent, it would be death by a million small cuts, and her rival's disdain would be impossible to bear.

Whatever could she do? Run away to London and follow her dreams? There was something very tempting about the notion of jumping onto a train and watching her heartbreak retreat into the distance with every clack of wheels and puff of steam. But Alice had no money and no friends in the city, and Elsie's idea of them sharing a flat had vanished long ago. Realising she was stuck in Polwenna made Alice cry even harder.

The sound of footfalls on the lane and a cheery greeting made her look up.

"Alice? I thought it was you. My goodness, whatever's wrong?"

It was Henry Tremaine, looking years younger out of uniform, and wearing beige cords, and a soft blue shirt rolled up to his elbows under a moss-green pullover. A black spaniel, all pink lolling tongue and floppy ears, bounced at his heels with its gazed fixed on the ball held loosely in his tanned hand.

Alice wanted to howl. What *was* it with this man that he always seemed to catch her at her very worst? "I'm fine," she gulped.

"Clearly," said Henry drily. "Good Lord, at this rate I'm going to worry this has something to do with me. Every time we meet you're in distress. Hanky?"

Alice laughed through her tears.

"My family already owe you two. Will you have any left?"

"Hundreds. Mother insists upon it." He pulled a pristine white square from his pocket and passed it to Alice. The dog jumped up, thinking this was a game.

"Sit, Milo!" Henry ordered, and the spaniel instantly obeyed. Alice, still trying to collect herself, wondered if tears would cease too if he ordered it … Probably. As before, she felt absolutely certain nobody ever questioned this man's authority.

"Thanks," she sniffed, blotting her eyes. "I'm so sorry to be such a wet blanket, but I just found something out that's really upset me. It's been a bit of a shock."

Unbidden, the image of Milly and Jonny leapt before her vision, and more tears threatened to fall.

"Poor old you," said Henry. "I know how ghastly it is to get bad news when you're not somewhere you can have a private howl. It's like being ambushed."

Alice was surprised. She couldn't imagine Henry Tremaine crying. Then she remembered that he was an officer in the army and had fought in the war. He must have lost friends and comrades all the time yet been expected to keep a stiff upper lip. That must have been hideous.

"That's *exactly* it," she said, cheered to know somebody understood.

"No one's hurt or worse, I hope?"

"Oh no, nothing like that," Alice said quickly. "Everyone's quite well."

She wondered whether she ought to tell Henry Tremaine what had happened. He must think her quite deranged, since each time they met she was in some kind of emotional freefall. There was also something about this man that invited confidence and set her at ease. Maybe it was his quiet strength. Or perhaps it was because he didn't press her, or appear to feel the need to fill silence with questions. Whatever the reason, Alice trusted him innately.

She blotted her eyes with the hanky. It smelt of Lux flakes and sandalwood.

"Somebody I love ... he's found somebody else."

"Then he's a bloody fool," said Henry shortly. "An utter bloody idiot."

Alice was taken aback. She wasn't sure what response she'd expected, if any, but it hadn't been that. She couldn't help rushing to Jonny's defence.

"It's not his fault. He's found somebody his parents approve of."

"Then he doesn't deserve *you*."

Alice stared at him, taken aback by the conviction in his voice.

"She's not a fisherman's daughter. She's from a suitable family."

"What does that matter? Love isn't about who is *suitable*. That isn't love. It's expediency," Henry replied. "*Let not the marriage of true minds admit impediments*. True love doesn't care about such obstacles."

"Sonnet 116," said Alice sadly. It was her favourite. *Love is not love which alters when it alteration finds*. Her love for Jonny had been steadfast in spite of everything – but now, knowing he was courting Millicent Jago had shaken her. He had certainly bent with the remover to remove.

"You know the sonnets?"

Alice bristled. "Why shouldn't I? Because I'm just a village girl?"

"That wasn't at all what I meant," Henry said gently. "I was surprised because not many people of your age are particularly interested in Shakespeare. My nieces are far more interested in Doris Day and going dancing." He sighed. "That young man's done some damage, whoever he is."

His cornflower-blue eyes were filled with compassion, which made her want to lean against him and sob out the whole sorry tale – but he was only being kind, and wouldn't want to be bothered with the woes of a seventeen-year-old.

Alice raised her chin. "I'll be fine."

Henry was studying her face intently, as though weighing up her strengths and weaknesses and drawing a conclusion. Although she barely knew this man Alice realised that he could see through her bravado and false smiles and into her soul where the truth was curled up, sobbing. She was surprised to find that she didn't mind this scrutiny in the slightest, because it was reassuring to be seen so totally and utterly. Once again Alice understood why Henry Tremaine's men would follow him anywhere.

"You will indeed," he said slowly. "You're a strong person, Alice, and you'll move forwards. I know it hurts like hell right now, and you probably won't believe a word I say, what with my being so old – but it *will* get better and your heart will mend. One day you'll look back and wonder why you were so upset. I also promise that your young man will live to regret letting you go."

Alice doubted this very much, because when Jonny had been kissing Milly he'd looked far from regretful. Henry

Tremaine had clearly never been in love, Alice decided, but she appreciated his kind attempt at a pep talk anyway.

"You're not that old. You can't be older than my father."

He barked with laughter. "That makes me feel so much better!"

Alice was mortified. "That wasn't what I meant! You're not *old*!"

"And there I was feeling a positively spring-chicken-like thirty-four! Fetch me a walking stick and a Bath chair!"

He bent his arms and pretended to hobble along, one hand pressed into the small of his back, and in spite of her misery Alice laughed. He been transformed from a serious army officer into a man who wasn't afraid to mock himself, and the years between them seemed to vanish. He was as daft as any boy her age!

"That's more like it," said Henry once she'd caught her breath. "There's always humour to be found somewhere, and laughter's healing. I learned that during the war, and it was why so much effort went into entertaining the troops. Hitler was a damn menace, but when there was a comedian to make you laugh and take your mind off the rest, winning seemed far more likely."

"Did you see much action?" Alice asked, thinking of Daniel and of Hugo's lost brothers.

A dark cloud passed over Henry's face.

"Enough to know I never want to see any more. Anyway, never mind that. How are you doing now?"

He wanted to change the subject, and Alice understood, because Morley Pendeen never spoke about the trenches, only saying he wanted to forget those dark days. She focused on Henry's questions and was startled to find she was actually feeling a little brighter. For a few blissful moments she had been totally distracted from her woes.

"Better, thank you," she said, surprised.

"Good," said Henry Tremaine. "Now in my experience there's only one thing better than laughter when you're blue and that's a slice of cake and a cup of tea. Cake always puts the world to rights, and I happen to know that Mrs Perran has made a very fine Victoria sponge. Would you care to join me on the terrace at Seaspray?"

Alice thought of her unfinished chores at Polwenna House and the pile of laundry she'd abandoned. She really ought to return or there'd be trouble, but she couldn't face seeing Jonny and Milly together so soon. Alice knew, too, that she that couldn't work there any more; it'd be far too painful. She would hand her notice in the next day and see what else she could find. Maybe it was time to enquire at the draper's shop in town, or ask about working for the milliner. Yet the idea of seeing inside Seaspray House was tempting; her mum had always said the views from it across the village and out to sea were spectacular.

Alice almost accepted – but then a thought occurred which doused her enthusiasm: what would Elizabeth Tremaine say when her son arrived at the house with a village girl? After her experiences with the St Miltons, Alice didn't think her self-esteem would survive another knock.

"I'd love to – but what about your mother?"

"What's my mother got to do with it? There's enough cake for her, if that's what you're worried about," said Henry, puzzled.

How wonderful it must be to be him. Henry Tremaine had clearly never been sneered at or told to use the back stairs in his life.

"I wouldn't want to make anyone feel awkward," Alice said. "Your mother's from a very grand family, isn't she? I'm not the sort of girl who has tea with ladies like her. I'm the one who serves it. I've delivered fish to your cook in the past, too, and *she* might not approve, either."

"I couldn't give a hoot what Mrs Perran thinks! You're my guest, Alice," Henry said. "Mother's out this afternoon – she's visiting a garden in Fowey – but I promise you she wouldn't care who you are. She isn't snobbish in the least. All right, so she doesn't suffer *fools*, but you're far from one of those, so there's nothing to fret about."

Alice, relieved to hear that Mrs Tremaine was out, said, "I'd love some tea. Thank you."

"Marvellous. Heel, Milo! Shall we?"

He offered her his arm and, feeling very grown-up all of a sudden, Alice took it. Although Henry was tall he didn't tower over her, and it was nice to lean on somebody strong and purposeful. As they strolled along the lane Henry chatted easily about his family, his soft voice soothing as gentle waves as he told her about his parents' romantic past.

"It's true what you said earlier, about my mother coming from a grand family. She's from a branch of the St Aubyns, but she isn't a snob. Quite the opposite! Ma was a deb in the twenties and could have picked anyone, but she insisted upon marrying my father, who was a sea captain's son. Her father disowned her, so my mother brought nothing to her new home apart from a holdall and a cutting from the rose which grew beneath the window of her childhood home. The Tremaine Rose, we call it now, and it covers Seaspray. It's glorious in June."

How Alice wished Jonny was a fraction as brave as Mrs Tremaine. She couldn't imagine him leaving home with just a bag and a plant cutting.

"Your mother married beneath her?"

Henry considered this.

"I suppose so ... not that she ever saw it like that. Not one bit! She knew my father was a clever man, and she believed that with her by his side he would be able to go on to do even greater things. When a man finds the right woman, Alice, he can truly do anything with her at his side."

The passion in these words snatched Alice's breath. Who would have thought emotion ran so deep in a man as reserved and as proper as Captain Tremaine? There was clearly more to him than he let most people see, and Alice felt privileged to be taken into his confidence. Would Milly be the right woman for Jonny? At least with Dr Jago's daughter at his side doors would open, that was for certain, whereas with a fisherman's daughter for a wife many more would have slammed in his face.

Deep in thought, she followed Henry down a narrow side lane, and together they threaded their way through the cottages via the old alleyways which wiggled and forked up to the cliff path or veered downhill to the abandoned sardine works. Keen to hear more, Alice increased her pace.

"During the war Ma filled Seaspray with evacuees and helped the war effort by turning our gardens into vegetable patches," he was saying. "She loved digging for victory – Ma's got green fingers, you see – and she had chickens too, and a pig. She looked after the lot while her men were away fighting. It must have been tough, but I never once heard her complain. She's an incredible woman, Alice."

Alice had been very young during the war, but she recalled seeing the upright figure of Mrs Tremaine striding through the village with six children following in her headscarfed wake as she swapped eggs for fish or a loaf. She also had a hazy recollection of seeing her planting out greens in Seaspray's steep garden, just visible in the distance from the village ... Sometimes planes had come over and then they had all been ushered into the Anderson shelter, which Alice had thought great fun. The skies above Plymouth had been red with fire, but this had seemed wondrous, and even the dogfights over the sea had looked exciting. And how she'd loved the Americans with their honeyed voices and gifts of gum and chocolate!

"When my father was ill, Ma nursed him until the very end. It wasn't always pretty, but I never once saw her flinch," Henry told Alice as they reached the cliff path. He opened a gate for her and latched it behind them with a firm click. With his hand resting lightly in the small of her back, he guided her up a narrow path which switchbacked through a steeply terraced garden. Swaying beds of flowers flanked each side, lavender filled the air and bees thrummed through early blooms.

"What a beautiful garden!" Alice said in delight. This luxuriant growth was better by far than the St Miltons' rather sterile beds.

Henry beamed. The joy in his face stripped away the years and the care, and he looked very young.

"All Mother's doing. She dug the beds and planted the lot herself. The cutting garden over there is all her work too. She's not afraid to roll up her sleeves. We have a gardener for the lawns, but he's not allowed anywhere else. Mother does the lot."

"That's incredible," said Alice. Like many of the villagers the Pendeens had a vegetable patch of land on the cliff, and she knew from experience how hard it was to dig the soil over and keep the weeds at bay. A garden like this was hard work.

"Ma often says her mother would be in despair at the state of her hands. I suppose what I'm saying is that my mother is a strong lady and an independent thinker, and she isn't easily shocked. But woe betide anyone who gets on her wrong side!"

Alice wasn't sure whether any of this made her feel better, but since Henry Tremaine appeared certain that inviting a fisherman's daughter home for afternoon tea wasn't a problem, she decided to relax. A nose around Seaspray and a slice of cake would certainly help distract her from her woes. Elsie would pop when she heard Alice had visited the house!

"So please don't look so worried," Henry Tremaine said. "I have a feeling Ma will like you very much indeed. Aha! Here we are at last. I think the climb's worth it for the view. When my father built Seaspray he didn't really consider the practicalities."

They had arrived at a large terrace, drenched in sunshine. Henry was right; the vantage point offered an unrivalled vista over Polwenna Bay, and butterflies of light danced over the water. The sun played hide and seek with clouds and flung deep shadows over the green folds of the valley where cottages scrambled up the hillside and lanes laced it all together like a set of stays trying to contain a buxom figure. Something squeezed inside Alice's chest as she drank in the living picture. It felt a little like falling in love, and she felt certain you could live here for a hundred years and never grow tired of this view.

Henry watched her reaction with pleasure. "Do you like it?"

"I *love* it!"

Alice couldn't believe how different Polwenna Bay looked from this angle. It was just a toy village from a fairy tale. The St Miltons had a lovely sea view, but Seaspray's aspect knocked theirs into a cocked hat, for it was a living painting. A visual work of art. A feast for all the senses. A wonderful way to watch the world go by while the people down below remained oblivious of the observation.

Way down on the harbour she spotted the tiny figures of her father and Sam mending a net. Far across the valley the black-cassocked vicar was wafting through the churchyard while in the Rectory garden his daily was pegging out his long woollen combinations. The Pollards, building a dry-stone wall by the harbour, were stopping to eat their crib and chat. Everyone down there was totally unaware that Alice was watching, and this made her laugh – and feel a little nervous! If she lived here she'd watch all day and never get anything done. Even the wireless would be ignored.

"I knew you'd like it," said Henry, looking pleased.

"I love it! You can see *everything!*" She turned to him as a thought occurred. "Now I feel worried. Do you watch everything that goes on?"

He laughed.

"Not me, although when Pa was very unwell he used to lie out here looking through field glasses, and I think he enjoyed passing the time that way. But the glasses have gone now, and I've no idea where they are. Don't worry, Alice! It's the background to our life, and I assure you I've never spied on anyone. Now, let's have tea on the terrace and you can enjoy the view – and watch your neighbours if you wish!"

He led Alice to a weathered wooden table, lichen-velveted and pooled in sunshine. Shading her eyes with her hand she made out the faint outline of the Eddystone Lighthouse, a smudge against the bright sky, and the triangular sails of yachts shark-toothing the horizon.

"I need sunglasses," she said, squinting.

"This'll help."

Henry fiddled with the large cream parasol sprouting from the centre of the table. As he wound a handle vigorously, deep shade spread slowly across the terrace and Alice relaxed her eyes. Oh. It was blissful here at Seaspray.

"I'll go and see what Mrs Perran can rustle up," said Henry. "Just take a few moments to gather your thoughts. I always find sitting here and looking out to sea puts things into perspective."

Alice nodded. Henry was such a kind man and he seemed to understand so much. Even though he was so much older than her, wildly glamorous and from a very different world, she felt totally at ease in his company. Although she sensed his eyes on her and realised that he was on some level attracted to her, there was no prickly sensation of unease such as she'd experienced with other men (boys, really) in the past. Henry Tremaine was a gentleman.

Before long he returned with a tray laden with tea things and a huge wedge of sponge cake. As he'd said, a cup of tea and slice of Victoria sponge did a great deal to lift her spirits. Sitting in such a glorious spot and chatting to him about his plans for a boat yard and marina also took Alice's mind off Jonny, and she became excited about Henry's plans. Seaspray was magical, she decided. It was a healing place.

"I love sailing," he was saying as he poured Earl Grey from a silver pot. "Something about being on the water makes me feel alive. It's probably in the genes."

"Mine too." Alice raised her tea cup. "Here's to Tremaine Marine."

They chinked teacups and toasted his new venture. Alice had a good feeling about Tremaine Marine.

"And who's joined us for tea this afternoon?"

A tall woman with silver hair styled in an elegant French pleat joined them on the terrace. She was dressed in a lightweight tweed suit which displayed her slender figure to perfection. Chanel, thought Alice, eyes wide – it had to be! The cut. The fabric. The way it was so simple yet so chic. These qualities were hallmarks of that house.

"Mother!" Henry rose to his feet and kissed her, then

turned towards Alice: "Ma, this is Alice Pendeen. Alice, meet my mother, Elizabeth Tremaine."

"Hello," said Alice. She wasn't sure whether to sit or stand, and the table was too big to reach across. She hovered awkwardly while Henry pulled out a chair and settled his mother.

"Don't stand on my account," said Elizabeth to Alice, helping herself to a teacup and motioning for Henry to pour. "Lemon, not milk, darling. Go and ask Mrs Perran for some. And another cup, for you, some more cake, and whatever else she's cooked up for us."

"Sorry, Mother. I'll fetch some."

Henry retreated as ordered, leaving the two women alone. Alice understood this was a tactical move by his mother and braced herself for an interrogation. She decided to make the opening move in this game of conversational chess.

"It's lovely to meet you, Mrs Tremaine. Captain Tremaine has told me all about you."

Elizabeth arched a fine eyebrow. "Then you have the advantage, my dear. He's never once mentioned you."

She was older than Alice had first thought, in her late sixties perhaps, with a tracing of fine lines around her lips and eyes like delicately cracked porcelain. She smelled wonderful, of a deep old rose perfume with undertones of Pears soap. The pearls in her earlobes glowed with a lustre that Alice's Woolworth's choker would never possess. Everything about Elizabeth Tremaine was elegant and classy.

"Henry and I have only met a handful of times," Alice said.

"And yet here you are having tea with him." Henry's mother sounded amused. "I'm intrigued. My son isn't usually sociable. In fact, he's quite the misanthrope."

Alice struggled to equate this version of Henry with the man she knew. His easy conversation and warm manner were hardly the stuff of brooding Brontë heroes. She searched for a reply, but Elizabeth wasn't looking for an answer.

She leaned forward and cast an appraising glance over Alice.

"Tell me, are you May Pendeen's daughter?"

"Yes, Mrs Tremaine. She's my mother."

Elizabeth nodded. "I thought so. You have a look of her about you. She's a good woman. She dug up all my ornamental beds in '41 to plant potatoes. It's heavy soil here. The rain was lashing down too – but not one word of complaint. People like your mother won the war, mark my words. It wasn't just our menfolk who fought." Sharp eyes, the same summer sky blue as her son's, scrutinised Alice over the bone china. "Are you like her?"

Alice considered this. Her mother was self-contained and hard-working, but she was also unambitious and only saw a woman's role as that of a wife. Alice wanted so much more.

"In some ways – but I'm my own person too."

"I'm delighted to hear it. A woman needs to have her own identity," said Elizabeth, and then pulled a face. "Dear Lord. I'll be asking where you were born next."

"In a handbag in a cloakroom at Victoria Station," replied Alice, unable to resist it. She loved *The Importance of Being Ernest.*

Elizabeth stared at her for a split second before barking with laughter. She appeared delighted with the reply. Alice was relieved – her mother had often warned her not to show off or have ideas above her station.

"*Now* I see why Henry has invited you here. Oh, yes. Indeed I do. So, enlighten me, Miss Pendeen, as to how you came to meet my son."

Alice explained how Henry had been kind enough to help her home on Christmas Eve.

"He rescued me," she concluded. "My knee was badly cut."

"Henry's very chivalrous. He gets that quality from his father," nodded Elizabeth. Her eyes flickered over Alice and amusement curled her mouth. "I imagine he was very happy to help you, my dear."

"I'm sure he would have done the same for anyone."

"Indeed," Elizabeth said, "but he wouldn't then invite them to Seaspray for afternoon tea. There must be something very special about you, Alice Pendeen – something far more interesting than your pretty face. Those are two a penny, and Henry could take his pick if he were so inclined."

Alice blushed. "Honestly, he was just being kind."

"My son *is* kind, it's true – but he's also single-minded and determined. When he sets his heart on something he gives it his all. He always has a strategy and a game plan. His kind heart is a good cover for his iron will – as I'm sure you'll have discovered already."

The message within these words made Alice's heart thud in a way that wasn't entirely unpleasant. She recalled how Henry had refused to accept her rejection of his offer to take her home last Christmas Eve, and shivered. She hadn't been mistaken. He *was* attracted to her.

"My son always plays to win," Elizabeth said softly as Henry crossed the terrace balancing a precariously laden tray. "Just remember that."

"I'm determined to carry the lot in one go, you just see!" he called.

His mother smiled at Alice.

"As I said, Tremaine men never, ever admit defeat. Welcome to Seaspray, my dear. I have a feeling I'm going to see a lot more of you!"

CHAPTER 14

1954

"The dodgems look fun – and the lad running them's such a dish! Shall we have a go?"

Alice gave Elsie a stern look. Her friend might be head over heels in love with Hugo, but she was still a terrible flirt.

"Let's try to hook a duck," she suggested, pointing to a booth where yellow bathtub ducks bobbed in tanks of water. "We might win a goldfish."

"Or that pink teddy," said Elsie, momentarily distracted by a lurid bear. "Go on, Alice. You're a fisherman's daughter. *You* should be good at this."

Everyone in Polwenna Bay looked forward to the annual Easter Fair. For Alice the smell of frying onions, jaunty strains of pipe organ music and lurid whirl of carousel gallopers always marked the start of the summer. The whole village attended, the men heading for the shooting range to try their luck, while the women attempted hoopla or tried hooking ducks. Young men strutted through the stalls, the soft toys tucked beneath their arms won for the admiring girls at their sides, mothers queued for the swingboats with excited children while fathers smashed coconuts or decamped to the beer tent. Young women peeled away from their parents to court their sweethearts or – like Elsie – make eyes at the thrillingly dangerous boys who ran the rides.

Last year Alice had attended with Sam, who'd soon abandoned her to impress Betty Penhalligan at the coconut shy. With her dad safely ensconced in the beer tent and her mum busy gossiping with her friends, it had been easy for Alice to slip away and meet Jonny. As evening fell they'd exchanged candyfloss kisses in the shadows and watched the field transform into a wonderland of lights. It had been cool that Easter, and Jonny had tenderly slipped his coat around her shoulders, whispering that he loved her and couldn't wait for them to be together. Alice had glowed with happiness, and truly thought it could have snowed and she wouldn't have noticed. Love had kept her warm.

Now, this year, was Jonny here with Millicent? So far Alice had failed to spot him in the crowd. Whenever she glimpsed a tall dark-haired boy her poor heart still skipped a beat – only to plummet when it wasn't Jonny. She still missed him terribly, and the smell of onions, jangle of organ music and shrieks of excitement tugged her back to the previous year in a way that was beyond painful.

Alice had tried her best to make excuses not to attend the fair, even pleading that she'd been offered extra hours in the draper's shop where she now worked, but her parents wouldn't hear of it. The Easter Fair was as much a mainstay of village life as the Midnight Mass and the Boat Blessing. Missing it would have raised so many questions that Alice had decided it wasn't worth the effort. The last thing she needed was a parental inquisition.

Defeated after several failed attempts to hook a duck, Alice was forced to admit she was a useless fisherman. Was she really a Pendeen?

"Sorry, Else. That was hopeless. The pink teddy bear isn't coming home today."

"The ducks are probably weighted," Elsie said kindly. "Anyway, never mind the bear. Dishy dodgems boy is looking our way."

"You think *everyone's* looking our way."

"That's because they are," said Elsie, shooting a dazzling smile across the fairground. "We look top-notch in these dresses, because you, Alice Pendeen, are a genius. Promise you're going to make my wedding dress and my bridesmaid dresses. Promise!"

Both girls were wearing the Dior-inspired summer dresses which Alice had run up on her sewing machine. With tight bodices and full skirts worn over several net petticoats, these looked expensive even though they were fashioned out of remnants gleaned from the draper's shop. As the girls rode the carousel, modestly sitting side-saddle and clinging to the barley-sugar twist poles for dear life while the grinning horses whirled, their full skirts billowed romantically and attracted great admiration. Alice had already been asked to run up several more, and was quietly hoping she might be able to save enough money to take an evening class in dressmaking. Perhaps she could start her own business from Cobbles? She might have lost her dream of marrying Jonny, but she held this one close to her heart.

"Promise!" Elsie pressed.

Alice shook her head. "You're not even *engaged* yet!"

Her best friend tossed her blonde curls. "I will be by harvest time."

And she would be too, thought Alice with total admiration. When Elsie put her mind to something she didn't stop until it happened. Poor Hugo didn't stand a chance. Alice often wished she could be more like her single-minded friend, and that Jonny's family were as Bohemian and easy-going as the Tregarricks. If wishes were horses, as her mum would say …

Over by the dodgems the youth manning the ride was smiling cheekily at the girls. Elsie gave him a coy wave and he winked back.

She giggled and nudged Alice. "I bet he lets us ride for free!"

"You're taken, remember?"

"I might be – but *you're* not."

"I've told you, Elsie, I'm not interested."

"Don't be such a wet blanket. It's only a ride on the dodgems. He's not proposing marriage."

Alice didn't care. If it wasn't for Elsie badgering her she would have slipped away and gone home hours ago. The fair was no fun without Jonny.

Life was no fun without Jonny.

"Buck up, Alice," Elsie said, towing her to the dodgems. "Just have some fun. Do you want to end up an old spinster? Give *you know who* the satisfaction?"

Elsie had been shocked when Alice told her about Jonny, and rather hurt not to have been taken into her best friend's confidence earlier on – but, sunny by nature, she was soon over her own injured feelings and determined to cheer her best friend up. Elsie's preferred method of doing this was to spend every spare moment pointing out the charms of all the other boys in Polwenna Bay. She was on a mission to fix Alice up, but

Alice knew it was a fruitless exercise since her heart still belonged to Jonny regardless of his being tightly clutched in the palm of Milly Jago's manicured hand. How *could* Alice think of anyone else? Elsie meant well, but she didn't understand.

She was on the brink of telling Elsie she had a headache and needed to go home when a brightly painted wagon caught her eye. It was more a work of art on wheels than a home, fashioned from polished wood and richly decorated with flowers and scrolls in ornate pokerwork. The iron wheels were scarlet, and matching wooden steps led up to a doorway hung with a midnight-blue curtain embroidered with silver stars. A length of bright green canvas was stretched over hoops to create a roof, and burnished pots and pans hung beneath a ledge where a shaggy lurcher snoozed in the shade. A piebald cob with shaggy feathers and one startlingly blue eye was tethered beside the caravan champing at the grass and swishing flies away with his long tail.

Alice's attention was drawn most of all to the gilded letters painted on the side of the wagon. *Madame Sienna – Fortune Teller.* A sign propped against the ladder promised that Sienna was a true Romany whose gift had been passed down to her from generations of women. Madame Sienna could read tarot cards and palms as well as consult her crystal ball and her guides.

"What does the future hold for you? Is there love? Health? Wealth?" read Alice out loud. *"Cross my palm with silver and find out!"*

At only seventeen Alice had never worried about health a day in her life. Wealth was an abstract concept. But love? Of course Alice wanted to know what her future held when it came to love! She *had* to know if Jonny would come back to her. Maybe Madame Sienna would be able to tell her?

She tugged Elsie's arm.

"Look! Shall we go and see her?"

"What for?"

"To have our fortunes read, of course! Wouldn't you like to know if you're going to marry Hugo?"

"I don't need a gypsy to tell me that! Of *course* I'm going to marry him."

Elsie's future was laid out before her like a delicious picnic, and all she had to do was pick what choice morsels she wanted to eat.

Alice felt a pang of envy; her best friend had no need to ask questions or seek reassurance.

"I'd like to see her, anyway," she said firmly. "Maybe she'll see my future."

Elsie grabbed Alice's hand and squinted at her palm.

"I see Jonny St Milton, long forgotten by you and married to Millicent. He's leading a life of hell. Give me a sixpence, then."

Alice snatched her hand back.

"It's not funny, Elsie."

"Who says I'm trying to be funny? Maybe I have the gift? My granny can read the tea leaves. Shall I ask her to do yours? Maybe she'll see a handsome captain and a big house?"

Elsie was obsessed with Henry Tremaine, and this was driving Alice crackers. Henry, having resigned his commission, had settled into Seaspray. He and his mother were now full-time Polwenna residents, and Henry was working long hours to establish his marine business in the old sardine cannery. He was employing Peter Pollard and a host of villagers to create a marina and the infrastructure for the boatyard he'd planned for so long. Alice had visited the site several times and was thrilled to see his dream taking shape. She knew how much it meant to him, for he had confided that it was all that had sustained him when he was away fighting.

He explained how he would visualise the finished marina when all around him was death and carnage, and he knew that to make his dream a reality he had to survive.

"I've never shared that with anyone before," he'd said, looking shyly at her from beneath the wheaten fringe that had grown since he'd abandoned his regulation haircut. "Does it sound insane?"

Alice couldn't imagine what Henry had endured during the war.

"I think it sounds as though you were being really brave and holding onto something that would draw you back home. It must be incredible to see your dream come true."

Henry considered this. "It is, yes. Tremaine Marine's been a dream of mine since I was a boy and my father first took me sailing. Even then I knew I wanted to work with boats. If we hadn't been an army family I'd have probably gone into the Navy."

"Like Prince Philip," said Alice. Now she thought of it, Henry Tremaine and the Queen's handsome husband were very alike. They shared the upright bearing, that air of dash, ill-concealed impatience with foolishness, and fair good looks.

Henry smiled. "I'll take that as a compliment. He's a well-respected commander and, in my opinion, rather wasted as a consort. He strikes me as a man who thrives on activity and purpose."

Like you, thought Alice suddenly understanding. Would Henry Tremaine become bored with a quiet life in a Cornish fishing village?

"Maybe the Queen *is* his purpose? She's dedicated her whole life to the country, and he's dedicated his to her," she said slowly. "That's service to the country too, isn't it?

Henry regarded her thoughtfully. "You never fail to surprise me, Alice Pendeen."

"Why?"

"You're wise beyond your years, that's why. I'd never considered it that way, but you're absolutely right. I imagine that's exactly how Prince Philip views his role; his duty is to serve his Queen. When a man has the right woman at his side he'll step up to take on all kinds of challenges."

There was an intensity in his eyes as he said this, and Alice felt he was going to say more, something personal and which might change the nature of their friendship. This made her flustered, so she swiftly made her excuses and left. She wasn't a fool; she knew Henry was attracted to her, and if she hadn't been hoping to win Jonny back, she might have allowed herself to be attracted to Henry in return. He was a handsome man – but more importantly she enjoyed talking to him and being his friend.

Elsie seemed to have a sixth sense for Alice's feelings, for when the girls were together the number of times Elsie needed to visit the quay was astounding. She couldn't have been more obvious if she'd tried, and Alice could only hope that Henry, much older and with a business to establish, didn't mind. He was always very polite and had even taken the girls out for a short sail on his lugger, but Alice was mortified by such blatant attempts at matchmaking.

She glared at Elsie. "I told you, we're just friends."

And she and Henry *were* friends. Sometimes they met for a walk on the beach with Milo the dog. On other occasions she would deliver fish to Seaspray, and stop for a chat and a cup of tea. Last week she had helped Mrs Tremaine in the rose garden, weeding the tricky parts the older woman struggled with, and learning a lot about soil and horticulture. Henry had been digging over the beds below, unaware of the two women watching from above, and his muscled arms were so tanned that the contrast with his white linen shirt was dazzling.

When he had taken it off to work bare-chested, Alice had forced herself not to stare at the glistening pectoral muscles which tautened and swelled beneath bronzed flesh dusted with golden hair. Henry was a man, not a boy, and the difference was marked and unnerving. What would it feel like to be kissed by him? Held by somebody so powerful and strong and determined? What would his lovemaking be like? Passionate and intense, Alice had thought with a shiver – and, with his attention to detail, utterly addictive. Gooseflesh rising on her arms, she had turned away, shocked at the trajectory of her thoughts and dismayed at such disloyalty to Jonny.

Now, back on the quayside, "I think he's sweet on you," teased Elsie. "He always says hello and seeks you out. Everyone's noticed."

Alice tried to laugh this off. "It's not *me* he's interested in. He wants to employ Sam to run the boatyard."

"Only because he's *your* brother! Henry's trying to win you over by being kind to your family. It's so obvious," Elsie said pityingly. "He could employ anyone he likes, so why *Sam*, hmm?"

Alice's cheeks flamed, because Sam had asked her the very same question. He hated fishing, he said, and would jump at the chance to earn a decent wage on dry land – but why did the Captain want *him*? Was there something going on between her and Henry Tremaine? Alice had assured him that this wasn't the case, leaving out the bit about still being in love with Jonny, but part of her knew that Henry wanted more than her friendship. She found this confusing, for Henry was so much older, was socially far above her and could have any woman he chose. Or maybe he was just being kind or wanted Sam because he was honest and quick-thinking, and she was misreading the situation …

This was why Alice needed to consult Madame Sienna. She

needed some insights into her future, because without the certainty of Jonny's love she was cut loose from her moorings and adrift in a sea of confusion. Maybe this fortune teller could help.

"Well, I'm *going* to have my fortune read," she told Elsie, who pulled a face but knew better than to try and change Alice's mind. Arranging to meet her best friend later on by the swingboats, Alice climbed the wagon steps and left Elsie contemplating the dodgems.

"Your path is not hers," said a slow and deep voice in heavily accented English.

Alice jumped. The curtain swung aside as though by magic to reveal an elderly woman standing to the side of the aperture, holding back pleats of fabric in a clawed hand. She regarded Alice with shrewd black eyes, and although she was small and wizened there was a regal dignity and raw power about her. She was richly dressed in a flowing scarlet skirt patterned with flowers and swirls of silver, and a black velvet bodice was laced tightly across her bony chest. A billowing snowy blouse and fringed emerald shawl completed the outfit, and her grey hair, plaited and coiled, was covered with a scarlet scarf. Gold coins hung at her throat, bangles chimed on bony wrists and heavy hooped earrings swung from stretched lobes.

Goodness! She certainly looked the part.

"Come in my dear," said Madame Sienna. "I sense you have many questions."

Alice ducked her head and stepped inside. The interior of the wagon was dark, and it took a few moments for her eyes to adjust to it. Then she saw a black pot-bellied stove at the far end. Bright rag rugs covered the polished floor. Lacy curtains hung over windows shaped like cough drops, and a lantern, positioned to light a small table draped in midnight-dark velvet, swung from the canvas ceiling. Narrow bunks covered in bright quilts lined either side of this small space and served as seats for the table, which boasted a crystal ball and deck of tarot cards.

"Sit, my child."

Madame Sienna indicated the left banquette, and Alice did as she was asked. The curtain fell and the fortune teller lowered herself opposite Alice.

"What's your name, my dear?"

"Alice, Madame Sienna," she said.

Her voice was a whisper, for she was suddenly afraid. What would Reverend Sharpe say if he found out Alice Pendeen had been to see a fortune teller? It would be fire and brimstone until Christmas. Or maybe burning at the stake. If Alice hadn't been so in awe of this regal woman she would have bolted.

"Call me Sienna, child. Do not be afraid or doubt me. I have the gift. Do you have a specific question?"

Alice nodded. Her mouth parched and she couldn't speak.

"Very well," said the fortune teller. "Let me see what secrets lie hidden within your palm."

Alice rested her shaking right hand in the old woman's veiny claw. What would the fortune teller see? Did Jonny still love her? Would he come back to her? Would they marry? She held her breath and hoped to hear the answers she so longed for.

Madame Sienna stared intently at the map of lines criss-crossing Alice's palm. She ran a bony forefinger across the callouses and over Alice's short, scrubbed nails and ragged cuticles. Alice pictured Milly Jago's cream-softened hands and polished nails, and felt ashamed. Even in her pretty dress she knew she was coarse and shabby.

"You are a young woman who gives her heart and soul when she loves and who is not afraid to face opposition or danger," Madame Sienna began in a low and throaty tone. "You work hard and you're not afraid to do so."

Alice was disappointed. Who wouldn't give all when they were in love? And one look at her hands betrayed how hard she worked.

"I have no choice. If I don't work hard we don't eat," she said with a grimace.

Sienna examined her palm more closely.

"There's always a choice in life if we look for it. You have dreams and you need to follow them. You have a path that is yours alone to tread – but take care, my dear, for you are ruled by your heart and it blinds you to people's true intentions. You love passionately, but I see you have been let down by one young man, and because you love so deeply you are very hurt."

Alice gasped. This was all true!

"I still love him. Does he still love me? Can you see that with your gift?"

The fortune teller raised Alice's palm closer to the light.

"There is much love between you both, that's clear, but you need to put him from your mind until he's worthy of you. Only when he is ready and deserving can you open your heart to him again. Not a moment before."

Alice leaned forward. "How long will that be? Soon? A few months? A year?"

She was eager to know just how much longer she had to endure Millicent Jago's jubilation. Alice thought she might just about manage a year of seeing Jonny and Milly together if she knew that an end was in sight to the torture.

But Madame Sienna shook her head. The gold coins on her headdress jangled.

"That I cannot tell you, for it is a part of *his* journey, and he has his own path to follow. See here? This is your love line. It breaks here, then forks off. Later on that line rejoins it after the second one."

"What does that mean?"

Sienna looked at Alice, long and hard. Her dark eyes were bottomless and infinitely wise.

"It means that you are a lucky woman who will be much loved in this lifetime. There are many that would like to win you, but you will not settle for anything less than true love, no matter what they might offer. You are not easily won, or impressed by worldly trappings."

Alice thought of Barry Penhalligan with his new boat and inside plumbing.

"You will know great love not once but twice in this lifetime," Sienna continued. "Both men will love you deeply, but you are linked with one of them not just in this life but in those that have come before. He is your soulmate and will be the great love of your life. He will sense this even if he doesn't understand it yet, or acknowledge it. The same is true of you, for although you and he may appear different you are two halves of the same coin. Together you will build a dynasty and a wonderful life."

This had to be Jonny! Alice was so excited. She *knew* he was the love of her life. The other man – the faceless one – she was far less interested in.

"How many children will I have?" she asked. Alice really wanted a big family; she had loved growing up with Danny and Sam but had always longed for a sister. Five children seemed like a nice number. She and Jonny had already picked their names, dreaming about the fun they would all have growing up in Polwenna Bay.

Sienna peered at her hand more closely and a frown creased her brow.

"I see only one, yet I also see many. How strange. Look at

how the lines bifurcate here. It could be one, or it could be at least seven. There are more in the future, too. A long line of descendants. They are like stars in the sky."

"Lots, then."

Alice was pleased. Jonny liked children and she knew he'd be a wonderful father – and then she urged,

"Tell me more about the love of my life." She wanted as much proof as possible to sustain her, already knowing she would be dwelling on the fortune teller's words in the weeks ahead. Jonny wouldn't stay with Millicent – that was clear now – and it was only a matter of time until he saw sense. Alice felt so happy that it was all she could do not to fling her money at Madame Sienna and run outside shouting with joy.

"He is wise and kind, but he can also be stubborn and self-destructive," warned Sienna. "You are in his thoughts, and he is drawn to you against all logic. I see a long life with him in a house by the sea, and a midsummer kiss will seal your union. The kiss will capture his heart for all time and will mark the start of your journey."

It *was* Jonny! Polwenna House overlooked the water, and Jonny could be very stubborn, as Alice knew only too well! All she had to do was make sure she kissed him at midsummer, and all would be well. Her future would be sealed and her happy ever after in the bag.

"The other man is a far lighter energy than the first, yet troubled in his own way. The two men are opposites, but each will love you and will bring great happiness in different seasons of your life. You are blessed – but oh—"

Madame Sienna stopped abruptly.

A finger of ice traced Alice's spine.

"What is it?"

The fortune teller shuddered almost imperceptibly –"A farewell lies ahead." Alice snatched her hand back. Suddenly she didn't like thinking of secrets hidden in the lines and whorls, or her future as written. It felt too sinister. Too inescapable.

"Who will I be saying farewell to? Will someone die?"

Sienna shook her head. The earrings brushed her cheeks as she rose to her feet.

"I cannot see any more, for the Sight has fled. All I can tell you is that this loss is linked to your destiny. It has to be. From deep sorrow will come deep happiness. Joy will rise like a phoenix from the ashes. Love shall bloom in the stoniest ground."

Alice shivered. She wasn't sure if she liked the sound of this.

"So it'll all be all right in the end?"

"There's a long life ahead of you, my dear. A blessed life, not without its sorrows, but long and filled with love." Madame Sienna looked exhausted and impossibly ancient. "That's what I can see for you. That and no more. Now cross my palm with silver, child, and may God bless you."

The sunshine and the noise of the fair had been absent from the van, as though the outside world had ceased to exist once the curtain had sealed the wagon door, and as Alice emerged she felt as though she was waking up after a very strange dream. Snatches of the conversation played through her mind, but it was hard to remember everything that Madame Sienna had said, and by the time Alice spotted Elsie giggling with the lad running the swingboats the entire reading had crystallised into one message: Jonny St Milton was the love of her life, and once she kissed him at midsummer all would be well.

All she needed to do now was find a way to make this happen.

CHAPTER 15

MAY 1954

"Alice! Wake up! Alice!"

In the first few seconds of swimming upwards from a deep sleep, Alice didn't know whether she was still dreaming, and this urgent voice was part of an unconscious landscape, or if her mother really was shaking her. The exhaustion of a busy day at work followed by an evening of lugging heavy boxes of fish on her delivery round dragged Alice backwards into her dreams, and she burrowed deeper beneath the blankets. Outside the wind was gusting and pummelling the village, and rain pattered against the window.

She turned away from the voice. It was so warm and comfortable in bed …

"Alice! Wake up!"

Fingers bit into her shoulder, and moments later the counterpane was whipped away. Cool air chilled her bare legs and all traces of sleep were ripped away with the covers. Opening her eyes, Alice saw her mother, already dressed, was pulling clothes out of the chest of drawers as though possessed.

She rubbed her eyes, confused. There was no light creeping in through the gap between the curtains and the dawn chorus, her usual alarm call, was yet to break the silence. Her small room was only lit with the lantern her mother had placed on the bedside table and her shadow loomed monstrously against the far wall, Nosferatu in curlers.

Alice sat up and rubbed her eyes. Her alarm clock read four in the morning. It was too early even for her mother to be awake, and Alice felt a prickle of irritation. She had a rare day off from the draper's and had been looking forward to a lie-in.

"Mum? What's wrong?"

Her mother was busy rooting through the top drawer and too intent on finding clothes to answer. She tugged out a thick sweater and tossed it onto Alice's bed. Moments later socks and slacks followed.

"Get dressed. We have to go."

She wore a flannel night gown teamed with gumboots. She had flung a raincoat over the top, but her curlers were still in and she wasn't wearing a scrap of makeup.

Unease crawled over Alice's skin.

"What's going on?" she demanded, swinging her legs out of the bed and reaching for the sweater. Although it was spring, Cornwall was cold this year with unseasonal storms, and heavy rain had been lashing Cobbles for most of the night.

"I'm heading out, love! Barry's going to launch his boat. We've put a shout out for the lifeboat."

Her father's voice rang through the small cottage, louder than Alice had ever heard it, and tight with urgency. If the call had been put out for the lifeboat it only meant one thing: a fishing boat was in trouble. This happened rarely, but when it did the whole village was rallied to help. Alice remembered the night Tommy Jago's lugger had gone down on the Shin-deeps, a bank of lethal rocks several miles out from Polwenna, and how she had stood on the quay with the women waiting for news while the men put out to sea. Alice had only been tiny, but the recollection of the long wait and the heavy silence which followed the dreadful outcome still gave her chills. Fishing was a dangerous way to scratch a living, and very few families in Polwenna were fortunate enough not to have lost someone to the sea. Alice sent up a silent prayer of thanks that her dad was home.

"Who's in trouble?" she asked, pulling on the sweater then hopping into her trousers.

Her mother was facing away from Alice. Her shoulders heaved and she made a strange strangled noise, halfway between a gasp and a sob.

"It's Sam."

Alice froze, one leg in and one out of her slacks. She caught sight of her mother's face in the mirror, haggard and prematurely aged with misery, and horror weakened her legs so utterly that she collapsed onto the bed. It couldn't be Sam. That was impossible.

"But Pa's here," she whispered.

"Your brother took the boat single-handed."

Their eyes met in the mirror. Both women were transfixed by terror. Taking a fishing boat out single-handed, in effect alone and with no crew to keep watch, was incredibly risky, and something the men only did when they were desperate. After a rough winter and an equally poor spring, and with Alice earning far less in the draper's than she had brought in from the St Miltons, the Pendeens' finances were in a desperate state. The previous day had brought strong gusts of wind and sharp squalls racing across the water. By suppertime the rain had been lashing down, and Morley had decided against venturing out to haul their nets. Sam had insisted they could make it out and back before the bad weather really hit, but Morley had put his foot down.

"It's too risky, son. I've seen it before. A spring storm'll turn on you like a stray dog."

Sam had scowled. "We need the money. If the nets stay out any longer the catch'll be ruined. We could even lose the nets, and we can't afford to risk that."

Morley had slammed his fist onto the table. Plates bounced and water sloshed from glasses.

"Christ! I said *no*, boy, and that's my last word on the matter. I'm the skipper, not you."

Nobody had felt much like eating after this exchange. Alice and May had cleared the table and washed up while Morley listened to the wireless and Sam had stomped off to the pub – or so they'd all thought. Tired from a long day at work, Alice had gone to bed long before Sam was expected home, but now she wished she'd stayed up to chat to him. That way she would have noticed his absence.

"Oh, Mum," Alice whispered.

May leaned on the dressing table and closed her eyes.

"We had no idea he'd taken the boat. The first we knew was when there was a knock on the door at four from Joe Levitt. He was fuming because the harbour gate had been left open and several tenders were loose. He tore a strip off me until your father appeared. Well, you can imagine Joe's shock. We soon realised Sam must have put out to sea alone – no wonder the gate wasn't shut."

Joe, who had captained the Polwenna Bay Home Guard with a rigour the army would have envied, was now the harbour master, and a stickler for procedure and rules. Henry often joked that he was jumping through so many hoops for Joe he ought to join the circus, not run a boatyard.

"Sam's bed was empty, and your dad flew down to the quay to find the boat missing. It's two hours, give or take, to make that trip to the Shindeeps, and Sam should've been back long ago. Your dad and Ed Penhalligan were trying to decide whether to put to sea themselves when Joe had a call from the coastguard."

"What did they say?"

Alice's mother looked at her for what felt like an age.

"You must be brave, love … news had come in of a gill netter hitting the rocks about a mile east of Adriatic Point. It was *Girl May*."

Alice felt the room recede. They both knew what this meant; Sam must have fallen overboard while hauling his nets, and the vessel had continued without him. If he hadn't been caught in the winding gear, a horrible fate, then he would have fallen into the water. When May held out her arms Alice flew into her mother's embrace and wept into her shoulder.

"Barry's going out to where our nets are in case Sam fell overboard. They've called the lifeboat out to Adriatic Point, but there's a lot of swell so they don't think it'll get close enough," said May, holding Alice tightly.

"Sam's a strong swimmer," Alice said. She was desperate to look for hope.

"He is," agreed May, but everyone in Polwenna knew that the icy water would soon sap a man's strength.

Alice wasn't giving up. "Or he might have clung to the wreckage. Sam's *tough,* Ma. He'll be fine."

May didn't reply, and Alice was searching for some words of comfort when there was a loud knock on the door followed by a greeting.

"Hello? Alice? May? Anyone at home?"

It was Henry Tremaine.

Alice flew down the stairs feeling ridiculously relieved to

find him on the doorstep. If anyone could help now and find Sam it was her friend. Henry, tall and solid and capable, was dressed for action in a windcheater and gumboots, and without thinking she sagged against him, choking out what had happened.

"I know, I know," he said, resting a gentle hand on the crown of her head. One arm held her up, and his quiet strength felt infinitely right in a way Alice that couldn't articulate.

"I'm heading up a search party to walk down the cliffs to Adriatic Point. The lifeboat crew can't get close enough, what with the breakers, so they're heading to the position where Sam was hauling his nets."

Henry didn't release Alice as he spoke and she didn't pull away from him. Something flowed between them, a close accord that couldn't wholly be explained in the context of such a brief friendship, and Alice realised she trusted him completely to handle things. As Henry explained how he would drive his Jeep across the fields and lead a team of men down the treacherous footpath to the rocks where *Girl May* was breaking up, Alice knew he'd leave no stone unturned. Henry was going into battle for Sam, and the manoeuvre would be executed exactly to plan.

"That's a big ask," May said, looking worried. "The path's dangerous enough and you might not like what you find."

Henry nodded, a grim expression on his face. He knew as well as anyone what might be waiting for him in the wreckage of the boat.

"If Sam's there we need to help him. Please don't worry on my account, Mrs Pendeen. Just look after yourself and Alice."

"I'm coming too."

Alice looked up at Henry, afraid she'd been lulled into

passivity. There was no way on earth she could stay in Cobbles while Sam was missing. She would go insane.

"It's too dangerous," Henry said. "Your father can come with us. You need to stay here with your mother in case there's news from the coastguard."

Alice crossed her arms.

"My dad's knee won't take that descent. He's much better off here with Mum, waiting to hear from the lifeboat."

Henry frowned. "No, Alice. I won't let you put yourself in danger."

His voice contained the same imperious note Alice recognised from Christmas Eve and hearing him organise his builders, but she ignored it. This was far more important than wrecked shoes or the position of pontoons.

"That path's lethal if you don't know it well. *Do* you know it, Henry?"

He shook his head.

"*I* do," said Alice. She had climbed down it many times with Jonny, for the hidden cove beneath was perfect for secret meetings. "I can lead you and the others."

Her mother looked aghast. "That path's dangerous at the best of times, Alice, and it's dark and wet now."

"The dawn's breaking and the rain's easing off."

Alice reached for the mackintosh hanging on the newel post. It was Sam's, last worn on the way home from taking Betty to the pictures, and as she shrugged it on Alice prayed it would bring her luck. She was hoping against all the odds that her brother was injured or trapped in the wheelhouse. He *had* to come home. Anything else was unthinkable.

"Come on, Henry. We're wasting time."

There are moments in life when time seems concentrated and it feels as though the future is balanced on the head of a pin. This was the one thing – maybe the only thing – Alice could do for her brother. She couldn't bear to be inactive or seen as less than Henry's equal. If he denied her this opportunity to act then he didn't understand her at all and their friendship was no more than an illusion.

But Henry nodded, even though he was clearly troubled.

"Very well. The Jeep's parked by the bakery. I'll meet you there."

"Be careful," May implored Alice. "I can't lose you both."

Her mother looked very small all of a sudden, and Alice hugged her tightly.

"Your daughter's safe with me, Mrs Pendeen," Henry promised. He glanced at Alice, and the admiration in his eyes made her breath catch. "Besides, she's the most capable woman I know."

Later, whenever she attempted to recall the events of that day, Alice would never be sure how long it took to reach the headland. She recalled squashing into the back of a battered American vehicle with the Pollard brothers and balancing a pile of blankets on her lap, but the journey itself was a blur of twisting lanes, men jumping out to open gates, and endless jolting over plough and tussocky pasture. Then they were spilling out into a grey morning, the sky pearly white with an over easy egg of sun poking through, while the sea hissed and spat below like fat in a pan.

Alice stood at the top of the path with the fresh wind whipping her hair into her eyes. At the bottom of a dizzying drop below was the battered hull of the boat, no more than blue and red splinters in boiling grey water, and her heart lurched at the terrible sight. If Sam was in that wreckage, how could he have possibly survived the impact and the cold, let alone the razor-sharp rocks?

He couldn't.

She blinked back tears. How was it possible that this place

– the setting for picnics, beach gatherings and her trysts with Jonny – could have turned on the Pendeens? She and Sam had swum here as children and flown kites on the small sickle of sand given up grudgingly at low tide by the covetous sea. She feared the same hungry water had claimed her brother … but she would not leave him there all alone. Come what may, she would do her best to bring Sam home.

"You don't have to do this," Henry said quietly. He was carrying a first aid kit, and behind him the Pollard brothers bore a stretcher.

Alice thought of her brother Danny, and of Henry's brothers and all the other young men who had done things they didn't really have to do but which they had known were their utter and certain duty. She thought of how she had watched Spitfires and Messerschmitts dogfighting above the sea, and she recalled all the brave women who'd waved their menfolk farewell at Polwenna Halt. Her tears over Jonny, and her obsession with winning him back, now felt childish. She was facing something far worse than a broken heart. How bitter it was to realise that all those times she had been sobbing into her pillow her life was actually wonderful, because all her dear ones were safe. When dreadful events swamped the everyday, how precious the trivial and mundane became!

These were split-second thoughts, as sudden as the bursts of frilled sunlight around dove-grey clouds, and as she looked up into Henry's blue eyes Alice was filled with a determination to never take anyone for granted again.

"It's the one thing I *can* do. I'm light enough not to dislodge the boat from the rocks when I climb onto the wreckage. That'll help. You know it will."

"I do know," he said grimly. "I just would rather you didn't have to, Alice. I can't lose you as well. I *can't*."

Alice had no idea what Henry was referring to. His brothers? His fallen comrades? Sam?

"You won't. I know the way. Follow me exactly, and don't step off the path I pick," she said, pushing away her fear. "Try to edge down sideways if you can. Pete and Ross, keep a few yards between you."

"I haven't been this way since I was a nipper," remarked Ross Pollard, peering down nervously and turning slightly green. "I didn't mind heights back then – but I'm not so sure I can do this now."

"Do it for Sam," said his brother.

Slowly and in single file they began the descent. Alice led with Henry close behind, and she heard him catch his breath several times when he missed his footing or slipped on scree. It was one thing to make the journey on a sunny day, laughing with Jonny and taking a leisurely approach, but another altogether to be battered by a strong wind, slithering on wet rock and in a hurry, for each minute was another minute her brother didn't have to spare if he was still on board that vessel. The path twisted and switchbacked, and as she edged her way along Alice tried not to look down at the snarling rock fangs and foaming water. Poor *Girl May* writhed with each pounding onslaught, and her hull splintered like matchwood. They all knew nobody within the boat could withstand such an assault.

Halfway down, the path veered to the left and plunged into emptiness, carrying the unwary into eternity. Alice turned sharp right. It was easier from this point onwards, because smugglers had hewn steps into the rocks to make landing their contraband less tricky. Only one last leap, and she would be on the same lip of jagged rock as the boat.

"Here, let me help."

Henry leapt down first, as lithe and agile as a panther, and reached for Alice. He lifted her easily and set her down as though she was made of china.

"Ready?" he asked.

Alice swallowed. Seeing *Girl May* so broken and battered was truly awful. The old boat was a part of the family as well as their only means of income, and she had been a faithful friend for Alice's whole life. To know her brother could be trapped in the wheelhouse or mangled in the winding gear made her stomach roil like the waves, yet she understood it was a better proposition than him being out in the sea somewhere.

Oh Lord. What might she find in there? What might she see?

Suddenly Alice was shaking. Her whole being was consumed with a dread so choking and visceral that she knew she could go no further.

"I can't go on board, Henry. I'm so sorry. I don't think I can do it."

He squeezed her shoulder.

"There's nothing to apologise for. You don't have to do anything more. Christ, Alice, you've done more than enough just getting us here – no, stay with her," he ordered the Pollards as Peter stepped forward. "The boat's only just balancing, and too much weight will tip her. I'll go alone."

Alice watched with a racing heart as he picked his way over the slippery, jagged rocks towards the boat. The currents were lethal here, and she was terrified he would be sucked into the water and dashed against the rocks, but Henry Tremaine was strong from hours of sailing and riding, and his balance was good. Somehow he managed to traverse the rocks without incident. She saw him grimace as he pulled himself onto the remains of the bow and edged towards the wheel-house, knees bent and hips supple, as the wreckage bucked and surged beneath his feet. When he almost lost his footing she cried out, her heart hammering so loudly she could hear it above the waves. The water tugged at his boots as though wanting to consume him, and he was soon soaked and in his socked feet.

"That was close," breathed Ross.

"I'm going inside," Henry called. "If I'm not back in five minutes, go back up and call the coastguard. Do *not* attempt to come and find me under any circumstances. Is that clear?"

Peter gave him a thumbs up. Alice said nothing. She knew if Henry didn't reappear she would do her utmost to get onto the boat. There was no way she would leave her brother and her friend out here. No way at all.

"Bloody hell, the Captain's got balls," said Ross, and then flushed. "Sorry, Alice,"

"No need to apologise," she said. Henry Tremaine was the bravest person she knew, and her admiration knew no ends. He hardly knew Sam, yet he was risking his life for him. That was brave and selfless, and she longed to thank him properly.

"Honest to god, I'd follow him into battle – and you as well actually, Alice, after you went down that path like you did. You and the captain are two peas in a pod," said Peter.

Alice wasn't sure about that, but there was a peculiar chord of sympathy between her and the Captain. What had Madame Sienna said? Something about a soulmate? Surely that meant Jonny. Alice wished she'd paid more attention, rather than making the fortune teller's every word point towards the boy she loved.

She'd been right all along about Henry's men following him willingly. Right now she'd have done the same. Not for the first time Alice wondered why there wasn't a Mrs Henry Tremaine. Once this was over and Sam safely home, she'd invite Henry to Cobbles for dinner, and maybe he'd tell her family a little more about himself. They'd talk about how he and Alice had rescued Sam, then Sam would be embarrassed at causing such a fuss, and then Henry would give Sam a job at the boatyard and he'd never be in danger again. All would be well.

It was a lovely dream – but Alice already knew a dream was all it would ever be. When Henry reappeared alone, what little hope she'd had was lost. Her brother – her hot-headed, brave, beloved and only remaining brother – was gone.

Sam Pendeen would never come home again.

CHAPTER 16

THE PRESENT

"What happened next? Did the lifeboat find him?"

Holly gripped the pew in her gloved hands. She must have been expecting this story to conclude with a daring rescue and an against-the-odds survival, Hollywood style.

How Alice wished she could tell the young woman that Sam had drifted home astride a piece of driftwood and all had been well. She'd wished it all those years ago as she, her mother and the rest of the villagers had waited on the quay-side for Barry's search boat to return, praying that against all the odds Sam would be found safe and well.

Silence hung over the village like a gill net that morning. Even the gulls had been quiet, as though subdued by the sombre mood. The gathered villagers were oblivious to the beauty of the bright new day, the glittering storm-whipped waves, wheeling gulls and sparkling sand. They stared ahead; all eyes trained on the sharp line of the horizon as though willpower was enough to draw Sam home. The collective gathering was instinctive and a part of life in a fishing community. Most of the villagers were descended from fishing families who had held this same bleak vigil for generations. As long as men had set out to sea from Polwenna, fishing boats had been lost and the families of those of board had waited on the quay for a vessel that would never return.

The only sounds were the slap of waves against moored boats and May's sniffs. Her son was missing and her husband sailing a rough sea to search for him. Mamie Penhalligan stood beside May while her daughter Betty wept into a hanky. Even Reverend Sharpe was present, and for once Alice had been pleased to see him; surely he would be able to persuade the Almighty to bring Sam home. Alice had given up bargaining with God a while back, since nothing she'd offered seemed to have enticed Him to change Jonny's mind – but now, as she stood on the quay, she promised that if God brought Sam home she'd never ever again moan about work or bleat on about her broken heart.

Once the silent ride back to Polwenna was over, Henry, Alice and the Pollards returned to the quay, but there was little to be done but wait. Henry fetched field glasses from the marina, which he trained on the horizon with a hawklike intensity. He passed them to Alice from time to time, and as she squinted against the glare of molten sunlight she had a premonition that she would look back on this enforced inertia with longing, since it was a time when there was still hope …

Now Holly asked quietly in the silence of the church, "Alice? Was Sam all right?"

"I'm afraid not," Alice said quietly. "They never found him."

She recalled the punching shock of hearing her father explain that there had been no sign of Sam by the Shindeeps. Not so much as a woolly hat or a boot bobbing, he had said hoarsely. They'd hauled the nets, Barry Penhalligan had added, but they'd been empty. The look in Barry's eyes had said *thank God*, but May had wailed at this revelation.

"Where *is* he?" she'd sobbed. "Where's my boy?"

There had been no answer. Sam Pendeen had been lost to the sea. The demanding, hungry water had claimed Alice's brother.

Grief cast a long shadow, and now, although Sam had been dead for over sixty years, Alice still caught herself searching for him on the quay or calling one of her grandsons by his name.

Holly's hand rose to her mouth.

"He *died?*"

"I'm afraid he did."

"But he was so young!"

"Far too young – but fishing's dangerous. I believe at least ten fishermen are lost each year in this country alone," Alice said.

"I get that your brother had no choice – but there must be safer ways to earn a living nowadays."

There was no way Alice could explain how fishing was in the blood or convey the passion with which the fishermen spoke of each trip, retelling every detail in the pub and talking of their catch with more passion than they ever spoke of their wives. Each man had no sooner moored up than he was yearning to put sea again. It wasn't a job but a way of life, and one which ran through Polwenna folk like the seams of pink and purple through the rocks on the beach. It wasn't so long ago that the trawler belonging to Alice's grandson, Nick, had gone down in the very area where Sammy had been lost. Nick, luckier than his great-uncle, had been rescued, but Alice had been a nervous wreck until he decided to hang up his oilskins.

"It's a well-paid job all year round – and there's not many of those about in villages like Polwenna," was all she said. "I know the village looks busy now, but as soon as New Year's Eve is over it'll be quiet, and all the gift shops and cafés will close until Easter. The fishermen know the risks, but they enjoy the work, and it's a way of life. We all live side by side with the fear, and everyone born in Polwenna has a healthy respect for the sea. My parents came from a long line of fisherfolk and knew the risks as well as anyone. The sad truth is that Sam shouldn't have gone to sea when it was rough – and he definitely shouldn't have gone alone."

Yet no matter how aware of the risks you were, nothing prepared you for the reality of losing someone to the sea. Alice's stomach still dropped when she thought of her brave and impulsive brother's final moments. And at home, another empty seat at the kitchen table had all but broken her parents. Without Sam clomping about and arguing with Alice, the cottage had breathed silence.

"It's so *unfair*. He only wanted to help your parents," Holly said.

Alice couldn't argue. She had raged at God for a long time.

"Life can be that way at times. Please don't be sad. It was a very long time ago. Why, Sammy would have been almost a hundred now!"

A lifetime had raced by since Alice had seen her brother's cheeky grin, but she still missed him. It wasn't the acute bite of new grief, but rather the ache of long absence. A background sadness of what might have been had Sam not put to sea all those years ago. Alice often wondered what his life would have looked like. Would he have kept on fishing? Married Betty, and provided Alice with lots of nephews and nieces? Or would he have followed his dreams of higher education as soon as finances had allowed? He'd dreamed of travelling, often talking about Australia, and Alice suspected that he and Betty might have set off for a golden new life on the other side of the world. How sad that his story was left unwritten, the sentence incomplete and the ink spattered across the page as his narrative was cut off before its time.

So much life and potential lost far too soon. Sam lived only in her memory now – and how long did she have left? His name, although etched in a memorial on the church wall, was rarely mentioned, and nearly all of their friends had already headed for the summer lands. Soon her impulsive, fiery brother would be lost to living memory. Alice could have felt sad about this too, but she was older now, and she understood that unless an exceptional life is led – one documented in the history books or perhaps on celluloid – every name eventually grows faint, and as children and grandchildren follow, the older faces and names slip into shadow. The oldest tombs in the churchyard with their time-blurred engravings and lichen-furred stones guarding soft grassy mounds were the resting places of folk whose memories had been long lost to time. In the end nothing remained of anyone but snatches of dreams and whispers. Alice took comfort in knowing that Sam's adventurous nature lived on in her own son, that his fiery temper was echoed in her granddaughter Mo, that Symon had Sam's sunset hair and that his loyal heart beat in the chest of her dear Jake. Nothing is ever truly lost, since everyone carries a little piece of those who have come before.

"So what happened next, if you don't mind telling me about it?" Holly asked.

The young visitor was clearly so engrossed in Alice's story

that she was no longer dwelling on her broken heart. That was a good sign. Alice would press on with the tale and do her best to leave this sad part behind. She'd had to revisit it because Sam's loss was instrumental in what was to follow, and a huge indication that the Romany fortune teller had been genuine.

"There was no body," Alice continued, closing her eyes. "We had to wait for the coroner to rule officially that Sam was dead, so there was no funeral. No closure, as we'd say nowadays. My father wasn't fishing since we had no boat, and poor Mum couldn't get out of bed. I tried going back to the draper's shop, but I was in a dreadful state – I could hardly string a sentence together, let alone serve customers – and they sent me home. So no money was coming in, and things were looking desperate for us."

"You must have been really stressed out."

"Fact! As my great-grandson might say," agreed Alice. "Why don't you have a look at the brass plaque we had made for Sam? It's beside the war memorial. And maybe ask Perry to find us some more hot drinks. There's always coffee on the go in the vestry."

Holly gave her a narrow look. "Are you trying to matchmake?"

"No – but if I was he's definitely one of the good ones," Alice replied. She could never understand why dear Perry was so unlucky in love. He was so sweet and kind and attractive in a dishevelled, floppy-haired way. Perhaps he just hadn't found the right girl? Alice often wondered what Elsie would have made of her great-grandson. She felt that the young Elsie would have chatted him up in a heartbeat, while the older version would tell him to tuck his shirt in and drag a brush through his hair. Didn't age do strange things to folk! Alice still felt just the same inside as she always had, but maybe she'd changed too. What would her younger self make of the woman she had become?

"If I were looking for a man I think I just might find religion if that's the vicar," Holly was saying. "I bet he's way hotter than your Reverend Sharpe."

Alice followed her gaze. Neil Cavendish, the curate, was putting the finishing touches to the pulpit that she and Elsie had decorated all those years ago. It was too cold for Neil's usual kilt, but skinny jeans showed off his muscled legs and the greens in his sweater set off his sherry-hued eyes to perfection. The dog collar worn at a rakish angle lent him just the right amount of dash. Neil was very *The Thornbirds,* Alice thought wistfully recalling one of her favourite 1980s bonkbuster novels. Ah well! She might be old, but she could still admire God's creation. Neil was definitely easier on the eye than Reverend Sharpe.

"Reverend Neil certainly is a handsome young man – and I imagine his husband thinks so too," she remarked.

"Can't I just *pick* 'em?" sighed Holly. She hauled herself to her feet and stretched. "I'll see what I can do about hot drinks."

Alice watched her cross St Wenn's and pause by Sam's memorial. Next to it was the Roll of Honour for those fallen in both wars. Daniel's name was on that, along with Perry's great-uncles, Henry's brothers and so many others. Life was fleeting and precious, Alice thought. If only Holly could see this and realise that what felt so unbearable now would soon pass – but this was a lesson she'd have to learn for herself. After all, would the young Alice have listened to anyone who'd told her that her heartbreak would ever lessen, or a day dawn when she no longer woke up thinking of Jonny?

She needed to compose herself before continuing with her story. Recalling these long-ago events was far more exhausting than she'd anticipated. How incredible that even though it was all such a long time ago these recollections possessed the power to whisk her back to the grieving girl she'd once been. It was as though the emotions had lain dormant all these years, waiting for the moment when she might feel strong enough to wake them. Now they were back and clamouring to be felt. It was shattering …

"Two coffees and half a packet of custard creams … Oh! Did I wake you?"

Holly was back and bearing two steaming mugs.

"I must have dozed off. What a bore it is, getting old."

"I don't want to keep you. You must have a lot to do since it's Christmas Eve."

"Nothing that won't wait a while," Alice said, reaching for her drink.

Holly sat down and blew steam from her coffee. Alice, knowing the church machine liked to serve drinks at molten-lava temperatures, balanced hers on the hymn book ledge to cool.

"So, you became friends with Captain Henry, who had a thing about you," Holly prompted. "What next?"

What next indeed? Alice was about to pick up her story when a loud clatter followed by a cry made both women jump. Coffee sloshed onto Holly's coat.

"Careful!"

In front of the bell tower a large scaffolding platform had been erected, draped in tinsel and set up as a stage for scenes from the Nativity to be acted out during the big Christmas Day service. A long pole with a huge star attached to it appeared to have fallen to earth, nearly impaling Jen Wheeler.

Jen glared up at the skinny young man in flowing white robes who was clinging to the top of the scaffold.

"You could've hit me, Roger! What are you *doing* up there?"

"I'm looking at the crib," the angel said. "I'm Gabriel."

"Not until tomorrow," Jen screeched.

Gabriel appealed to the portly man standing by the improvised stage.

"I'm getting in role, aren't I, Dad?"

His father flourished a thick sheaf of papers.

"That's right, my boy. We're going through his lines, Jen. Practice makes perfect as the good book says."

"It doesn't say that – and he only has one line! *I bring you glad tidings of great joy.* Why would you need to practice that?"

"To get it right," said Gabriel, as though this was obvious. "And to make sure the star's in the right place. It has to be right above the manger, doesn't it, Pa?

"That's right, my boy, that's right. It would be a sad thing for world religion if the angel put the star on the wrong building."

"Or if it fell off," chipped in Gabriel. "Else the shepherds and wise men will never find Baby Jesus."

"That's right, my boy, that's right. They'll get lost, and we can't have camels and sheep marauding through the village. There'll be hell up."

"It's not the *real* stable! It's for a play!"

Jen was beside herself, but nobody was listening. They were far too busy discussing how sheep might best be herded into St Wenn's. Lambs were mentioned too, and pigs. The nativity area would be a busy place, thought Alice, and somebody would need to muck it out. She hoped Jules and Neil had a fork and barrow on standby.

Holly was watching this exchange with great amusement.

"Brilliant! Is this part of a sketch?"

Alice smiled. "No, this is for real. Meet Big and Little Roger Pollard."

"Pollard! Like the brothers who climbed down the cliffs with you?"

"They'd have been Big Roger's uncles."

"Wow. People really do stick around here, don't they?"

"They do – and they marry one another too," Alice said. "This can make life pretty complicated, especially when rival families are feuding. Well, anyhow, Barry Penhalligan's great-granddaughter is my grandson's partner, and Barry's sister Betty eventually married Elsie's brother, Davey Rowe."

"Pollard, Penhalligan, Rowe … names I've seen on the war memorial," said Holly slowly. "It puts things into perspective, doesn't it?"

"It does," Alice agreed. "And time does heal, or maybe it's more accurate to say that life moves forward and gaps open up to admit new experiences and people. Things are never static, and emotions, no matter how painful they are, can't stay acute forever. Sometimes they ambush you, but mostly they recede. Sometimes you feel guilty for moving on and leaving loved ones in the past, but that has to happen so wonderful new times can happen."

"I hope you're right," said Holly doubtfully.

Alice touched her hand. She was still thinking of Sam.

"It's true. Everything passes, impossible as that seems sometimes, and life has sunshine as well as clouds."

Existential thoughts had to pause at this point while Little Rog attempted to rearrange the star without skewering himself in the groin and bringing the Pollard line to an abrupt end.

"So … what happened?" Holly asked Alice once the Star of Bethlehem had been safely positioned. "Did Jonny see sense and win you back? Or did the dashing Captain sweep you off your feet?"

Alice thought about this. The answer was both – but not in the way anyone, least of all her, had expected. Life was, as Holly would soon discover, far, far stranger than fiction.

She sipped her coffee and settled into her seat.

"To answer that I need to take you back to the day when Sam was lost and we'd been left waiting in hope and fear. I didn't know it then, but that was probably the moment that everything changed for me. Let me tell you what happened next ..."

CHAPTER 17

1954

The crowd was silent. Everyone knew that the absence of a body was no cause to celebrate. The Pendeens would forever, unless Sam was found, look out to sea and wonder. Each winter storm would render them queasy with a sickening concoction of hope and trepidation, each report of a recovered body would be accompanied by a cold clutch of dread – and, perhaps cruellest of all, a small flame of hope would always burn in their hearts.

"I'll call off the search," said Joe Levitt quietly. "If that's our decision?"

He looked at Morley, who didn't reply. Never a well man since his ordeal in the trenches, he clung to May's arm as though he had aged decades in hours.

"We *can't* give up!" May cried. "Sam's still out there. I *know* he is."

Joe cleared his throat.

"I'm so sorry, May. There was no sign of him, and we hauled the nets too. There's no way he's still a—"

He caught himself, but the unsaid word hovered in the air like an evil spell, transforming their worst fears into ugly reality. Mortified, he turned to Morley.

"We're going to have to make a call, mate. I'm so sorry."

"He might be clinging to some flotsam. Don't call off the search," begged May.

Morley bowed his head. He knew Joe was right; it was only a matter of time before the coroner was involved.

Alice glanced at Henry Tremaine who had remained at her side, a quiet and reassuring presence. Nothing could make this awful day less horrendous, but the Captain's quiet strength made her feel less alone.

"I'll take my boat out and search the coastline. There's lots of inlets and coves. We'll not give up, Mrs Pendeen," Henry said firmly. Authority rang from his voice, and several fishermen nodded and offered to do the same.

"What if he's still out at sea?" May asked, clutching Joe's arm frantically. "The lifeboat needs to go back in case he's swimming home."

This was the only glimmer of hope in a world turned dark. Sam *could* be clinging to some flotsam. Or perhaps a passing boat had picked him up. Maybe they oughtn't to give up hope just yet? She looked at the faces of the gathered fishermen and knew that if she allowed these thoughts to take root she'd only be fooling herself.

"He won't be, love," said Morley. "There's no way he could have survived for long in that cold water. He's *gone,* love."

His voice cracked and his face crumpled. May collapsed against him.

"I could search again," offered Barry. His big frame was

slumped inside his oilskins, their cheery egg-yolk yellow as out of place as the bright blue sky and the sunshine.

"I'll radio the coastguard," said Joe quietly. "I'm so sorry."

Events gathered pace at this point as logistics took over. Calls needed to be made and officials contacted. Henry offered to make these from Seaspray on their behalf, since Cobbles didn't have a phone line, then he accompanied the Pendeens to their cottage as though this was the most natural thing in the world. The truncated family sat at the kitchen table, stunned beyond tears and too dazed to drink the sweet tea Henry brewed for them. Eventually, when it had got cold, he poured it down the sink and asked Alice to dig out the dusty bottle of brandy that May kept for feeding the Christmas cake.

"For the shock," he said, sloshing large measures into glasses and setting one before Alice. "It will help. Trust me."

Alice did trust him, and Henry was right; the burning liquid ignited her into action and even seemed to revive her parents a little. He refused a glass, saying he needed his wits about him if he was to navigate the rocky stretch of coast between Polwenna Bay and Fowey. He was also keen to organise a team of men to tow home what was left of the boat.

"We can't leave *Girl May* to smash to nothing on the rocks," he explained when Alice ushered him out of the cottage and into the lane outside. "The coroner will need to see her too, I imagine. If we can limp her home, I'll make sure she's kept out of sight at the boatyard until that part's done."

He didn't elaborate, and Alice was grateful. She couldn't imagine how she or her parents would have made it through the past few hours without his support.

"Thank you, Henry."

"You don't need to thank me. It's what anyone would do for a friend."

Tears misted her vision. They were in danger of overflowing down her cheeks, and Alice blinked them away. She couldn't afford to fall apart.

"You've been so kind."

He took her hands in his. His presence was so warm and protective that she longed to beg him to stay. No matter how dark things were, Alice had a conviction that with Henry Tremaine at her side she would make it through anything. She'd instinctively felt this way about him since that cold December night when he'd driven her home.

"It's not kindness, Alice. I'd do anything to spare you this pain. *Anything.*"

Now she couldn't remember who'd moved first. Maybe they'd both stepped towards one another at the same time. Henry pulled Alice to him and folded her into an embrace, placing a tender hand against the back of her head as she buried her face in his coat. Held and comforted, she felt the adrenalin which had propelled her forwards ever since May's early wake-up call, subside, and a wave of grief knocked her off her feet. It was safe to cry in the circle of Henry's arms and as he held her against his heart Alice wept for her brother, for her parents and for a life that would never be the same.

Henry said nothing, simply allowing her to cry. Even in the midst of her grief, she was struck by how this man had always made her feel seen, and how being close to him felt safe and natural. It was as though they were two beads of mercury that after being long divided had instinctively rolled back into one. She never needed to explain herself to Henry or hide her feelings. She was always open with him and able to be herself, for he had seen her at her very worst and never once criticised her.

"You're going to have to be strong," Henry said, once the storm of weeping had past.

"I'm not sure I can be."

Alice felt wrung out and weak, wanting nothing more than to collapse into bed, pull the covers over her head and shut out this waking nightmare.

"You're stronger than you know – and you have friends to lean on too. Elsie. Me. And my mother thinks the world of you – and you know I do too. If you need anything or any help, all you have to do is ask. There's an awful lot to be done now, and your parents aren't in a fit state. They're going to lean on you, and you'll have to be strong, for them and for Sam."

She gulped, knowing there'd be legalities to attend to and mountains of paperwork, and at some point a funeral to arrange. How would May and Morley cope? Especially when the mourners began to arrive with cards and condolences. Reverend Sharpe was bound to be first, wanting to pray with her parents, and there would be no shortage of men keen to distract Morley with a trip to the pub and women wanting to comfort May. Betty, sweet on Sam and hoping for a ring, would want to visit. So would all those who wanted to drop in with food and a kind word. The unstoppable machine of loss was already in motion, and Alice would be very busy ensuring that her parents weren't overwhelmed.

"They just want Sam back," she whispered.

Saying his name made her feel as though she might collapse. How could her brother be *gone*? It was unbearable. First Danny, and now Sam. This savage wave of grief made all the tears she'd shed over Jonny seem foolish and indulgent.

Alice had, like her namesake, stepped through the looking-glass. The girl she'd been before the boat had been lost was a silly creature, blissfully ignorant of what really mattered, a person she barely recognised. How had she not realised she was already living in utter paradise? Money might have been scarce, but her family had been safe and well. So what if Jonny proved faithless, exchanging Alice for Milly as though she were no more than a toy he'd tired of? Alice wouldn't care if he never looked her way again if this meant Sam was still alive. Even the mundanity of her previous daily life was bathed in a golden glow. But now, a treasure of great value, that life was lost for all time, and no regrets or wishing or tears could ever bring it back.

"How can I help my parents?" she whispered.

"Help them by being you," Henry said simply. "Don't you know how incredible you are, Alice Pendeen? How strong?"

He regarded her steadily with his lapis lazuli eyes. In them she saw such belief and admiration that it snatched her breath. She was nothing special. She was just a draper's assistant. A nobody from a poor fishing family. Mrs St Milton had left Alice in no doubt as to her own insignificance.

"Me? I don't think so."

He tilted her chin up so that she was looking into his eyes. They were as dazzling in their intensity as light swords through dark clouds.

"You *are*, Alice. You're loyal and brave, and you give all of your heart to those you love. Anyone fortunate enough to spend time with you is blessed, and I feel honoured to be one of them. If anyone's ever led you to think less, then they're a fool and very wrong." He paused, as though he wanted to say more but had thought better of it. Then he shrugged. "One day they'll realise it and appreciate what slipped through their fingers, and they'll be too late."

He meant Jonny. Alice was touched. They'd never spoken in depth about her broken heart, but to Alice it meant a great deal to be reassured that Henry thought Jonny had been foolish. Like Elizabeth, he wasn't dazzled by flashy looks or impressed by social status, and she liked him even more because of this.

"Thank you," she said. Courage flashed through her like lightning.

He kissed her cheek. "It's the truth. You're wonderful, Alice – and I promise you'll find the strength to navigate what comes next. Because it's already in you."

Then he turned and walked away, leaving Alice on the doorstep. She touched her hand to her cheek wonderingly. The spot where his lips had brushed her skin was as warm as sunshine. In a world plunged into darkness, Henry's friendship was the only glimpse of light.

CHAPTER 18

1954

During the bleak days which followed Sam's loss the chances of finding him alive receded with each turning tide. May refused to leave her bedroom window, where she sat in a wicker chair nursing one of Sam's blue smocks to her heart and scanning the horizon. Morley took to walking the cliffs for miles, leaving at first light and not returning home until the pub had closed, when his friends half-carried him back.

As Polwenna was such a small, close-knit community Cobbles was constantly filled with people as friends and neighbours rallied around to support the Pendeens. The kitchen table groaned with donated cakes and stews, enjoyed mostly by the gulls since none of the family had much appetite. Alice was surprised to discover that not just their own friends but also the most unlikely folk wanted to help during such a difficult time, and she was touched by their kindness. Reverend Sharpe was, of course, a constant visitor. Mrs Tremaine called in with a cake baked by her daily woman. Lady Tregarrick brought flowers from her hothouse. Even Mrs St Milton called to offer her condolences, and insisted upon paying May's full wage until she felt able to return to work. Alice's boss at the draper's shop had been understanding as well, offering to keep her position open until the funeral was over.

In stark contrast some people shied away, as if believing bad luck was contagious, or perhaps because they were afraid of saying the wrong thing. Elsie called in several times but, full of happiness herself and sporting a new engagement ring, found it awkward to be faced with utter misery and struggled to make conversation. The once garrulous Barry Penhalligan could barely grunt out a hello, and several of Alice's friends would duck into the village shop to avoid her. The tragedy had made the Pendeens a source of embarrassment to some, and Alice was increasingly thankful for the steady friendship of Henry Tremaine.

The Captain was a rock for the family, helping Morley navigate the overwhelming bureaucracy, and driving Alice to Truro to meet with officials and sign the necessary documents. He dealt with the recovery of *Girl May* and made sure that what wreckage remained was examined by the coastguard then discreetly placed out of sight in the boatyard, so the Pendeens weren't confronted with that reminder of all they had lost. Alice appreciated his support and the way he offered it, quietly and without foisting his opinions on anyone or being overbearing. After that dreadful morning when they had scrambled down the cliff face to reach the wreckage, she sensed a shift in her relationship with the Captain. That day they had become comrades – comrades sharing an experience which would bind them together for the rest of their days.

Who else would ever understand the sheer dread of standing on snarling rocks hoping and dreading they would find Sam inside what was left of the *Girl May*? That moment was imprinted inside them both, a haunting memory that would become part of their internal landscape and which was voiced in a language only they could speak.

Her parents had disintegrated and so, as Henry suspected, it was left for Alice to talk to the officials and liaise with the coroner. It wasn't only Sam who had been lost that morning; the carefree Alice was gone forever, too. It felt as though she'd aged decades, no longer recognising the person who had daydreamed about Jonny and harboured ambitions of being a fashion designer. That Alice felt like another girl who had lived another life, a life which now seemed as remote and fantastical as any novel Daphne du Maurier might pen.

When Alice looked in the mirror her reflection was similar to her old self, yet there was deep sorrow and weariness in her eyes and their sparkle had been extinguished by grief. The worries that had preoccupied her during the time before Sam's loss seemed trivial when contrasted to weeping parents, death certificate and memorial service. It was no longer Jonny who featured in the very first thoughts flying to mind when she awoke. Hours could pass now, days even, without her thoughts straying to him at all.

Alice hadn't heard from him. He hadn't sent his condolences, save a card sent on behalf of the St Milton family, and Alice knew that if the situation had been reversed nothing would have prevented her from being beside him. She would fly to Jonny's side, regardless of what his parents thought or whether Millicent was incensed. Alice was sure she still loved Jonny in spite of everything – yet she feared that, like a flower denied light and water, her love, without word from him, would wither away.

Henry had also been correct in believing Alice would be able to draw on a strength she hadn't know she had possessed to carry her through these hard weeks. She made decisions on her parents' behalf, set in motion the plans for a memorial service and agreed with the harbour master that there was not enough of the fishing boat left to repair. Without the boat and the fishing income the family's finances were dire, and so to help make ends meet Alice took in mending and alterations, stitching into the small hours and only giving up when her eyes could no longer focus. These things were all hard, yet when it came to agreeing with the coroner's ruling that Sam was dead they were as nothing, for Alice was tormented by the guilt of being the one to officially give up on her brother. Until this verdict had been written down and stamped, she could still fool herself there was a faint hope that Sam might return – a hope the Pendeens clung to as tightly as Sam might have clung onto a piece of wreckage.

While hope was alive then so was Sam, yet as time marched on with no news Alice also knew that the family and the community needed resolution. Existing in limbo was excruciating, and every time there was a knock on the cottage door she leapt up as though scalded. Her heart would drum against her rib cage, and her entire body was awash with a cocktail of dread, which subsided when the caller was revealed as a neighbour or Reverend Sharpe. Alice feared that without a body to lay to rest the torturous uncertainty would never end.

Although in most people the hope of Sam's survival faded fast, Alice refused to give in. She visited St Wenn's several times to plead with God, promising she would never complain about her lot in life again or waste another moment on Jonny if only He would return her brother. But this bargaining proved fruitless, for still there was no news. Kneeling at the altar rail, Alice studied the stained-glass window depicting the church's namesake saint floating into Polwenna on her miraculous millstone and wonder why the Almighty would have chosen to consign such miracles to the past.

Reverend Sharpe had said Sam was with God now, and the Pendeens needed to trust in His will. May seemed to find this comforting, but Alice found it hard not to be consumed with rage. *They* needed Sam. How could she trust a God that had stolen both of her brothers? How could it be His will to take them both? Hadn't her mum and dad suffered enough? Why was God so cruel?

Alice couldn't listen to Reverend Sharpe, and whenever he popped in to speak with her parents she made her excuses to leave. She knew the vicar meant well, but his platitudes about Sam going home to his Maker didn't offer her any comfort. Quite the opposite; they filled her with a dark fury. Sam was full of life. He hadn't wanted to leave them, and had only gone to sea because he was worried about supporting his family. As for going home to his maker, she had never once heard Sam mention any kind of religious conviction; if anything he was usually frustrated that Sundays were given over to church when they could have been spent in The Ship or walking out with a pretty girl. If God cared for Sam so much, thought Alice savagely, He could have given her brother a huge catch and calm seas, and brought him home safely. Why steal him from them and put the family through this hell? Alice's grief deepened with each angry question. Would she lose her faith completely, as well as her beloved brother?

Alice didn't voice these dark thoughts to anyone except Henry Tremaine. She'd taken to hiding away at the boatyard, watching him work on a boat, or sitting on the quay beside him, drinking tea and sharing a pasty. Henry would gaze out across the water while Alice choked out her anger. He only rarely told her what he thought and never offered platitudes, but simply allowed her to talk.

"I've learned not to search for meaning in these things," he'd said quietly one afternoon when Alice had been raging about the vicar's latest lecture on God's plan, "and if there is meaning, maybe we aren't equipped to see it. It could be years and years on until events make sense."

"You think Sam's death will make sense in years to come?" Alice tossed her wind-tangled hair and scowled. She was so angry she thought she might combust.

"No. It'll never make sense. Neither will Dunkirk or Normandy. Not to us, anyway – but if there is a broader canvas? Then maybe."

He stared across the harbour and at the beach where children were building a castle in the sand. Their laughter and squeals floated on the breeze as they tipped pails of water into moats and then kicked down their turrets with glee.

"Not long ago this beach was all barbed wire and tank traps, while not very far across the sea the waves exploded with bullets and my men fell around me like scythed wheat. It was hell, Alice – but without that hell and without their falling, would there be all this? They died for this, and for the generations that follow."

Alice felt he was missing her point …

"Their deaths," he went on, "had meaning, because the Nazis would have invaded otherwise. Those soldiers died for a reason and a purpose. They were heroes."

His fists were clenched. He was clearly reliving the scenes that Alice had seen only in newsreels, whose horror had been overlaid by the excitement of watching their troops pushing the enemy back. But Henry could obviously hear the splinter of bone, the crack of gunfire and the screams of the dying. He had witnessed his comrades in arms falling and had seen their blood turn the Normandy sand scarlet.

"They still died," he said quietly.

"To stop Hitler. They were heroes."

"True – but I don't think many of them were thinking about Hitler or being heroic when they fell," he replied. "They screamed and bled out into the water and called for their mothers and wives as they died. We knew we were there for a purpose, sure, but the longing to survive soon takes over. Trust me, when I was there Hitler was not on my mind. All I wanted was to survive. That instinct surpasses all ideologies – right and wrong."

Henry always talked to Alice as an equal, neither glossing over details for fear of upsetting her nor being condescending by refusing to argue. Alice thought this was one of the things that she enjoyed the most about his company. He was thoughtful and sincere, and a true friend.

She shook her head. "All that aside, there was still a purpose to their deaths."

"True, and everyone knew that – rationally, at least – but their ending was still bloody and brutal. Back then, we had no idea whether or not we'd win, remember, and if the Allies had been defeated that effort, that agony, would have all been in vain. It's only when we look back from this present perspective that the loss makes sense, is justified and seems worth it."

"It was a glorious victory," she insisted, recalling the celebrations in Pendeen House as the family gathered around the wireless listening to the BBC broadcast which announced the start of the push-back. "Everyone says so. People will talk about it forever."

Henry smiled rather sadly. "Yes indeed. The offensive *was* a huge success – in the end. But there's no real glory in war. Ask your father about. I'm sure he will tell you the truth about

Owen's 'old lie', *Dulce et Decorum Est, Pro Patria Mori.* People forget the sacrifices, too, as time passes and everyday life takes over. We have to, or we remain trapped in the past."

"You fought the enemy, Henry! You're a hero. You have the medals to prove it!"

"I did what I had to do, no more and no less. We were fighting a great evil, no doubt about that, but not all the enemy soldiers were bad men and not all of ours were good ones. That's far too simplistic. War is more nuanced."

Alice was shocked. The Germans were the enemy. Of *course* they were all bad! Back in the early days of the war, she and Sam had planned how they would kill a few themselves if the invasion happened. And when an enemy plane had crashed into the sea the whole village had rejoiced.

"They were also husbands and fathers and brothers and sons," Henry continued, almost to himself. "They were far from home and many were very young. Like us, they were swept up by ideology and rhetoric, or conscripted. They fought because that's what soldiers do; they follow orders. Those men also fell and bled and died, and their loved ones cried for them just as ours did for our men."

"So you're saying that even the *Germans* died fighting for something they believed in?" Alice was outraged. She kicked the harbour wall with the heels of her boots, and the unyielding stone beneath made her feel even angrier. "Fine. All soldiers are heroes. Danny died a hero. Your brothers. Even a load of Germans. But Sam died for nothing. Absolutely *nothing.*"

Henry whipped round. His blue eyes were bright with anger.

"I'm saying that men die. Good and bad and indifferent. Some for reasons they believe in, and others because they are swept up in events beyond their control. I'm saying that I've learned not to try and judge them or to find reason in utter chaos. But don't you *dare* say that Sam wasn't a hero. Your brother went to sea because he wanted to take care of his family. He took a risk because he loved you all and believed it was the right thing to do in order to provide for you when times were hard. That's heroic, Alice. Sam died for his loved ones. He gave his life for you and your parents."

Alice felt ashamed. "I never thought of it like that. I thought it was a meaningless end."

Henry exhaled. The anger seemed to slide from him.

"It wasn't a meaningless end at all. You don't do Sam justice if you believe it was."

On the beach the children were now dancing in and out of the waves. Others clambered over the rocks with nets and bright buckets. To them, the cruel water that had stolen Sam was heaven, and the rocks where they fished for shrimp weren't sharp teeth to snare boats but treasure troves filled with wondrous sea creatures. It was all about perspective and timing, and suddenly Alice understood what Henry was trying to show her. Her rage evaporated because her friend was right: Sam *had* been brave. He had made the ultimate sacrifice because he loved them. Maybe God or Fate had no say in it at all? Perhaps everything was down to choices and timing. Or maybe it was all just dreadfully random?

Alice stole a glance at Henry from beneath her lashes. He had seen the very worst and the very best of humanity, yet he clearly wasn't bitter or angry. She thought he was the most remarkable person she knew. Just being in his company soothed her fury. Recalling how safe she had felt when he'd held her in his arms, Alice was filled with an overpowering longing to experience that sensation again. What would his mouth feel like on hers? What would it be like to kiss this deep and thoughtful man and lose herself in his embrace? To become a part of him utterly and completely …

Jolted, she scrambled to her feet, cheeks turning pink at the images which had slipped unbidden into her imagination. What was she thinking? Although he was undoubtedly handsome, Captain Tremaine possessed an edge of danger which although attractive was also a little unnerving. Unlike the boys Alice was used to spending time with, Henry Tremaine was a man and experienced. He would want far more than snatched kisses and moonlit promises. He would want a woman who was prepared to share with him her mind, body and soul.

Henry was attracted to her. Alice, no fool, knew this – but she also knew he was much older, and she suspected, too, that by spending so much time with her he was just being kind. Anyway, she loved Jonny, and Henry knew this. Jonny had yet to get in touch, but Alice felt sure he would at some point. He was probably waiting for the right moment. Jonny and Sam might not have seen eye to eye, but Jonny would know how sad Alice was. He would want to comfort her, Millicent Jago or not.

Of course! *This* was the higher meaning that she had been looking for! Sam's death would bring them back together, her brother realising from the afterlife that he had misjudged Jonny and cosmically influencing events in order to reunite them. That was what would happen in a novel, and it seemed as good a notion as any other. Alice realised she had to make sense of something that made no sense at all. If she didn't she'd go mad.

She made her excuses and hurried back to Cobbles, scolding herself for her unsettling thoughts about Henry and blushing at how vivid these were. She could only conclude that she was behaving strangely due to shock and grief. By the time she let herself into the cottage Alice was convinced this was the case – but even so she couldn't help wondering why Henry didn't have a wife, and over the days ahead was alarmed to find her thoughts turning to the Captain far more often that they did to Jonny.

Grief had some very strange side-effects.

CHAPTER 19

1954

The Pendeens needed to bid a proper farewell to Sam. Superstitious by nature, the fishing community believed that if Sam was to rest in peace there had to be some kind of service. Although there would not be a body to bury, the Pendeen family would pour all their love and grief into this memorial service. It would be the very last thing they would do for Sam, and they were determined to do him proud.

Since there was no coffin as the focal point for the mourners, a table was set up by the altar, draped with a simple white cloth and bearing two pillar candles which flanked an enlarged and coloured photograph of Sam. As the photos of him trussed up in his Sunday best were all dreadfully stiff, Alice had struggled to find anything that reflected the lively lad everyone had known. Henry, waiting for the green light to take a picture into Truro for enlarging, worried that they were cutting it fine and warned Alice that they could be left without anything to display.

"I'd rather have nothing than a picture of Sam that doesn't feel right," she told him when the Pendeens had exhausted every avenue but a few baby pictures. She rejected another picture a sigh. "He hated wearing Sunday best. He once said that in this photo he looked like one of those Victorian pictures of dead people. If we show everyone him wearing a tie he'll haunt us forever."

"I saw what Sam did to Jonny on Christmas Eve. I don't think I'd like to be haunted by *him*," said Henry wryly, making Alice smile. It was good to talk about Sam, and better still to talk about him as he had really been – irritating, hot-headed and impulsive – rather than as some saintly version of himself. When she and Henry spoke together she felt closer to Sam than when her parents turned him into an unrecognisable paragon.

Then something strange happened. The morning before the memorial service Barry Penhalligan called at Cobbles bearing a photograph. Fancying himself as Polwenna's answer to Cecil Beaton, Barry was well known for taking random shots of all and sundry, though with varying degrees of success. Seagulls on lobster pots were a speciality, as were blurry pictures of girls sea-bathing unawares – and he'd once earned himself a big telling-off from Elsie's mother. Sam had recounted tales of how Barry had driven them mad at sea as he'd attempted to document every haul or shoved them out of sight to better frame a shot. Yet it was Barry who, when he presented them with an image that distilled everything Alice's brother had been and had hoped to become, was able to give the Pendeens one last and very special memory of Sam.

It was a simple black-and-white head-and-shoulders shot of Sam in his fisherman's smock and with his wild hair ruffled by the sea. He was gazing beyond the camera with a wide joyful smile, eyes filled with wonder while behind him a doily wake laced the water, gulls peppered the sky and the sea spread out to infinity.

"He was up on deck watching dolphins," Barry recalled as he stood on the doorstep, shyly offering the photograph. He'd taken it on a trip to the Scillies the previous summer when Sam had been hired as extra crew, but Barry had only recently got around to developing the negatives, and seen this image.

"Sammy always did love to watch dolphins," May nodded, peering at the picture. Her blotched face crumpled and she pressed the heel of her hand to her chest. "Oh my goodness! He's so happy – look, Ally."

Alice took the photograph and felt tears rise, but bitter-sweet ones this time, because Sam was clearly in his element. He had told her that he'd loved the trip west. The open sea and the potential of a life beyond had thrilled him, and he had talked to her about the freedom displayed by the dolphins, struck as he was by how easily they sliced through the water, and saying they'd made him feel it might be possible to journey beyond Polwenna. He just needed to make the leap into the unknown …

He'd certainly done that now, Alice thought.

Barry studied the toes of his boots. His face was pink and his feet shuffled awkwardly.

"Don't laugh – but when I was out fishing today a bleddy pod of them followed the boat for nearly the whole trip. They wouldn't leave us alone. It sounds barmy, but I'm sure it's a message from Sam, because he wants you to have this picture. I fetched it as soon as we moored up."

Fisherman were superstitious – maybe rightly so – and neither Alice nor May were laughing. Quite the opposite. They knew Barry was right. Sam was telling them this was how he wanted to be remembered – free and smiling, and with his whole life spread before him like a net set to catch all manner of wonderful experiences.

Alice ran to Tremaine Marine with the precious image tucked in an envelope, hoping desperately that they'd be in time to meet the photographer's deadline, and Henry instantly abandoned sanding a yacht to drive to Truro.

"I don't want to inconvenience you," she'd fretted, for he was clearly busy.

But Henry wouldn't hear a word of protest.

"You're never an inconvenience. I want to help. Besides, it's a small thing to do. I only wish I could do more."

It might have been a small thing for Henry, but for the Pendeens a trip to Truro was akin to organising an expedition to the moon. Not owning a car, they needed to take a bus to the railway station in town, then the branch line train, and a change to the main line … Alice could count her trips to the city on both hands. She guessed that when you were wealthy the things that caused her family huge logistical problems didn't even register. The relief of this final burden being lifted was overwhelming.

"Thank you," she said, tears starting to fall. They were never far away nowadays. "You've been so kind. Everyone's been kind."

Alice supposed it was inevitable that the strain of the past weeks had caught up with her.

Henry held her while she cried.

"Hey, hey. I've got you," he said gently. "Don't hold it in."

After keeping herself together for so long it was such a relief to be given permission to cry that she sobbed even harder. She buried her face in his overalls.

"It's just so awful. How can I ever bear it?"

Henry stroked her hair, gentling Alice as though she was

an injured bird, broken wings flapping and poised to launch into disastrous flight:

"There's nothing I can say that'll help, other than you *will* bear it, because there's nothing else you can do. It's an old chestnut, I'm afraid, but time will help."

She looked up at him. His face was grave but his eyes were warm with sympathy and understanding.

"Is that how you felt about your brothers?"

"Well … yes. It's true that time has eased their absence. It helps that we were often apart – well, as children anyway, with school and Oxford." He paused before adding quietly, "I was actually thinking of my fiancée."

Alice was shocked. Firstly that Henry Tremaine had been engaged, something he'd never mentioned, and secondly by the hatpin jab of jealousy which accompanied this revelation.

"*You* were engaged?"

He nodded. "Rose and I were engaged for three years. She was killed in one of the bombing raids on Plymouth. She was hoping to surprise me there, when I was due back on leave. Wrong place, wrong time, I suppose."

Alice looked up at him in shock.

"I'm so sorry, Henry. I didn't know."

"Of course you didn't. I hadn't told you. I should have done, I suppose – but to be fair, I never talk about it."

Alice felt dreadful. She'd always assumed Henry was a carefree bachelor by choice. Busy dwelling on her own broken heart, it hadn't occurred to her that she might not be the only one in pain.

"You don't owe me any explanations. You don't have to talk about her, not if it's too painful."

"That's the thing. It isn't painful now. Not like it was. Now I find I want to talk about how we met. Her brother and I were at school together – she was Diggory's little sister – and that when I first saw her I was so tongue-tied she must have thought I was an imbecile. I want to laugh at the foolish boy I was and how I spent that first visit to her home trying to impress her. I showed off out hunting, only to fall off at the first gate and break my collarbone, while Rose led the field. I want to describe how her hair was a mixture of marmalade and damson and peach, and tell you how it glowed like flame in the sunshine. I want to talk about the ball where we first danced, and how she looked like an angel all dressed in white."

His eyes contained a faraway expression and his smile contained such tenderness that Alice felt an unexpected knife-twist of jealousy.

"Whenever I think of Rose now, the memories make me happy, and I'm so thankful for the time we did have, however short it was. Grief still ambushes me, though. A bar of music will move me almost to tears because she once hummed it, or I'll catch sight of the back of a woman's head in a crowded place and my heart lifts – only to stall when a stranger turns around and it's not her. Somehow it's forgotten that she's gone, and I lose her all over again."

It was the most revealing speech Alice had ever heard Henry make. Suddenly she understood so much more about him. This complex, private man had offered her the key to his soul, and she saw him properly for the first time; his reserve was self-preservation, and his serious nature hid a heart bruised by pain. Henry was unmarried not through choice – or indeed, because he was (as they whispered in the village shop) a 'terrible philanderer' – but because he had lost the girl he loved. Although Alice knew Jonny was lost to her, at least he was alive and well. Alice's heart broke for her friend.

"I'm so sorry," she said again, and the words had never sounded more inadequate. Henry had lost the woman he was planning to marry. Rose had been his soulmate. She had been his fiancée. How could anyone ever recover from such a loss and remain as kind and as balanced as he was? *How,* when he must be filled with sorrow and emptiness?

She studied him anew. His face was an experienced one, though he was not so much older than Barry or the Pollards. It was a taut face with fine lines marking the corners of his mouth and starring those bright blue eyes. Henry had suffered dreadfully and never uttered a word.

"Losing my Rose was the most exquisite pain I could imagine," he continued, more to himself now. "Men aren't meant to cry, are they? Especially not officers. So I refused to believe it was true. She would be there in the rubble, buried and waiting to be rescued. God wouldn't have given her to me only to snatch her away. Why would He do that?"

"I have no idea," said Alice quietly. She didn't think God had much of a hand in any of it. The Allies had won, so God was on their side, she supposed – but why He had allowed Hitler to do such terrible things in the first place was anyone's guess. Far easier never to have allowed any of it to happen in the first place. So, was God in charge of everything? Or nothing? Alice had no idea, and trying to unravel this was like trying to salvage a tangled fishing line; it caused even more knots. She'd leave the theology to Sharpy.

"Of course she was dead," Henry continued. "We found her on the third day. Christ, Plymouth was a mess. That beautiful city was reduced to rubble. I spent day after day helping the ARP to dig, even with my bare hands at times. They told me there was no hope, but I loved her and it was my duty to help, or so I said. The truth was I wouldn't believe Rose was gone unless I saw her body with my own eyes. I knew I'd be living in hell otherwise. Without seeing her for myself, I knew I wouldn't be able to believe it."

Alice recalled how Henry had been the one to check *Girl*

May while she had shrunk from that duty, and was filled with admiration for him.

"I understand," she said.

But Henry was far away, in a city devasted by war and where sirens wailed and ARP wardens struggled to bring order from chaos.

"We buried her, in her wedding dress, at her family's church in Sussex. Then my leave was over. Back then there was no time to mourn, and I couldn't allow myself to fall apart. There was a war on. Practically everyone was carrying a personal tragedy, and in the scale of losses like Dunkirk and, later, Normandy, my own tragedy seemed on a small scale. I resolved to never speak of Rose to anyone, for what good could that do? I didn't need pity or comfort. Rose was gone, and she was never coming back. Harping on about myself wouldn't change that."

His voice was hoarse, and now it was Alice who held him. Henry Tremaine had built a wall around his loss and defended it for over a decade. She felt humbled to have breached it.

"I'm so, so sorry," she whispered into his navy-blue overalls, knowing that for the rest of her life the smell of two-stroke oil and sawdust would reel her back to this moment. "How do you bear it?"

"At first I didn't. I pretended I did, but the truth was I went into battle with little care for my own life and probably with the unconscious intention of ending it in a glorious way. In the end my superiors told me I was reckless and risking my men, so I was given a medical leave of absence. To cut a long story short, I was sent to Northfield, where I was lucky enough to meet a forward-thinking chap who talked to me, and talked a lot of sense too, rather than a quack who wanted to slice my head open and fiddle. I was lucky."

Henry was being so honest that Alice was plucked from her own grief and parachuted into his.

"What happened after that?"

He raised his eyes to the sky and pulled a face.

"Something of an epiphany. I went back to my regiment knowing that Rose wouldn't have wanted me to throw my life away. She had been brave, and I knew she would have carried on if the situation had been reversed, no matter how painful it might be – because life is beautiful, Alice. It really is. There are still sunrises and sunsets. New friends to make. Happiness to be had ... Life goes on. It has to, and so must we. That's how we best honour those who no longer journey with us."

"Why does it all have to be so *painful*?"

Henry smiled sadly. "If I knew the answer to that, I'd be a wise man, and I'm definitely not one of those. Why, everyone in Cornwall knows that a man who buys a boatyard and thinks it can make money is the biggest fool going!"

She squeezed his hands and laughed, knowing this was an attempt to lighten the atmosphere and close the topic, but also sensing that something had shifted between them. Nobody in Polwenna Bay knew Henry Tremaine like Alice did now, and she felt honoured that he had chosen to confide in her. Their friendship felt far deeper than earlier, because now it was rooted in mutual sympathy and understanding.

Henry duly set off for Truro, leaving Alice mulling over their conversation and seeing her friend in a new light. Did she like him more because he'd had his heart broken, or did she simply understand him so much better? She wasn't sure, but she felt a new tenderness towards Henry Tremaine – and a fierce protectiveness, too. She was also filled with a burning curiosity to know what the mysterious Rose had looked like, but having read *Rebecca* several times she suspected that this would be a dangerous path to follow. Besides, she wasn't in love with Henry, just plain nosey.

Later that day Henry returned with the charismatic photograph, enlarged and beautifully hand-coloured, and framed in dark oak. Sam stared out of the image and into eternity, forever young and startlingly vital. Alice knew it was the perfect homage to her brother. This photograph was, Henry insisted, a gift from him and his mother rather than flowers, and May and Morley (who had paled at the mere thought of the expense of an enlarged photograph, let alone a coloured one) were speechless with the kindness of this gesture. Henry really was the kindest man, May remarked once he had gone, and why he was unmarried was a mystery. A girl could do a lot worse than the Captain, she added pointedly, and Alice couldn't help agreeing. Beneath the austere and enigmatic façade, Henry Tremaine had a tender heart. It was quite alarming how often he was starting to slip into her thoughts.

The day of the service dawned warm, with flat calm sea and powder-blue skies. Sunlight bounced from the rooftops, and the morning light threw a milky haze over the still waters of the bay. The hedges were white with may blossom and threaded through with dog roses; daisies were scattered against emerald grass, and high above it all the skylarks sang their hearts out. The whole world was made new and beautiful. Bright and fresh and brimful of life, the vibrant morning was a stark contrast to the sombre colours worn by the villagers as they trudged up to the church. Alice thought this made saying farewell to Sam even harder. He would have hated to have been cooped up in St Wenn's when he could have been outside. She wished they could have held a simple outdoors farewell on the quayside with beer and pasties served in the pub, as her brother would have liked. But tradition decreed otherwise.

As the bell tolled and her mother gripped her arm tightly, Alice forced herself to step forwards and to keep her gaze fixed on the path, away from the pitying eyes of her neighbours. Today they would do Sam proud, and she was determined to be strong for her parents. It felt a little like a bad wedding, she thought as she followed Reverend Sharpe's narrow frame along the aisle, for the whole village was in attendance and everyone was dressed in their finery. Alice had hacked an old blackout curtain into pieces to create a full-skirted dress, and had dyed her mother's wedding veil black, then stitched it to a little black hat she'd once unearthed at a jumble sale. Clothes were always Alice's armour, and at least she felt properly dressed for this role.

As they reached the front of the church, Sam's clear-eyed gaze staring beyond the congregation and into eternity, Alice was startled to see a tall, dark-haired figure sitting to the left of the aisle.

Jonny.

Her heart fluttered; shouldn't he have been off on his Grand Tour by now?

Their eyes met briefly. The pain and longing in his deep green gaze said he still loved her. She'd needed him desperately these last few months, but only now, at last, was he present Alice felt so angry she could have swung at Jonny St Milton there and then. Where had he been when she needed him? How could he have abandoned her? Why did he think it was fine to turn up now without warning her? As if she wasn't under enough pressure already, duty-bound to hold herself together! The tears she'd wept over Jonny since Christmas Eve could have filled an ocean. Then the torture of imagining him kissing Milly, making love to Milly, telling Milly he loved her …

Knowing that Jonny was seeing another girl had been akin

to having her skin peeled away, piece by tiny piece. It was agony. It was cruel when he'd promised so much – and taken so much, too. To have had him by her side over the last agonising weeks would have meant everything. But there had been no word from him, not even as much as a card. How *dare* he arrive now in a show of sympathy and wrongfoot her when she most needed to keep her chin up and her heart steady?

Maybe it was disloyal, but she thought of Henry Tremaine spending days digging through rubble with his bare hands for Rose, refusing to stop fighting for her until it had become clear that there was absolutely no hope left. A bitter sense of disappointment swelled in Alice's chest, sweeping away any anger and leaving her so weary she could have crumpled onto the flagstones and slept for a hundred years. She simply didn't have room in her thoughts for Jonny today. She needed all her strength for what lay ahead.

Sensing her distress, if misinterpreting it, her mother squeezed her arm.

"Be brave, Ally," she said softly. "We're Pendeens. We'll do Sam proud."

Alice raised her chin; Mum was right. The Pendeens might be humble fisherfolk, but they were well respected in Polwenna Bay. How *dare* Jonny have made her feel worthless? Henry Tremaine had never once made her feel anything like that, and as though her thoughts drew her eyes to him she caught sight of the Captain and Mrs Tremaine in the second row, both ramrod straight and dressed in black. When Henry gave her an encouraging nod – the kind she imagined he might have given his men before battle – Alice felt heartened and no longer as afraid, for she knew that in this man she had an ally and true friend.

The church was packed, and people wept openly. The Pendeens were seated in the very front pew for this special occasion, and as Reverend Sharpe intoned the familiar words of the funeral service Alice wished there was a pew in front to cling to and keep her steady. She would get through this, she promised herself. Henry and so many others had managed to survive loss, and she would take them as her examples. She might be battered and bruised, but Alice Pendeen was far from broken.

The service seemed to flash by in a blur. How many times had she sat here with her family daydreaming about Jonny or listening to her mum tutting when Sam had drummed his heels impatiently against the pew? Now, as Alice she stood up to sing hymns and listen to Bible readings, she felt as though she was drifting outside herself, for these past occasions seemed like carefree vignettes of another life. If only she could travel back in time and warn her younger self not to fall in love – and then tell her brother to follow his academic dreams and not set so much as a toe on the deck of a boat! 'If only' … they had to be the saddest words in any language.

Later on, when everyone was streaming out of the church and making their way to The Ship, Alice slipped away to catch her breath and gather her thoughts. Once she went into the pub everyone would want to talk to her, telling stories about Sam or offering their condolences, and there would be scarcely time to draw breath, let alone compose her thoughts.

Her feet walking through habit rather than direction, she followed an unloved track past the newer graves and into the overgrown part of the churchyard, where ivy scrambled over listing headstones and briars lay traps for any feet which dared stray from the scythed paths. This was where she had used to meet Jonny – and now, as she caught sight of him leaning against a caged memorial, she realised that a part of her had been expecting this meeting, had always known it would come. It was as inevitable as the tide returning to the shore, hissing pebbles and flinging salt spray over rocks in a violent rage, and always forgiven mere hours later. Was this when she would forgive him?

"Ally! I hoped you'd come."

Habit and love still made her shoulders melt with relief to see him, but their landscape had changed in every way. Once she would have flown into his arms, but now she was uncertain how to react.

"I was catching a few quiet moments before my brother's wake. I wasn't looking for you," she said. Her tone was curt, and Jonny gulped.

"I'm so sorry about Sam, Ally. Truly I am. He was a sound chap."

"You couldn't *stand* him," said Alice. "And he hated you. Remember Christmas Eve? After you broke things off with me?"

Jonny's pale skin flushed. "I know that he and I didn't exactly see eye to eye, but he was your brother and he was looking out for you. Christ – if I'd had a sister who was being messed about by me, I'd punch me too. If that makes sense?"

This typically convoluted Jonny logic made Alice smile in spite of everything. He always could make her laugh.

And cry. She mustn't forget that bit.

"He wasn't your greatest admirer," she agreed.

"No – but he was a loyal chap, and he has a wonderful sister. A sister I'm crazy about. Who I should have never let go." Jonny's eyes sought hers, and he added softly. "I'd take a thousand beatings from Sam if it would make up for how I let you down. I'd give anything for him to be here now and thrash me all over again."

"Me too," said Alice.

"Are you doing all right? You look absolutely beautiful, by the way. Utterly breathtaking."

He stepped closer but she held up a hand to ward him off.

"Don't, Jonny. You can't say things like that to me any more."

"Why not? It's true. You *are* beautiful, Alice."

"Stop it, Jonny! Sam's dead, and today's about *him*. Not you and whatever games you're playing now. Have some respect."

Her vehemence startled them both, and Jonny hung his head.

"Yes, you're right, but for the record I've never played games. I did love you. I *do* love you. I think about you all the time. Lack of love was never the issue, was it? Lord – what a mess. Can you ever forgive me?"

These were words Alice had longed to hear for so long, yet now they failed to fill her with the joy she had anticipated. Instead she felt desperately sad. He meant it, she was certain – but could he put his feelings into action? Was Jonny enough of a man to stand up and fight for the girl he loved and the life he wanted? Would he dig through rubble with his bare hands for her?

"Jonny – stop!" she said.

"I can't, Alice. I have to tell you how I feel. I know I've messed up, but I still love you and I think you still love me."

Alice did still love him, but it was hard to untangle love from this knot of anger and hurt. The tighter those emotions pulled the more twisted out of all shape and recognition the love became.

"Do you love me enough to stand up to your parents?" she asked.

He flushed. "It's not that simple. I can talk them around eventually, once things are more settled. I do think that in time they might agree and accept you."

Alice didn't want to be *accepted.* She didn't want her future husband's family to be *talked around*. She wasn't a guilty secret or something to be ashamed of. She was any man's equal, and a woman to be proud of.

Nevertheless, kicking herself, she asked, "And how long's the timescale for this?"

He shrugged. "I'll find the best time. After Oxford and National Service, anyhow, and ideally once I'm twenty-five and have inherited. We'll be home and dry then."

"That's seven years away," said Alice.

"The years'll fly by," he insisted. "Especially if we see one another in between. What's time, anyway, when you love someone?"

Alice trailed her fingers over a headstone. It felt warm and curiously alive. She wondered who lay beneath, and who had once sat inside the church to pray for them and to weep in this spot. Everything came full circle in the end. Eventually it all ended up here.

"One thing I've learned about time is that none of us know quite how much is allocated to us," she said quietly. "The best time to do anything is now, because it's all we have."

"What are you saying?"

"That we shouldn't waste another moment being apart. Let's walk into the wake holding hands, and show the whole world how we feel. Never mind what your parents think. It's time to tell everyone how we feel. Walk into the wake with me. Show the world that you love me."

It was a gamble, and for a split second Alice truly believed it might pay off – but Jonny's silence told her all she needed to know.

He looked utterly dismayed.

"You know I can't do that."

"You can if you love me as much as you say you do."

"I do love you! Christ! I'm miserable without you."

"Yes, you and Milly looked very unhappy when I saw you last," said Alice wearily.

Jonny threw his hands up in despair.

"Milly doesn't mean anything, Ally. I love *you*. I always will. Of course I want everyone to know you're my girl. I see how that man looks at you, and it's agony. I want to bloody kill him!"

His face was white and his fists were clenched. Alice had never seen him so agitated.

"What are you talking about? What man?"

"The Captain," Jonny spat. His whole frame was grey-hound-taut. "Don't deny it, Alice. You must know. He can't take his eyes off you."

"Do you mean Henry Tremaine?"

"You *know* I do," Jonny hissed. "Don't deny it."

"For heaven's sake! Henry's just a friend."

"A friend? He's fifteen years older than you."

"Thirteen," she said – but her quick response only poured fuel on the fire of Jonny's jealousy, and his top lip curled.

"So you've thought about the age gap."

After her first doubts about it Alice hadn't even considered it. The years between Henry and herself had never seemed an issue. They had always talked easily and openly.

"He's a friend, and shall I tell you how we met? That night you broke things off at the Manor, when I had to walk home in the dark and in my party shoes. You had abandoned me and broken my heart, Jonny – and Henry happened to be driving by. He rescued me when I was at my lowest."

"The perfect Prince Charming," he said bitterly.

"Funny – until that night I'd always thought that was *you*," said Alice sadly. She stepped forward and kissed his cheek, aching at the familiar scent of his skin and the texture beneath her lips and feeling her heart shatter all over again.

"Goodbye, Jonny," she said.

Alice walked away through the ancient tombstones and long grass. She felt the warmth of his gaze on the back of her neck and knew that he was willing her to turn around, but she didn't fly back to him, no matter how very much she ached to do so. Jonny St Milton had made his decision.

So much for Madame Sienna's talk of midsummer kisses and true love. As she walked down the hill and prepared herself for the onslaught of the wake, Alice Pendeen felt quite sure she would never, ever love again.

CHAPTER 20

THE PRESENT

"Jonny wanted you back," said Holly. Her voice bright with satisfaction, she leaned back in her pew and beamed at Alice. "You must have been over the moon. The Captain made him jealous. Genius!"

"Although I thought about making Jonny jealous I never actually tried to do it," said Alice.

"Come on! The Captain was wealthy, handsome and a war hero. Nobody would blame you. Maybe it was even subconscious?"

"Are you asking me to psychoanalyse my seventeen-year-old self?"

"Maybe a little?"

Alice laughed. "Deep down, I probably did feel a little pleased. Jonny had hurt me a lot, remember?"

"Maybe I should look around for a handsome local to make Jamie jealous?" said Holly.

Alice shook her head. "That's a dangerous game. People's feelings aren't toys to be played with. In my book those who play games with emotions are best avoided."

"You're so right. Jamie was always playing games. He loved nothing more than making me feel insecure and jealous. It was almost a relief when I found out that he really was cheating on me. I'd started to think I was going mad."

"Only insecure people like to make those they claim to love feel that way," Alice said firmly. She'd seen enough of life to feel confident on this score. Watching her grandchildren having their hearts broken (or in her grandson Nick's case becoming a game-player and becoming increasingly unhappy) had only cemented her opinion. "Henry Tremaine was always honest – and so was Jonny, come to think of it. He was just young and confused."

"And scared of his mother."

"Absolutely," agreed Alice. "Never underestimate just how formidable a man's mother can be. Oh, it's hard to remember just how scared we Pendeens were of the St Miltons. It must seem daft now, but in those days that family really did have the power to ruin people."

"It was a long time ago."

"Indeed, although sometimes it could be yesterday. Quite often I'm shocked to see an old woman in the looking glass. That's not *me* – how can it be?"

"So we always feel the same inside?"

"I think the essence of who we are is pretty much constant," Alice replied. "Maybe the past and the present are just illusions; overlapping circles in Venn diagrams."

"You've lost me now," said Holly. "That sounds way too complicated."

Alice stared past her and through the church, where the buffed pews and time-smoothed flagstones decorated with coloured ribbons of light were the same today as they had always been; in the old church time dissolved and the years blended. The emotions and faces of the past and present melted, and it seemed as perfectly possible that Sam could come striding in – late as always and glowered at by Reverend Sharpe – as it did now for Jules to be scrutinising the crib while Perry struggled to explain why there was a T Rex by the manger.

Where had the years gone? Had they gone anywhere at all? In the ancient building, time seemed to have lost its power, and in her mind Alice was seventeen again. Her hands were smooth and white, her hair thick and dark, and Jonny St Milton was about to follow her into the churchyard while Henry Tremaine watched thoughtfully, so strong and vital that it was unthinkable he could ever rest beneath a headstone. Surely if she left St Wenn's right now she could walk home to Cobbles and find her mum presiding over the range or her dad snoozing in his armchair? The cottage would be just as it always was – a family home filled with love rather than an expensive and empty second home – and her parents would be there, the reassuring safety net that would always catch her, and which at seventeen she'd thought would remain in place forever.

The landscape of the past was so vivid that Alice's throat tightened with a sudden surge of grief for all that had been lost by the slow erosion of the years. Maybe this was why we spent more time looking back as we aged. In memory it was possible for anyone and anything to still exist, and for nothing to have changed. The past might well be a foreign country, as L. P. Hartley said, but whenever Alice dreamed, she could visit it at will. And when she was awake the past and the present were a strange mixture, faces and voices and settings all chopped and sliced and blended and familiar, yet strange.

Alice sighed. Maybe the answer was that there was no answer?

"You must have been a bit pleased he'd noticed the Captain liked you?" Holly pressed. "I know *I* would be."

Alice tugged her thoughts back to the question. Could she really trust her memory to be honest about how she'd felt back then? She remembered being furious that it had been the Captain's attention to her that had been Jonny's main concern on the day she'd been bidding farewell to her brother. Perhaps she might have felt a ripple of satisfaction that he was jealous – but …

"I was sad and tired," she said. "It was a dreadful time. Anyway, bad times pass … Now, what happened next?"

Holly glanced at her watch. "We've been talking for over an hour. I don't want to keep you."

Alice smiled. "It's the other way around. You're being very kind letting an old lady ramble on."

"Not at all. I'm loving hearing your story, and especially seeing how it ties in with this place and the people."

Holly glanced across the chancel as she said this, and her gaze lit on Perry, who was attaching a tinsel-clad Barbie to the roof of the nativity scene. Barbie, looking like a stripper doing parkour, had clearly insisted on sitting with her legs at a very inappropriate angle. Reverend Sharpe, in the churchyard, must be spinning.

Sensing Holly's attention on him, Perry turned around and grinned.

"Almost there!"

"Looks like Barbie won't listen to you," observed Holly.

"Story of my life," Perry remarked. He tried to reposition the doll, which insisted on moving again. "Fine, Barbie. You stay like that if you must. Anyhow, just the wise men to sort, and I'm done. I've spotted two Action Men and Buzz

Lightyear in the toybox. Perfect."

"He seems nice," said Holly, once Perry had departed to rummage through the toys in the Sunday School area.

"He doesn't take after Elsie, that's for sure!" said Alice. "She had absolutely no patience. Perry's more like Hugo. He's hosting Christmas lunch for my family this year, as he's in the restaurant trade with one of my grandsons." Then an idea occurred which she felt had to be divine inspiration – two ideas, if she was honest: "Why don't you join us?"

"I couldn't possibly do that."

"Why not? Do you have plans?"

"Hardly. A bottle of wine and a big tub of Pringles is about it for me."

"Then join us," Alice insisted. "Wouldn't you like to see the place where I was meant to dance all those years ago, and the grand house Elsie got her mitts on?"

"That'd be fascinating – but I'd be imposing on your family Christmas."

"It's more of a rugby scrum than a family. One more won't make any difference at all, I promise."

"Would there be enough food?"

"Trust me, Symon will've cooked so much food you'll be doing us a favour, because otherwise we'd be eating leftovers until New Year. Besides, you might enjoy putting some more names and faces together and seeing the manor."

"Well …"

Sensing Holly weakening, and excited about her new – and, she had to say, utterly *inspired* – idea, Alice decided it was time to press on with her story.

"Wonderful! Well now, you really need to know what happened next. I can't have my bunch spoiling the ending for you. That'd be like reading the last chapter first."

"Or cheating with a box set," nodded Holly. "Jamie was always doing that. He ruined *Game of Thrones.*"

Alice had no idea what Holly was talking about, but the more she heard about Jamie the less she liked him.

"Let's press on to the end of my story, or it'll be next Christmas," she said.

Holly worried her full bottom lip with her top teeth:

"Please tell me that you and Jonny got back together and lived happily ever after. I want you to have lived the fairy tale. I need to believe it exists."

"It exists all right," Alice assured her. "It might not have happened in quite the way you expect, though, so my advice about arriving at happy endings is to be open to all possibilities. Fate has a way of changing your life for the better just when you think things are at their darkest and your life's over."

"That's just how I feel right now," Holly said sadly.

Alice patted her hand. "Maybe we've met for a reason, then? Now, where was I? Ah, yes. The service for Sam had taken place, and my life had shifted into a new pattern …"

CHAPTER 21

1954

Alice still loved Jonny, but her sadness over losing him was over shadowed by Sam's death and Jonny's abject failure to be supportive to her. As life settled into a new rhythm, she attempted to sift through a pile of jumbled thoughts and feelings. Hurt from Jonny's betrayal was coloured by a newly fledged anger with him. When Alice prodded the pain of their separation as a tongue tentatively tests the spot vacated by a pulled tooth, she was taken aback to discover the pain was less acute. Had Jonny's failure to put his own feelings aside when she was grieving for her brother blunted the razor's edge of loss? Or was she still reeling from the shock of losing Sam and unable to identify her feelings?

Alice was willing to admit she was flattered by the possibility of Henry Tremaine harbouring romantic feelings for her. He was a very handsome man, and she saw how the eyes of women of all ages were drawn to him whenever he walked into a room. His confident air of authority was very attractive too – but more importantly he was kind and loyal and fair. Alice appreciated the support he had given to her family on that terrible morning when the boat had washed up, and the support he'd continued to offer ever since. He was brave too, not hesitating to risk his own life to search for Sam, and Mrs Tremaine once let slip that he'd been awarded the Victoria Cross for his gallantry in combat. Alice concluded that since Henry wore his achievements lightly he could add modesty to this list of personal qualities, and for that she liked him even more. He was a quiet hero. A man whose strength wasn't flaunted or put on show, but which underpinned his whole person just as the granite hidden beneath Polwenna prevented the village from slipping into the sea.

Quiet and reserved in manner, Henry was often perceived by some in the village as aloof and haughty. He never drank, confiding in Alice that he had seen what alcohol did to men who returned from battle, and for that reason he missed out on the camaraderie the village men found in the pub.

"He thinks he's better than the likes of us," was how Barry Penhalligan had once put it, but Alice understood Henry's darkest fears and, having witnessed them take hold of her own father, was admiring of his resolve. She also appreciated that his reticence to socialise was the manifestation of shyness and past hurt rather than superiority, and her kind heart ached for Henry Tremaine. All in all he was a good and honest man. He was also in possession of a fortune and, as Jane Austen had said, must be in want of a wife. Alice was certain that any young woman would be thrilled to catch his eye.

Or they would be if they weren't in love with somebody else, and in spite of everything Alice was sure she still loved Jonny. Of course she did. Whenever her thoughts strayed to the Captain she would scold herself, and remind herself of the promises she had made to Jonny. He might have forgotten them, bending with the winds of parental pressure, but she was made of sterner stuff. *Love is not love which alters when it alteration finds,* Alice reminded herself. Even if things with Jonny were complicated, she wasn't ready to forget him. Hearts didn't work like that, no matter what Elsie might think with all her advice of there being plenty more fish in the sea. Alice was not inclined to cast a net any time soon.

Still, Alice was aware that older than her or not, Henry Tremaine was what most women would consider a catch. Elsie was certainly of the mind that Alice should plump for the Captain and forget all about Jonny. Although Alice was sure that Elsie loved Hugo, Alice knew too that Elsie's pretty face and blonde curls disguised determination and pragmatism. From shop girl to Lady of the Manor was some leap, after all. Elsie's will of iron was famous amongst all her friends – and a cause for some envy too. Alice longed to confide in Elsie, but was aware that if she breathed a word of her own secret suspicions to her best friend she'd never hear the end of it. Jonny would be consigned to history and Elsie would suddenly be Henry's biggest advocate, dragging Alice around the bridal boutiques of Truro in a heartbeat and not resting until the ring was on her finger and Alice was Mrs Tremaine.

Alice Tremaine.

Mrs Henry Tremaine.

The name, even played silently in her own mind, sounded so ludicrous it made Alice laugh out loud – but in an uneasy way, for she sometimes sensed that a future very different from her past might lie ahead. The thought of this new path, however unlikely, made her feel as though she was standing on the deck of a ship pitching and tossing in rough waters. What were her feelings for the Captain? If there was no hope of reconciling with Jonny, would she want to walk out with Henry?

He was intelligent, serious and articulate, and she loved talking to him, long and intense conversations which she had to admit (with a little prickle of disloyalty) were very different from those she'd had with Jonny. It was hard to imagine Jonny wishing to explore the merits of the National Health Service or to discuss the Civil Rights Movement in the United States – almost as impossible as picturing Henry shimmying up the drainpipe to tap on her bedroom window or feeling embarrassed about an outbreak of spots.

No, Henry Tremaine was a *man* – a man who'd seen active service and had suffered great loss, whereas Jonny, still to see the world, was just a boy. Comparing them was neither fair nor kind, yet once she'd started Alice found it difficult to stop. But then she would cut her thoughts off quickly, telling herself sharply that Henry deserved better than to be second choice – and then, even more firmly, telling herself that she was simply daydreaming anyway.

Raw and grieving, Alice needed understanding and support from Henry; anything more would have looked like taking advantage and would have ruined any friendship, so she was glad he had never overstepped their relationship As for Jonny, whether he truly wanted her back or was simply peeved that she might have moved on, Alice never knew, for he went off to Paris and Italy then, she heard later, stayed with Mrs St Milton's family in Cannes. It was to be months before he returned to Polwenna Bay and although Alice, to her chagrin, still flew down the stairs to check the mat when the post came there were never any letters from him. She supposed all his letters were written to Milly these days.

The weeks following the loss of Sam were dark in every way. The summer seemed to retreat and storms battered the village, rain running down the window panes like tears, and the wind howling through empty streets like a thousand souls in torment. Without Sam's noisy presence Cobbles was eerily quiet, and the family withdrew into themselves. May worked long hours at Polwenna House, and Morley's knee, swollen in the damp, caused him so much pain that he spent most of his time, and what little money the family did have left, in The Ship. Without Sam's wages, and with Morley out of work, the Pendeens' fragile finances were soon so desperate that May too took in mending to make ends meet. She grew thinner by the day, often falling asleep over a pile of garments, and Alice, fearing for her mother's health, knew she needed to do more.

In the absence of a handsome prince riding along the quay to sweep her away and solve all her problems (Jonny was allergic to horses) Alice abandoned all hope, however tenuous, of working in fashion, and exchanged her job at the draper's for housekeeping for Lady Yelland at Polwenna Priory. It felt to Alice as though the young girl she'd once been, so full of excitement for the future, had died with Sam, and life held nothing but heartache.

As the world slowly came back to life Alice's dreams of fashion design and freedom had never seemed further away, and the vibrant hedgerows and wedgewood skies were almost a mockery of her sadness. When her own heart was so heavy, it felt jarring to look at sunlight and bright green leaves. Alice sometimes found her own thoughts meandering down paths that led to a very dark place, just as her feet would follow the treacherous path down to the rocks where the boat had washed up. She would stand and watch the boiling water, seduced by its siren call to slip into the depths and let it wash away her care. Only the knowledge of just how much her mum and dad needed her, and how another loss would break them, made Alice turn her back on the water and climb back up the cliff path. The siren voice was her shameful secret and its whispers a peculiar comfort; they suggested there was still one choice left if she really couldn't bear to continue.

Although the draper's had never been her first choice of employment, Alice truly mourned for her job, because it had at least been a tie to an old dream. The fabrics and textures had been a joy to work with, and her daily trip into town a welcome escape from a village where everyone, with the exception of Elsie, seemed content to follow in their parents' footsteps, pick up the family mantle and stay in their place. Pollards were builders. Penhalligans fished. Rowes baked. Pendeen women went into service.

At least while she'd been cutting fabric and snipping ribbons Alice had remained part of the world she longed for. She could chat at lunchtime with the other girls about music and Hollywood stars, or pore over fashion magazines to glean ideas for new designs. There was even the benefit of being given scraps of fabric which she could cobble together into aprons and boleros if she was feeling creative, and her sketch books had overflowed with ideas. While she'd worked in the draper's shop Alice could pretend she was still on her way to becoming a designer – but once she was cleaning and polishing and boiling laundry she had no choice but to accept that her future had taken a very different turn. Her sketch books were soon untouched, her designs abandoned and the film stars long forgotten.

Alice Pendeen was in service again. For six and a half days a week she worked at the Priory, scrubbing and sweeping and trying to remove centuries of grime from a house filled with dark corners, eerie cold spots and spiders' webs. If she fell into bed each night almost fainting with exhaustion, at least she knew she was able to ease the burden which had fallen onto her mum's slender shoulders. Her mother had suffered enough, and it broke Alice's heart to see her mother hunch over the copper as she pounded washing just as much as it hurt to see her once proud father a broken man. More often than not a Pollard or a Penhalligan would help him to stagger home, caps twisted awkwardly in their hands as they delivered a swaying Morley over the threshold and apologised for not being able to stop him drinking.

May always stopped her work to help her husband to bed. She was never harsh with him, and Alice never once saw her lose her temper. Although May too, heartbroken, was working hard while Morley drank himself into a stupor and wasted their money, she was as tender with him as though he was a child, undressing him, washing him and helping him to bed. His load had simply become too heavy to carry, she explained one evening when Alice became angry. The first war had taken his health and youth, the second had claimed his first-born, and now the sea had stolen Sam. He could bear no more. He had nothing left to give. He couldn't carry on. Alice understood. But also she wondered why it was that women had no choice but to carry on …

As the summer shrugged off the last remnants of spring and dark mornings left in a heap for the autumn to pick up, Alice tried hard to shake off her heavy mood and look for positives. The Priory was a beautiful house only a mile inland, through woods and bluebell dells. Centuries-old, the ancient house had seen more wars and deaths than Alice could imagine, and she drew comfort from its timelessness. Set against the years all her problems were, she felt, placed into context. In a hundred years who would care about them, or even know?

Once a monastery, the Priory had been a dwelling since the Reformation and was currently home to the elderly Lady Yelland. During the war it had been a hospital for convalescing airmen, and Alice vaguely recalled them, bandaged and brave as they'd strolled through the village, many of them looking dazed as though they couldn't quite understand how they had found themselves in Polwenna Bay. Perhaps some of them were truly puzzled? Henry had tried to explain the disconnect between active service and being on leave. He said it had left him reeling to find himself in a place where there was no sudden rush for action, no sickening adrenalin surge as you reached for a rifle or crawled on your belly, praying the enemy didn't spot a tell-tale glint of metal.

The airmen were long gone now, back home with wives and sweethearts who would never understand their silences or faraway expressions, and since Lady Yelland was too old to walk up the stairs the men's empty rooms were filled with dust and silence. Alice's duties mostly involved keeping the parts which were inhabited as clean as possible. As she scrubbed and polished and mopped she sometimes thought she caught the strains of swing music from a gramophone and would pause for a moment, certain that it was footsteps making the floorboards above her creak rather than the old timbers expanding in the summer heat. The Priory was an atmospheric place, and she would scold herself and return to work, trying hard to put aside a growing conviction that many of these unquiet walkers predated Spitfires and Hitler.

There were worse places to work, she knew, and the money was, if not good, more than she had earned at the draper's. Leaded windows framed trees and sky, and inside the house the still air hung heavy with the scent of age and lavender. When the wind blew ivy tapped at the glass like fingers and the old house shivered with memories. Although Alice only worked there in the daytime she still felt as though the place was filled with dark corners, and would shiver at the half-remembered legends of weeping ladies and ghostly monks which Sam had teased her with when, as children, they'd dared one another to creep though the trees to look at the house. Several times a day Alice would be cleaning a room and, thinking her employer had walked in, turn around to find herself alone.

Lady Yelland was frail, and seldom strayed from the house. A distant relation of the Tregarricks, she was old but as sharp as a knife, regularly sparring with Reverend Sharpe and terrifying the WI ladies who took it in turns to visit with scones and jam – and, the old lady observed dryly, big dollops of condescension. She loved to read, but as her eyesight was failing it often fell to Alice to read to her, and together they were working their way through Austen and the Brontës. Alice was head over heels in love with Heathcliff, drowning in the fiery passion between him and Cathy, but Mrs Yelland scoffed at this, saying it would never last. She was a firm advocate of Mr Knightley, and argued that he and Emma were a far preferable combination.

"You'll understand why when you're my age," was all she would say. "There's far more to love than dramatic declaration and wailing. Take *Emma* home and finish it. *Then* tell me you prefer that madman Heathcliff."

Alice, who had done her fair share of wailing over Jonny, hadn't agreed. What was more important than passion? Besides, she couldn't imagine ever being as old as Mrs Yelland. Her employer had to be at least eighty. What did *she* know about being young and in love? Not wanting to look rude, she'd taken *Emma* home and read it from cover to cover, to be surprised at how many similarities there were between Austen's thoughtful hero and Henry Tremaine. By contrast, Brontë's Heathcliff did indeed appear rather unbalanced. Maybe Lady Yelland had a point?

In a gesture that Austen would have approved of, as soon

as Tremaine Marine opened for business Henry called in at Cobbles and offered Morley a job.

"You know I was always planning to employ Sam. I'd promised him that he could come and help me once the boat-yard was running," he explained, sitting at the kitchen table while May flapped about, trying to tidy washing and gather mending into baskets. "Mrs Pendeen, please. Sit down! Stop worrying about the washing. It's only me! I don't give a hoot how tidy the house is."

She sat down. It was, Alice thought, a real sign of how accepted he was by her parents that Henry was no longer escorted into the chilly formality of the front room and offered tea and cake served from the best china, but ushered into the heart of the cottage and plied with a mug of builder's tea and buttered wadges of saffron bun.

"But Sam's ..."

May's tears, never far away, made her eyes shine.

Morley, still sober because it was Sunday afternoon and the pub was closed, reached for her hand and held it tightly.

"He's dead, Captain," Morley said harshly to Henry. "You don't have to feel obligated to keep that promise, and you don't need to give me charity. We're proud people and we don't want your pity."

Henry bowed his head. When he spoke again his voice was hoarse, and Alice knew he was struggling to keep his emotions in check.

"There's nobody I can trust with the business like I knew I could trust Sam. Nobody but *you,* Mr Pendeen. This isn't about being obligated or, God forbid, pity. If anything it's self-ishness on my part. You know the coast here better than anyone, and there's nothing you don't know about engines and rigging. I know who taught Sam, remember? I need somebody I can trust to help me with Tremaine Marine. I need *you,* Mr Pendeen. You'd be doing me a favour."

He held out his hand and Alice held her breath. This job could change everything for her parents, and for her too. Alice also knew that Henry understood that. He could have employed anyone – of course he could. People would queue up to work at the new marina. Henry hadn't needed to make good on his promise to Sam, but he knew her father needed a focus.

The whole cottage seemed to hold its breath. Even the gulls nesting on the chimney stopped squabbling and the old clock on the mantel seemed to tick a little less heartily. Then a smile split her father's face, the old smile Alice hadn't seen for so long. It was the smile which used to make dimples dance in his cheeks and his eyes crinkle when he came home from sea and swung May into his arms while Alice and her brothers hugged his legs. It was the smile that came from her father's heart and which Alice had missed as much as she'd missed Sam and Danny.

"Well, if I'm needed, Captain, I can't see how I can say no!" he said, shaking Henry's hand. "I won't let you down, I promise."

Alice and her mother exchanged a look across the kitchen. They were both thinking about the bouts of drinking and the bleak moods that submerged Morley for days at a time, but as Henry clapped him on the back and arranged to be at the boatyard for eight the very next morning, Alice felt sure those dark days were behind them.

And she knew who to thank.

Once the Pendeens had recovered from the excitement, and May from the shock of hearing just how much her husband would be earning (*and on dry land too, and without any danger*, she kept saying in disbelief) Henry made his farewells.

Alice let him out of Cobbles, but as he turned to leave she caught his sleeve and tugged him around to face her.

"Thank you," she said softly.

"What for?" Henry asked.

"For what you've just done for my parents."

He looked down at her steadily.

"I didn't do it for them, Alice. I didn't even do it for me. I did it for *you*."

Alice's throat constricted with a rush of emotion. As Henry took her hand and raised it to his lips she lifted her eyes to his and saw such love and kindness there that she couldn't speak. Then he turned and walked away, leaving her staring after him as though she was waking up after a very long sleep.

Henry Tremaine, the handsome Captain and decorated war hero, was clearly in love with her.

CHAPTER 22

1954

Unsure what to do with this new knowledge, Alice pushed all thoughts of Henry Tremaine aside and threw herself into her work at the Priory. As though physical energy could banish her confusion she took to cleaning with such energy that Lady Yelland said she felt utterly exhausted and begged her to slow down:

"The dirt's all that holds this old place up, dear. Please go steady! Come and read to me."

Alice laughed, but she was so full of energy she couldn't bear to sit down for long. Instead she drafted Elsie in to keep the old lady company. With Hugo up at Oxford, Elsie, engaged to him, was at a loose end and keen to escape the bakery. In spite of the great disparity of their ages it was soon clear that she and Lady Yelland were kindred spirits, and they spent most afternoons settled down with gin, gossiping about the Tregarricks and comparing notes on their romantic conquests. While Alice cleaned and prepared meals she smiled to hear their laughter echoing through the old house, and once Elsie had discovered the airmen's old gramophone, her feet tapped to the strains of the swing music which twirled with the dust motes and thick pollen.

"I want to be just like her when I'm old," Elsie declared one evening as, arm in arm, the two girls walked back through the woods to Polwenna. "She's so young at heart you soon forget she's ancient, and she doesn't give a hoot about anything – oops!"

She tripped on a tree root and pitched forward, only staying on her feet because Alice was holding her up.

"She drinks too much gin," Alice said sternly. "And she'll rob you at cards, so be warned."

Elsie grimaced. "She thrashed me at poker. Apparently one of the airmen taught her during the war. As for the booze – well, what else has she got to enjoy in life? All her friends and family are gone and she's all alone. That must be the worst thing ever. Maybe I hope I don't get old at all."

Her heel caught on a bramble and she lurched once more.

Alice tightened her grasp.

"If you keep tripping like this we won't make it back to the village, never mind into old age!"

"We'll *never* get old," Elsie said firmly. "We'll always be young, Ally, and we'll always be friends."

"Even when you're Lady Tregarrick and I'm just a fisherman's daughter?"

Alice was realistic enough to know how Elsie's life would change. Although the St Miltons thought they were above the Pendeens, the Tregarricks were in a different universe altogether. As was Henry Tremaine.

Not that Alice was thinking about him at all.

Elsie turned to look at Alice and for once her merry face was serious.

"You're my best friend, Ally. Nothing's going to change that, I promise. You'll be the guest of honour at every party we throw! Besides, Hugo isn't a snob, and class doesn't matter to him. He chose *me*, didn't he?"

There was no denying it; Hugo *had* chosen Elsie – although once she'd set her sights on him he'd had very little choice. Luckily for Elsie, her beloved's parents, although titled, seemed far less concerned about social class than the St Miltons, which Henry explained was because they were established and didn't need to worry about proving themselves to have arrived – unlike the St Miltons. Class was, Henry had added wearily, a very British preoccupation. In the heat of battle bullets didn't care where you went to school or whether you said 'serviette' or 'napkin'.

But what about Henry? His mother came from a very grand family. Henry was well educated and well spoken. Surely in his circles a friendship with a fisherman's daughter would be frowned upon and marriage would be utterly impossible?

Henry again! She wasn't thinking about marriage to Henry; it was just a hypothetical question, and another example of him sliding into her thoughts. She might not have seen him for weeks – another reason for working long hours was because it meant she could avoid Henry without it looking obvious – but he was often on her mind. Things he'd said and observations he'd made would pop into her head at the oddest times, and she'd find herself thinking of things he might find interesting or that she'd like to discuss with him. In truth, her thoughts were now turning to Henry far more often than to Jonny, something she was trying very hard not to dwell on.

She smiled at Elsie. "Hugo's lucky to have you."

"I know," said Elsie. "I tell him that all the time. And Jonny would be lucky to have you if he finished with Milly and you could forgive him for being such an idiot. Hugo says Jonny knows he's made a big mistake."

Alice couldn't help herself.

"Is that what Jonny said?"

Elsie's golden curls bobbed. "So Hugo tells me. Jonny still loves you, Ally. Hard cheese, I say. We all prefer *you know who*."

Alice rolled her eyes. "I've told you a thousand times, he's just a *friend*."

"An unlikely one for you, though."

"You just said that class doesn't make any difference."

"I didn't mean that. I meant that he's …" Elsie paused, searching for the right words. "He's old."

"He's thirty-three! Hardly ancient."

"That's a proper grown-up man."

Alice grinned. "Agatha Christie's got nothing on you!"

Elsie elbowed her in the ribs. "You know what I mean. Henry's a proper grown-up. Jonny can't compete with him."

"Jonny never had to compete with anyone. He finished with me, remember?"

Elsie nodded. "I know, but the Captain's a totally different kettle of fish, and Jonny knows it. You know it too."

Elsie was right; Alice did know it. She said nothing.

"He's very handsome – but he feels dangerous."

Alice was shocked. "Henry Tremaine?"

"Maybe 'dangerous' is the wrong word? There's something a little brooding, you must admit. There's a dark edge to him."

Alice nodded. Henry had talked to her of the dark moods that swept over him and the dreams which left him sweating and afraid. He had seen – and done – things in the name of King and Country which he could never undo, and they haunted him. She suspected this was one of the things which had brought him closer to her father.

"He's seen war, Else, and it's changed him. Nobody comes back from conflict without losing a little of their soul. My dad still won't talk about what he saw in the first one. Jonny – and Hugo for that matter – are too young to have been affected. Of course Henry's not like them. His innocence must have been shattered on the Normandy beaches."

Elsie looked chastened. "You're right, of course. It's just that you can't play games with a man like that, Alice, so be careful."

"I'm not playing games with anyone. Now let's get home before my mother sends out a search party." Alice took Elsie's hand and helped her to navigate a stile, hoping the firm tone of her voice had made it clear the discussion was over. She really didn't want to continue – mostly because a lot of what Elsie said had been a little too close to the bone.

Henry Tremaine didn't play games. He was a serious man, and although he was reserved Alice knew he felt things deeply. She owed him a great deal, and she wouldn't toy with his heart.

If Elsie often needed a little more holding up than normal on their walks home, Alice didn't mind lending her assistance, for since her friend's arrival at the Priory her elderly charge had taken on a whole new lease of life. Even the old building seemed to be waking up, as though it had been slumbering for too long. The leaded windows twinkled like Lady Yelland's beady eyes, the old floorboards glowed in the slanting summer sunshine, and roses scrambled over the old walls with renewed vigour. That was Elsie's gift, thought Alice. She brought fun and energy with her and always made people smile. No wonder Hugo was smitten.

With Morley's new job had come a new lease of life. His

visits to the pub were now confined to a Saturday evening, and the pressure on the household finances was finally starting to ease. So May had suggested to Alice that she should think about returning to the draper's or even resume her studies, but as much as Alice was tempted, the idea of the family being reliant on Henry Tremaine didn't sit well with her. She feared it would make her obligated to him. Allowing his kindness to affect her employment would place their friendship on a new, and different, footing. It also seemed perilous, in case he was hoping their friendship turned into something more.

If this was the case Alice knew that Henry would deserve an answer. Although she had feelings for the Captain and couldn't deny she enjoyed his company and was attracted to him, she was still in love with Jonny. Of course she was.

Wasn't she?

As she tried to work through these questions, each one as knotted as salt-soaked and wind-whipped hair, Alice cleaned even harder. Soon Polwenna Priory was gleaming and as dust-free as such an old building could ever be. In an attempt to calm her down, Mrs Yelland announced she wanted to play cards with three people and set about teaching Alice how to play poker. While she played, Lady Yelland smoked like a navvy (another thing she blamed the convalescing airmen for) and told the girls wonderful stories of her life growing up before the first war – tales of great country houses and hunting and extravagant balls. Elsie and Alice loved hearing these stories and picturing Lady Yelland as a debutante in her feathers and silks. She thought the girls should be dancing and having fun too – and Elsie, who needed no encouragement, agreed.

"The St Miltons are holding a masked ball on Midsummer's Eve," she said one afternoon as the three of them played poker on the terrace beneath a *trompe l'oeil* sky of bright blues and lazy clouds. "It's going to be a big occasion. Everyone's invited. It'll be so exciting!"

Not *everyone,* thought Alice, who had already heard about this party from May (who was tearing her hair out at the thought of all the organising that would ensue); and Alice knew that her name would most definitely not be on the guest list. Elsie had only made the cut because she was engaged to Hugo. Already Alice sensed how their lives would bifurcate over the coming years. She studied her cards carefully, and hoped she'd cultivated enough of a poker face for her companions not to know her much her heart was aching at being excluded.

"How *exciting,*" said Lady Yelland. "There's nothing like a *bal masqué* for getting up to all sorts of mischief. I recall one at Hampton Court when I was a girl, and I slipped into the maze with a very handsome young man." Her eyes went somewhere far away down the decades and to a place where she was young and beautiful, laughing and running hand in hand with her masked lover through privet corridors before they fell into one another's arms to kiss in the darkness.

"Then what happened?" demanded Elsie, wide-eyed. "Did you *do* it?"

"Elsie!" gasped Alice. "You can't ask her *that*!"

"Why not?" grinned Elsie. "Lady Y was young once!"

"I was indeed – and suffice to say it was a *memorable* night," laughed Lady Yelland, not offended in the least.

"Oh, girls, how I envy you! Make the most of being young. Youth is so fleeting. You'll have a wonderful time at the party, of that I have no doubt. Take the whole weekend off, dear Alice, and have fun."

But Alice knew that her days of having fun at dances and slipping into the shadows to kiss Jonny were no more than sun-filled snapshots from another life. Those kisses belonged to Millicent Jago now.

"I won't be going to the party," she said. "The St Miltons haven't invited me. I'm just their housekeeper's daughter. I'll come here as usual, Lady Yelland."

"Hasn't the Captain asked you to be his partner?" Elsie asked, looking surprised.

"Of *course* he hasn't," snapped Alice.

That would have been a step too far. Henry knew it, and Alice certainly did. For Captain Tremaine to be accompanied to the St Milton's party by Alice Pendeen would set tongues wagging, raise eyebrows and raise all kinds of questions. Henry, always so thoughtful and so proper, wouldn't dream of putting Alice in such an awkward position. *He* had been invited, of course, and according to May would be escorting Mrs Tremaine.

"Dear God," said Elsie. "I despair, I really do. So how will you go to the ball?"

Alice shrugged. "I won't be going."

"Not *going*?" shrieked Elsie, who had quickly forgotten she had only been invited as the future Lady Tregarrick. "But that's not *fair*! You should be there, looking absolutely beautiful and showing Jonny just what he's missing. You know I'm right, Alice! It's the perfect way to win him back."

It would be a lie if Alice said she hadn't lain awake in her small bed beneath the eaves and dreamed about a scenario where this was exactly what happened. In her mind she saw herself floating across the velvet-smooth lawns, silken skirts whispering behind her and all heads turning as the guests wondered who the beautiful masked stranger was. Only Jonny would recognise her, because he loved her. He would step forward to ask for a dance, and realise he could never let her go again.

Alice had pictured how he'd take her hand and lead her into the rose garden, where shadows purpled the grass and the sea whispered below. Then he would sweep her into his arms and tell her how sorry he was. He would swear he loved her and kiss her beneath the stars, a kiss that promised he'd never let her go again.

Her skin was dusted with goosebumps at the mere thought of this, for hadn't Madame Sienna told Alice she would kiss her true love at midsummer and this would seal their bond? The ball was the perfect time for this prediction to come true!

This was a Cinderella dream, and one Alice had cherished ever since learning about the party – but in the cold light of day she knew it was no more than a childish fantasy. She had no invitation and no costume. Unlike Cinderella, who had a fairy godmother on her side, Alice Pendeen would not be going to the ball. The midsummer kiss would never take place, and Jonny would be lost to her for ever.

She swallowed the knot of grief in her throat and glared at Elsie. She never spoke of Jonny by name.

"I'm not going and that's the end of the matter. I'll be working as usual."

Elsie looked mutinous. "Well, I think that's unfair. J— I mean a certain person should have made *sure* you were invited."

Alice loved Elsie for her loyalty, but they both knew that Jonny wouldn't have been in a position to add Alice Pendeen to the guest list. The elaborate fireworks display Mrs St Milton had arranged for the evening would have nothing on her explosion if she spotted Alice socialising with her guests.

Lady Yelland peered at Alice over her cards like a shawled tortoise peeping from a sun-bonneted shell.

"You shouldn't be shut away here with an old fossil like me! A pretty young thing like you should be out and about at parties and breaking hearts. Why, I broke a few in my day! Not that you'd believe it now to look at me, but they were queuing up for the slots on my dance card. Even the Prince of Wales booked a dance with me. I could have been a royal mistress!"

Alice smiled. "I don't doubt it for a minute."

"Oh yes, those were the days! I was in love every five minutes back then. Quite a dish, I was."

She flickered her eyes back at her cards, and Alice swiftly held her hand closer to her chest; her employer wasn't above using distraction as a strategy.

"I thought I would die of love for one young man. He was a curate and so very handsome, but my mama said he was not at all suitable and forbade us from meeting. I almost wept myself sick when he left to be a missionary – until I met my Lawrence. Then I didn't give a fig for poor Reverend James!"

Sir Lawrence Yelland had been the big love of her life. She mentioned him at least once an hour and, just like the old queen she remembered so well, she had only worn black since he had passed away.

"Oh yes, indeed," Lady Yelland said, more to herself than to the girls, "Once you meet the one, you *know*."

"That's true," Alice agreed, still thinking of Jonny. She had known with every cell of her body that she loved him. She wondered whether she could ever forgive him, or whether their relationship was poisoned beyond any cure.

"No. I mean you really know. In *here*." The old lady slammed a clawed hand against her concave chest and coughed violently. A cigarette was curling to ash in a saucer, and she reached for it, inhaling frantically. She always swore that smoking helped her to breathe easily, but Alice wasn't convinced – unlike Elsie, who smoked with great enthusiasm and film-star dash.

A few puffs later Lady Yelland had recovered sufficiently to continue with her lecture.

"True love isn't a sudden passion, girls. Those flare and die. *Violent delights have violent ends*, as the Bard said. Love's not all excitement either, but a quiet and calm certainty."

Elsie pulled a face. "That sounds dull to me. Who wants calm?"

"The heart does," said Lady Yelland firmly. "The heart yearns for tranquillity above all."

Her filmy eyes met Alice's, and it felt as though the old lady was speaking only to her. Elsie, who was all about the excitement of her romance with Hugo, would never understand – or maybe not for a long, long time – if Lady Yelland's predictions were to come true. Alice's poor trampled heart certainly longed for tranquillity, but she wasn't sure that Jonny would ever be able to offer this. He was too tempestuous and changeable. Too uncertain in his own mind to be her ballast. Alice had a horrible premonition that no matter how much he loved her, Jonny St Milton would only ever let her down. Her vision blurred, and she looked back at her cards.

"Love is only true when it's quiet in your heart," continued Lady Yelland. "Love is knowing that your lover always puts you first and wants nothing more than your happiness and security. All the moonlight kisses and sweet words soon dissolve in the sunlight of daily life. There's nothing romantic about bills and babies, you mark my words!"

Elsie tossed her curls and put down a ten of hearts with a flourish. "I'll take passion over serenity, thanks!"

Lady Yelland looked at Alice. "Will it be Knightley or Heathcliff? I've seen you moping about, my dear, and it's a wicked waste of your best years. My advice is to get yourself to that ball, and find out who and what your heart really wants."

Alice focused on her cards. She laid down the jack in the suit, only to be trumped by her employer's king.

"There. I'm *never* wrong," Lady Yelland crowed. "In love or in cards! You'd thought you'd got enough with the knave, Alice, but it's the king you need. You bear that in mind."

Alice shivered at her words, recalling Henry's expression as he'd stared down at her the day he'd confessed that he'd helped for *her* sake. He'd looked as though he was drinking in every detail of her face. Beyond the terrace the sun had twinkled through the trees and cast dapples to dance on the lawn, but she'd barely noticed. All she could see was the Captain, gazing down at her with such intensity and that understanding, as though they shared a secret. There was an accord there which she couldn't deny.

She stood up abruptly. "I'll clear the table and then see about preparing your dinner, Lady Y."

Lady Yelland flapped a ringed hand. "Soup will suffice. There's far too much to do to waste time cooking!"

Alice gathered up the cards and shuffled them into a neat pile. "What would you like me to do instead? Weed the lavender bed? Or shall I scrub the doorstep?"

The elderly lady caught Alice's hand and halted her flight from the table.

"None of those, my dear, because there's something far more important to do first. We've got to find a way of getting you to that ball. Now, stop protesting and listen to me, both of you! This is what we're going to do ..."

CHAPTER 23

1954

The St Miltons' masked ball was the most talked-about event of that summer, and Alice knew it would be an event the villagers would always remember. Everyone was involved in some way, for even those who didn't possess a coveted invitation would be busy providing food and drink, or employed as extra gardeners in the rush to ensure the flowerbeds and lawns were perfect, or had been drafted in to serve refreshments.

May was so busy she was seldom home before sunset, and with Morley putting in long hours at Tremaine Marine there was nobody at home to wonder why Alice was spending most of the day in the kitchen glued to her sewing machine rather than working at the Priory. Even Henry was flat out with the amount of boat work, and apart from a few brief chats at the marina when she dropped by with her father's lunch, Alice had hardly seen him. She wasn't sure whether she was sorry or relieved about that; she missed their easy chats but she also suspected that if they did talk at any length she'd find it impossible to keep her plans a secret; Henry was so warm and so easy to confide in that she would have blurted the whole idea out in seconds. She suspected he would have been dismayed and would have warned her that she was setting herself up for heartbreak.

Henry might have been right – but by now it was far too late for Alice to back out. Even if she'd wanted to do so she doubted that Elsie or Lady Yelland would have allowed this. Both of them, giddy with excitement at their clever plan, were counting down the minutes until it was put into action at the ball, Elsie because she thought it would be an 'utter gas', and Lady Yelland because she was living vicariously through the girls. From the moment she had mooted her plan the old lady seemed to shed decades, and the closer the day of the ball drew the more animated she became.

The idea was simple, in theory at least, and involved Alice and Elsie both wearing exactly the same costume. They were of a similar height and build, Lady Yelland had pointed out, and if both girls had masks on and made sure they kept apart nobody would ever guess they weren't the same guest. The only person in on the secret would be Hugo, since he would have to escort both girls, one at a time, into the house.

Elsie had been certain this wasn't a problem, and Alice had believed her since everyone knew Hugo was so in love that he hung on her every word – but Alice hadn't been convinced by the rest of the plan:

"We have different-coloured hair," she pointed out.

Lady Yelland, who had read *The Man in the Iron Mask* several times, wasn't so easily put off.

"Then wear big hats. Or headscarves. Or dress in the style

of Marie Antoinette and powder your curls. Be creative, Alice! Now do buck up, dear. This is *so* exciting!"

Alice wasn't convinced. It sounded like a hare-brained scheme:

"But what about costumes?" she fretted. There was no way she could afford to hire something elaborate.

"There's no one better at designing outfits than you!" Elsie had said excitedly. "You're brilliant. Let's go as Madame de Pompadour, with powdered hair and velvet masks! Come on, Ally! Wouldn't it be fun to dress up like that?"

Alice had to agree it would be, and somewhat against her better judgement found herself agreeing to the scheme. It would be worth all the nerves, the fear of being caught and the sheer hard work of sewing two dresses to be able to see Jonny again, she told herself, as Elsie and Lady Yelland fleshed out their plan. Once Alice and Jonny had kissed and sealed their love all her worries would be distant memories. Knowing, though, that if she thought too hard about this plan she would see the flaws in it, she decided it was best not to examine the logistics too closely.

Over the course of the next few weeks Alice designed and created two identical dresses. Vaguely in the style of Marie Antoinette, they were cut from a pair of beautiful rose and gold curtains that Lady Yelland insisted they take down from a seldom-used drawing room. Tight bodices were cobbled together from her old whalebone corsets, garden wire utilised for hoops, and old net curtains snipped up to become foaming underskirts. Elsie raided trunks of old clothes in the loft to liberate lace and ribbons. Alice fashioned black masks from one of Lady Yelland's old mourning dresses, and trimmed two cartwheel-sized and very moth-nibbled hats with ostrich feathers plucked from a balding boa. This, combined with the fittings and her day job, was a lot of work, and Alice sewed every spare moment she possessed, telling her mother she was making a dress for Elsie – which was true, she told herself guiltily.

"You'd think Hugo's family could afford to buy Elsie a dress rather than expecting you to work your fingers to the bone," her mum had sniffed, offended on Alice's behalf.

"I don't mind, Ma. I like sewing," Alice protested. She wasn't surprised that her mum thought she was overdoing it; making two such detailed dresses from scratch was a huge task.

"That's not sewing, love, it's slave labour."

"I see Elsie's taking to being lady of the manor," said her dad. "That one always did have ideas above her station."

This was hugely unfair on Elsie, who had never once boasted about the way her life was changing. Alice couldn't bear the way her parents were resigned to everyone having their place, but she bit her tongue and said she was happy to help her friend.

"It's not as if Hugo's parents can't afford to buy his fiancée a costume," her mum muttered, but although she hadn't said much more that time, Alice, rather than hear the same conversation over and over again, carried her sewing to the Priory and continued by hand while Elsie took over her chores there.

The Priory grew a little dustier, and Lady Yelland ate more eggs on toast than usual, but nobody was complaining and the dresses took shape rapidly, soon looking every bit as glamorous as Alice could have ever hoped. By the time of the final fitting both girls were clad in sweeping gowns fit for a queen, and Lady Yelland clapped her hands in delight as they twirled before her.

"I can't tell who's who!" she cried. "Bravo, Alice! Those dresses are marvellous. You're a very talented young woman."

Alice blushed. She'd loved making the dresses. Although

they were costumes rather than couture, created from bits and bobs and best viewed in the soft evening light, she was proud of her handiwork. As she spun around she felt elegant and beautiful – and, best of all, hopeful. Catching sight of her reflection in the age-spotted mirror over the mantelpiece made hope flare in her heart. Surely when he saw her dressed like this Jonny would fall in love with her all over again? How could he resist?

But even as she thought this a small voice whispered to her that if Jonny had ever truly loved her, she wouldn't need to win him back. *Love is not love which alters when it alteration finds,* she recalled again – and, unbidden, Henry Tremaine came to mind, a man who once he gave his word kept it – and who, Alice felt certain, would be steadfast. He would never let down the woman he loved, for his heart, once given, would be hers for life.

What will Henry Tremaine think when he sees me dressed like a queen? Alice wondered as she studied her reflection. Would he think she looked older and more sophisticated? Less a girl and more of a woman? Would he admire her handiwork and ingenuity? Or would he say there was no need for her to pretend to be anything other than she was in order to be thought worthy? He certainly never gave any indication that he minded that she was a Pendeen or flinched at the shame of an association with a fisherman's daughter. He had never made her feel anything less than valued and respected. Unlike Jonny, Henry Tremaine had always treated her like a lady.

Thinking this way made Alice feel disloyal and guilty as well as sad; loving Jonny had once been as natural to her as breathing, for she had given her heart to him gladly and without conditions. Even though she appreciated the pressure he was under, Alice didn't understand his response to it because she could have never forsaken him. As the day of the ball grew closer she began to wonder if it was worth winning back a man who had treated her so badly, and she found herself comparing Jonny's conduct to Henry's – and, more importantly, her own.

How she wished she could confide in someone! But there was nobody who would understand. Elsie was so caught up in the romance of the plan it seemed unkind to disillusion her; Mum would have been horrified and forbidden the whole escapade; and Henry, who had somehow become her main sounding-board, was too caught up in her dilemma to become a confidant. All Alice could do now was hope for the best and hold tight to Madame Sienna's prophecy. If she kissed her true love at midsummer all would be well. The rest she would fret about later.

Midsummer's Day dawned with cloudless blue skies, a soft breeze and gallons of golden sunshine which poured over the village and made the sea glitter with harlequin diamonds. Mrs St Milton couldn't have ordered better weather, Morley remarked grudgingly, and by the time May had departed for a very long day laden vans were already trundling up the hill to deliver flowers and food, gardeners were mowing perfect stripes on the lawns, and the gulls' cries were competing with the banging of hammers on marquee frames. It would be the perfect evening for a masked ball, and even those who weren't invited – most of the village – found the excitement contagious. But to her great surprise Alice felt flat. She almost wished she wasn't going at all, and could spend the evening watching her father mend boats instead.

This reluctance made no sense; she'd worked so hard for this moment. This was the night when she'd finally win Jonny back for good, and she ought to be *fizzing* with excitement. Instead liquid dread flowed through her veins and she found herself wishing she'd never agreed to the whole idea. All the hours of sewing and the strain of being forced to lie to her parents had taken the gloss off the adventure. Hopefully once she was gliding down the elegant staircase – as she had so many times in her dreams – and was in Jonny's arms her spirits would rise.

In direct contrast Elsie was excited enough for both of them, and as the girls got ready at the Priory she chatted away merrily while Alice could barely speak. Her stomach curdled with dread and she felt queasy with the responsibility of what might happen if she was discovered. Her mother would lose her job for certain – and then where would the Pendeen family be? As the girls dressed Alice teetered on the brink of telling Elsie she'd changed her mind, and several times found herself wondering, disloyally, whether Jonny St Milton was worth the risk.

Of course he was! Alice gave herself a mental shake. She loved Jonny. Hadn't Madame Sienna said she would find her true love after much heartache, and that if she kissed him at midsummer their future would be sealed? All she had to do was keep the faith, and this secret, a little longer for the old wise woman's words to be proven true.

By the time Hugo arrived to collect them in the estate's shooting brake – the only vehicle which could make it along the rutted track to the Priory – Lady Yelland had sworn she couldn't tell the two girls apart. When they admired their reflections in an age-speckled looking glass even Alice struggled to identify herself. As long as they kept apart and didn't remove their masks there was no reason why their plan shouldn't succeed. With her full skirts, black mask and huge plumed hat, Alice also knew that she looked ravishing because Elsie certainly did. Everything was perfect.

So why wasn't she more excited?

"Ready, Alice?"

Hugo, transformed into a dashing cavalier complete with dark ringlets and feathered hat, offered his arm gallantly. His kind amber eyes twinkling behind his mask, he added mischievously, "I say! Even I can't tell you two girls apart this evening. That could get me into all kinds of trouble!"

Elsie whacked him with her fan and he yelped.

"I was kidding, Else!"

"You'd better not forget who you're engaged to, Hugo! Now, are you clear about what to do? We can't afford to make any mistakes."

Hugo nodded, serious all of a sudden. Even the jaunty plumes on his hat seemed to droop as though weighed down by the gravity of his task.

"I know the drill," he said. "Fifteen minutes between you both and all that. Trust me."

"Hmm." Elsie looked doubtful, for Hugo was famously scatter-brained. She and Alice had been through their plan with him several times, and now there was no more time to repeat it. They'd stressed the importance of timing, for Hugo had to make certain that by the time of Elsie's arrival Alice was as far away from the guests as possible. The girls couldn't be seen together, or the game would be well and truly up.

"I'll escort Ally in, circulate for 15 minutes, and then slip out again to collect you, my love," Hugo repeated. He tapped his head. "It's all safe in my noddle."

"It had better be," said Elsie darkly.

Alice was worried. "Do you really think this'll work? I mean, won't people think it odd that Hugo arrives twice?"

Hugo grinned. "One of the good things about being a Tregarrick is that nobody ever questions you, no matter how barmy you appear. My grandfather used to ride a horse into church – and don't even get me started on Tally Ho Tregarrick. He used to sleep in the kennel with his hounds."

Hugo was right; nobody ever questioned the Tregarricks, and for once Alice was glad that the village was so positively feudal in outlook. She pushed down her nerves, checked her mask was in place and raised her chin.

"Let's go to the ball," she said.

CHAPTER 24

1954

"The Honourable Hugo Tregarrick and Miss Elsie Rowe!"

The booming announcement made Alice start as she and Hugo were shown into the flower-filled entrance hall of Polwenna House. There were masked guests everywhere she looked! Knights, highwaymen and Egyptian queens thronged the room. Footmen glided through the press of guests, one hand behind their back as on the other they balanced a tray bearing ice-cold glasses of champagne. Music drifted in the blossom-scented air alongside the sounds of light chatter, laughter and the chink of ice against glass. It was so elegant and extravagant, and for a moment Alice froze, unable to believe she was really here.

"Everyone's looking at us," she whispered to Hugo. Eyes were trained on her and there was a ripple of interest. It took all of her courage not to turn on her heel and run.

"Chin up," said Hugo. "You're Elsie, remember? Of course they're gossiping – but she doesn't let that upset her. I rather think she enjoys it."

Alice laughed in spite of her nerves and pushed her shoulders back, channelling her inner Elsie, who would certainly revel in such attention. She knew she looked beautiful in her costume, and as they crossed the chequered floor she felt the gazes of all those present rest on her as light as butterflies – while whispers deadly as daggers were, she felt sure, being uttered behind raised hands.

Clutching Hugo's arm tightly, it was all Alice could do not to gape at the transformation of Polwenna House. No wonder her mum had worked such long hours! The place had been magicked into a midsummer wonderland. Always impressive, the cavernous entrance hall was filled with hothouse blooms, potted palms and even two giant orange blossom trees with their branches threaded with fairy lights and twined with white ribbons. Music swelled from the ballroom, each tread of the sweeping staircase was flanked with flowers, and at its foot was a table dominated by a vast ice sculpture surrounded by ice buckets filled with bottles of champagne, and glasses which sparkled in the candlelight.

Relieving a passing footman of two glasses of champagne, Hugo offered one to Alice and chinked his against hers.

"To finding true love at the Midsummer Ball."

Alice raised hers. "I'll drink to just surviving it!"

"To Dutch courage then."

Alice took a gulp, spluttering when the sharp bubbles danced a tango across her tongue and hurtled through her bloodstream with alarming speed.

"Steady on! That stuff's stronger than Pol Brew," warned Hugo while she blinked and coughed. "Come on, let's circulate for a few minutes before I meet Elsie. See anyone you recognise?

Alice scanned the hall. It was thronged with men and women dressed in the most spectacular costumes, some which must have cost an absolute fortune. Napoleonic-era officers chatted to ringmasters while butterflies smiled up at vampires. All were masked and utterly glamorous. She couldn't identify anyone. Alice wondered where Henry Tremaine and his mother were, and what costumes they had chosen. Somehow she couldn't imagine either of them entering into the frivolous spirit of this party. Tall and with such a powerful presence, Henry would stand head and shoulders above everyone and wouldn't be hard to spot. She craned her neck, but there was no sign of him.

"See anyone *special*?" Hugo asked.

She was meant to be looking for Jonny, not for a tall man with powerful shoulders and sea-shimmer eyes. What was the matter with her? It must be nerves.

"Not yet," Alice replied, flushing guiltily.

"He won't be far. Let's have a gander in the ballroom."

Glad her mask hid her consternation, Alice allowed Hugo to lead her through the hall and into the drawing room, transformed for the evening into a ballroom. With the French windows thrown open to the terrace, it was lit by candles held in chandeliers glittering above, flickering flames reflected into infinity in the jewels strung around elegant throats and polished boots of highwaymen and hussars. A string quartet played from a dais at the far end, and maids clad in black-and-white uniform offered canapés and delicacies to the guests seated around the edge of the dance floor or gathering in flocks by the door.

Alice spotted Mrs St Milton instantly. She was dressed in a regency-style costume of emerald green silk which drifted around her in soft folds as she presided over the ballroom, surrounded by a group of friends. At her side her husband was a flamboyant ringmaster complete with whip and a scarlet-and-gold jacket which strained across his tummy when he laughed loudly at something one of their inner circle said. Alice scanned the rest of their party for Jonny, but there was no sign of him.

"Hugo! There you are! Welcome! And Elsie too, of course."

A twenties flapper girl stepped forward and air-kissed them. It was Millicent Jago, looking stunning as always, and only given away by the petulant droop to her mouth. Alice's heart raced. Would she be recognised? She stayed silent as she knew that the moment she spoke the game would be up, but luckily Milly had no interest in Elsie and turned the full beam of her attention onto Hugo, simpering up at him and making polite conversation about absolutely nothing.

"Where's Jonny?" Hugo asked when she eventually drew breath.

Milly shrugged. "He's about somewhere dressed as Al Capone. He's wearing a black hat and a stripy suit. You can't miss him."

"You haven't lost him already, surely?" Hugo teased.

"We're not joined at the hip like you two lovebirds," Milly said lightly, but Alice saw her jaw tighten a fraction. Was Jonny avoiding Milly? And if he was, did that mean he was changing his mind about where his heart might lie? In the past this would have been a heady thought, but tonight it made Alice feel strangely empty.

Maybe she needed some more champagne?

Hugo drew Alice against him, every bit the devoted fiancé, and smiled.

"I'm not letting Elsie out of my sight. Somebody might steal her away."

Although Milly laughed, her top lip curled and she regarded Alice balefully. Then, looking back at Hugo, she said, "I shouldn't worry too much on that score. Elsie won't want to let *you* go. We all know that."

The unmistakeable implication was that Elsie was a gold-digger. This sudden insight into the barbed comments and snobbery that Elsie must meet daily made Alice seethe on her friend's behalf. Only the knowledge that speaking out would give her away prevented her from making a sharp retort.

"Good-oh," said Hugo cheerfully. With a social ease born of generations he placed his hand beneath Alice's elbow and nodded at Milly. "If you do come across Jonny, please be so good as to tell him we're here. Now, if you don't mind, there are some people I'd like to introduce my fiancée to. Darling, I think I mentioned Lady Robartes, my godmother? Shall we?"

Milly, glaring, was left alone, while Hugo and Alice stepped onto the terrace, now the hinterland of a magical kingdom peopled by fairytale characters and filled with bowers and arbours. The gardeners had worked wonders, thought Alice. Fairy lights were strung in trees, flares lit to mark where the neat gardens plummeted away into the thin air of the cliff edge, and hundreds of white candles in jars illuminated the ornamental paths and marked where steep terraces dropped into one another like horticultural Matryoshka dolls. The strains of Bach drifted into the garden, mingling with cigarette smoke and the rise and fall of laughter. Guests strolled through the grounds and gathered around a buffet table groaning with laden platters, and Alice's eyes widened. It was all so glamorous.

Hugo, very used to such occasions, was complaining about Milly.

"What a nasty piece of work. She looks like an angel but

she's a scorpion underneath. Please rescue Jonny from her, Alice. She'll give him a life of hell."

Alice refrained from pointing out that Jonny, far from needing rescuing, had chosen Milly Jago of his own accord; Hugo was a romantic and it seemed cruel to disillusion him. Instead she took another sip of her drink and studied the garden, still seeking the fair head and upright carriage she needed in order to calm her racing heart. Henry was her ally. He was her friend, and even if he was oblivious to her plan and her presence, the sight of him would be enough to lend her courage.

Hugo was still grumbling about Milly. Alice tuned out while she scanned the guests. There was only one face she was intent on searching for in the throng, and it wasn't Jonny's. Henry possessed a presence that she would know, whether he was dressed as a Roman or as a pirate (although for the life of her Alice couldn't imagine him deigning to don such costumes) and she was starting to wonder whether he had decided to give the masked ball a miss when she spotted him at the farthest end of the terrace, part of a group clustered around the buffet table.

Her heart leapt. Although he had his back to her and was dressed in a leather flying helmet, silk scarf and long leather coat, Alice would have known him anywhere. She laughed to herself, suspecting that he had simply unearthed his father's old flying gear from a trunk and flung it on moments before leaving Seaspray – unlike the rest of the guests, who would have been planning their costumes for weeks. His lack of interest in Polwenna's most talked-about social gathering made her like him even more. She knew that were she beside Henry now he would roll his eyes at the extravagance and make a dry remark. He would far rather be out at sea or at the marina with his sleeves rolled up and working on a boat. If it had not been for his mother, who liked to be polite to their neighbours, Alice knew that Henry would not have gone to the ball.

She wondered where Mrs Tremaine was. The group clustered around the white damask-clothed table were younger in bearing and costume choice. Maybe she was seated and Henry was fetching her some food? That must be it, Alice decided, watching him select swirls of tissue-thin ham and glistening slices of smoked salmon with the same intensity he applied to his work or their conversations. He would be seeking the choicest cuts for his mother and ensuring she was looked after. He was always so considerate and gentlemanly, and Alice found herself wishing she was at the party with him rather than with Hugo, who was counting down the seconds until he would be reunited with Elsie.

Her eyes still drawn to Henry Tremaine as if by a magnet, Alice made the right noises in response to Hugo, but her thoughts started whirling, because Henry turned and handed the plate to a woman at his side. Hugo's chatter rolled off Alice like raindrops, for there was no mistaking the connection between those two. Her face was turned up to his like a flower seeking the sun and although she was too far away to hear their conversation Alice heard Henry's roar of genuine laughter. He seldom laughed as much. Who on earth had amused him so greatly?

Heart thudding, Alice studied the mysterious woman. She was struck by her elegance, which was emphasised by the simplicity of her costume, a diaphanous Grecian affair whose flimsy folds clung like a second skin to her willowy figure. Jet-black curls were piled up on her head and pinned with a coronet of vine leaves, and her ocean-green eyes were shown off to full advantage by a simple white mask. She was the epitome of class, and Alice's home-made costume – the pitiful attempt of a humble fisherman's daughter to ape her betters – suddenly felt theatrical and clumsy in contrast, and she burned with shame. This woman was obviously Henry's equal in every way. There was no way he would ever have looked at Alice with anything other than kindness. Everything she had quietly believed was no more than a schoolgirl fantasy. He was only being kind to her, and she'd been fooling herself to imagine he might think otherwise.

Who *was* this stranger? They seemed to know one another well, and as Alice watched, Henry placed his hand in the small of the woman's back and escorted her to a stone bench beneath one of the ornamental trees. They shared the food and talked as they ate, heads bent close together, and seemed closer than words. Was she a family friend? A new acquaintance? Or somebody he had once shared a romantic history with? *Maybe I'm not the only one attending the St Miltons' party to pursue a deeper agenda,* thought Alice. For some reason she couldn't articulate, this notion was too much to bear, and she yanked her attention back to Hugo, who was still listing Millicent Jago's faults. There were an alarmingly large number.

"… and she'll make his life an utter misery," he concluded. "You have to talk some sense into him so he stops his folks announcing the engagement. Otherwise it'll be too late."

Alice was jolted out of her misery. "What?"

"Milly and Jonny *can't* get married, can they? It's a huge mistake, and Jonny will be desperately unhappy with her. He loves *you,* Alice, I know he does. As soon as he sees you tonight he'll remember that."

Hugo's words seemed to come from far away, and as the truth seeped into Alice's understanding it felt as though the ground was dissolving beneath her feet. This masked ball, then, was in honour of Jonny and Milly's engagement? The expense, and need to invite the great and the good from miles around – that all made sense now. She waited for the stab of misery that should surely accompany this devastating news, but it was curiously absent. Across the lawn the mystery woman had her hand on Henry's arm and her face still raised to his, and Alice's stomach flipped with jealousy. Who was she?

"Alice? Are you all right?" Hugo said. "You *did* know? Didn't you?"

Alice turned to him. She needed to focus. She was here to win Jonny back.

"This is Jonny's engagement party?

Hugo gulped.

"Not exactly, but they're going to announce their engagement before the fireworks. I thought you knew."

"How could I possibly have known?"

Even as she spoke Alice realised why Hugo had assumed she would have known. If Jonny had told Hugo of the pending engagement, Hugo would have told Elsie and expected her to pass on the news to her best friend. But maybe Hugo didn't know his fiancée as well as he thought he did, because although Elsie might enjoy a gossip, she was kind-hearted and loved Alice. This was why she'd have kept the engagement to herself, no doubt fearing that for Alice it might be the last straw. Now her friend's devotion to their plan, willingness to involve her fiancé and the urgency with which she insisted Alice *must* attend, made perfect sense. Elsie had known all along this party would be Alice's one chance to win Jonny back before it was too late.

"Oh Christ," said Hugo, ashen. "I'm so sorry, Alice."

Alice was shocked. Jonny had asked Milly to marry him. She would be his wife. The promises he'd made to Alice, and the life they had planned together and dreamed of, clearly meant nothing to him. Maybe they never had. He'd thrown her love away like it was worthless.

She waited for the sense of plunging disappointment and the knife-twist of pain which always accompanied the thought of Jonny and Milly together –

– but to her great puzzlement it failed to materialise. Maybe she was in shock? The betrayal too much to bear?

"I know his heart isn't in it." Hugo was tripping over his words now in his haste to attempt damage limitation. "He's in too deep, and he's been a fool."

Alice nodded. "I won't disagree with that."

Together they walked down the steps and onto the lawn. Alice forced herself not to look back at Henry and the mysterious woman, still deep in conversation beneath the tree, and followed a path edged by lanterns which led away from the crowds. Once certain they were sufficiently far away from the entrance hall, Hugo settled Alice onto a cushioned seat and urged her to seek Jonny out. Then he slipped away.

Finally Alice was alone with her thoughts. She took a deep breath and waited for tears. She thought about Jonny and Milly planning to announce their engagement, but remained curiously dry-eyed. Maybe she'd cried herself out when it came to Jonny St Milton? Alice's eyes only filled when she recalled the beautiful woman talking to Henry and the way their heads were so close together that they almost touched. Something about the way Henry had taken care of that woman was too much to bear. Was this because Alice had become used to him cherishing and caring for *her*?

Alice wasn't sure how long she sat alone in the darkness. Across the garden the party continued, but it seemed a world away and she felt no desire at all to be a part of it. Lantern light flickered, and she heard snatches of laughter and music as the night breeze rose and fell, but the scene felt distant and Alice no more than an observer. She pressed her palms against the bench, surprised how real the rough stone was to the touch, for the whole night had now seemed to assume a dream-like quality.

She no longer possessed any desire to seek Jonny out and win him back. Those plans seemed to belong to another life, and the girl who'd laid them with such care was a stranger to the one who sat in the shadows. From the house came the faint strains of a waltz. Alice imagined Jonny and Milly twirling across the ballroom, smiling into one another's eyes, and knew that everything had changed forever, because the idea of Jonny with another girl no longer carried the old pain. It barely even registered.

She closed her eyes, perplexed by this sudden change of heart. The plan that she and Elsie had hatched with such excitement seemed childish now, ridiculous. If Jonny had loved her, truly loved her with his heart and soul, none of these machinations would have been necessary. If Jonny loved Alice he wouldn't have let her go for a single second. Henry had never abandoned his beloved Rose. Even when there was barely any hope, Henry had refused to forsake the woman he loved. So whatever Alice had been fighting for, it wasn't true love. It was a dream. A mirage. An infatuation. It was smoke and mirrors in contrast to Henry's love for his Rose.

Maybe she should slip away through the garden gate and take the cliff path home. It was time to admit the truth; their love affair had run its course. Madame Sienna had been wrong; no great love would be sealed with a kiss this midsummer.

"Ally! There you are. Hugo said you would be."

A lanky figure clad in a stripy suit, black fedora and jazz-era white shoes slipped through the dusk. Silhouetted against the failing light he was all charcoals and greys, and as he sat beside her his body seemed to fold in on itself, a study in angles and tension. The green eyes behind his black mask devoured her with a longing she had been dreaming of for weeks.

It was Jonny, of course – but he was too late. Alice understood now that it had been too late for them from the second he had walked away from her on Christmas Eve.

"You look beautiful, Ally," he said. "My God. So beautiful. Please tell me it isn't too late to put things right?"

Alice said nothing. 'Too late' had joined 'if only' in the lexicon of saddest words. This was the moment she had been waiting for and had worked so hard for. It was, Alice already knew, one of those pivotal moments she would look back on in the years to come, and know she had consciously picked a direction that would change the course of her life.

Jonny still loved her. He wanted to be with her. If she kissed him now, beneath the moon and on this magical midsummer night, Madame Sienna's prophecy would be fulfilled. But now the question was: did she want to be with Jonny? Or had her heart changed? Did it now yearn for the man who filled her thoughts and whose friendship had come to mean more to her than she had ever expected? The man who filled her with peace and who was kind and steadfast.

The man who now appeared to be falling head over heels in love with a Greek goddess.

Was she in love with Henry Tremaine?

CHAPTER 25

1954

This was the moment she had dreamed of and had lived for these past six months. Jonny was taking her in his arms and murmuring endearments into her hair before pressing kisses onto her cheeks and lips.

But Alice's heart didn't even flutter. As Jonny's lips trailed to the hollow of her throat, she felt detached and very uneasy. How could something so familiar feel so strange and so wrong?

Jonny was looking up at her as though she was much-needed oxygen after a deep, deep dive into icy water.

"I've missed you so much," he whispered, his hands cupping her face. "I love you, Ally. I've never stopped. Can you forgive me? I've messed everything up, and I can't begin to tell you how much I've hated myself for that. It's been awful being apart from you."

Alice said nothing. If their separation had been awful for

Jonny, it had been a thousand times worse for her. She recalled how he had abandoned her on Christmas Eve and left her alone and broken-hearted in the darkness, and of how she'd thought she would die of the pain in her heart when she'd seen him kiss Milly. And most of all she thought of the dark days which had followed Sam's loss, when Jonny's love might have helped her to keep her own head above the churning sea of despair. She remembered how even in the churchyard following Sam's memorial service, Jonny's pity had been all for himself.

He was young, she realised with a flare of understanding. Too young to empathise or to appreciate what she had needed. Jonny St Milton wasn't a bad person. He was just a boy. And Alice needed more. She needed the love of a man. A man who would love her through the best and the worst that life had to offer, and whose first waking thought was of her rather than himself.

Jonny didn't seem to notice that Alice hadn't responded. He was busy whispering into her ear about what a fool he'd been and how hard it had been to know he had lost her. He had, he said, been devastated.

You didn't lose me. You threw me away, thought Alice. Indignation and anger reared in her chest – emotions she had never imagined might be linked to this much longed-for moment of triumph – and it was now that tears filled her eyes. Once upon a time the slightest brush of his lips or fingertip touch would have caused her to melt like butter on a hot saffron bun, yet she felt nothing. It was as though her heart was filled with ice where before an all-consuming and white-hot fire had raged. This was Jonny, her beloved Jonny, and he was saying so many of the things she had dreamed of hearing – but it was too late. Something had changed between them.

Or perhaps it was more truthful to say that something had changed in *her*.

As Jonny continued to murmur endearments and trace the curve of her cheek with his forefinger, Alice waited for all the old feelings to surge back like the tide flooding into the harbour, but there was only a trickle of fondness clogged with the bittersweet flotsam of sadness. Although there was a part of her that would always love this boy for what he had once been to her, Alice could no more fool herself than she could lie to him. Something precious had been lost – and this was, Alice realised with a pang, her trust in him. Like the vase her mother had once dropped and which her father had so painstakingly glued back together, the love that Alice and Jonny had shared might look the same – but there would always be cracks in the porcelain which no amount of glazing could conceal. Their love would always be flawed by the past.

How could Alice ever trust Jonny again? When he said he loved her, how could she believe him? As he continued to tell her how hard it had been to watch her from afar and see Henry Tremaine by her side, Alice waited for him to acknowledge the pain he had caused her and to explain why he was kissing her now when he was planning to announce his engagement to Milly. She waited for him to voice guilt for betraying her, and say that he was going to call off their relationship. But those words never came, and now Alice knew they never would. Jonny was too young to know his own mind.

"I love you, Ally," he said, and his voice, still new to that deep timbre, squeaked with emotion as though a fiddler was drawing a bow across his vocal cords. "Can you still love me?"

Her heart sank, for Alice knew what she would need to say and what it would mean.

Jonny hadn't been there when she had needed him most,

and he had stepped away during the darkest time of her life. She could make excuses all day long for him if she really wanted to. She knew she could tell herself he had been under huge pressure from his parents, was afraid of a future without the safety net of money, that he was young …

She could go on and on and on, but in the end she was only fooling herself. Jonny was eighteen now. It was not so very long ago that many of the same age – her brother among their number – had set sail for France to fight for their country. They had been prepared to lay down their lives, and far too many had done so. All Jonny had ever needed to do was fight for the girl he loved and maybe sacrifice an inheritance. The harsh truth was, she realised, that he hadn't been brave enough because he hadn't loved her enough.

He was emotionally young, Alice concluded as she studied at him with the cool distance of removed love. Henry and those of his generation had had to become men before their time, whereas Jonny, too young to fight, had been cossetted by privilege, and protected. He had never been asked to sacrifice anything until she had asked him. So of course he had struggled.

Her anger seeped away like the sea into sand and was replaced by a deep tenderness. She would always treasure Jonny, but for the two of them love had come too soon. It had been rooted in shallow soil and couldn't flourish. Jonny needed to see more of the world and grow into the man he was destined to become, for only then would he be ready to love another with the passion and devotion which gave a man the strength to dig through rubble with his bare hands.

"You're my first love," she said softly, transported to those blissful moments at St Wenn's Well. "I'll always love you, Jonny."

His hands sought hers in the darkness, gripping them tightly as though he sensed her slipping from his grasp.

"But you do still love me?"

"Love has never been the issue," she said sadly. "I never stopped loving you."

"Nor I you!" he cried, anguished. "I know I've let you down, but I never once stopped loving you. I swear it on my life, Alice! You have to believe me. Please forgive me for being such an idiot. For being so weak!"

Alice believed he meant every word, but she felt a deep sadness, for he had uttered them far too late. During the months apart she'd grown to understand – and without fully realising it until this night – that Jonny's definition of love was a world away from hers. What she needed and what he could offer were not the same. Like repelling magnets, they simply couldn't meet one another now, no matter how hard they might long to. Maybe their timing was all wrong, or perhaps the stars hadn't aligned for them in this lifetime, because every fibre of Alice knew that Jonny St Milton was not the man who would hold her heart and keep it safe.

He was not the love of her life, the soulmate, that Madame Sienna had seen.

She pulled her hands from his tight grip.

"There's nothing to forgive."

"There is," he insisted. "I let you down, Ally. If you give me a second chance I swear I'll make it up to you. I'll show you I love you. Name what you want! I'll do it."

Alice took a deep breath.

"Will you call off your engagement to Milly? Tell your mother you want me?"

She knew his reply would make no difference to her feelings now. Jonny St Milton loved her, but he didn't love her enough.

He exhaled slowly. "Ally, it's complicated. That's all got out of hand. I don't love Milly. Oh Christ, Alice. You don't understand what it's like for me."

No, Alice thought, *I don't.* He had kicked aside the sacred promises their bodies had made to one another, had trampled all over the unquestioning love she'd so freely given, and he'd made vows to another woman. What had meant the world to Alice seemed inconsequential to Jonny, and she simply couldn't understand how he had put their love aside. Not ever. He and Milly had chosen a ring together. Champagne would have been opened, kisses and congratulations exchanged, and this extravagant midsummer party planned with the sole purpose of making the happy announcement to all their friends and neighbours. As these images cantered through her imagination Alice felt bone weary.

"I wish I'd heard the news from *you*, Jonny."

He gulped.

"I knew if I saw you I wouldn't be able to go through with it, and my parents are pleased with me for once. Pathetic as I am, I've liked having their approval. Oh Christ, it's such a mess. What can I do?"

"You can't marry Milly. Not if you don't love her with heart and soul. That isn't fair – and you have to call it off right now. Before it's announced."

He paled. "Ma will be even more against you if I ruin her precious party. Better I go through with it tonight then break it off with Milly later on, –maybe a few months down the road. Christmas would be good, when I'm home from Oxford. I can say the distance was too much. In the meantime we can out work a way of you coming to visit. Nobody needs to know the truth. That way we can keep things secret a little longer …"

Alice stared at him. More lies. More deception. More

refusals to acknowledge her. Jonny really didn't understand why this wasn't enough.

She asked,

"More hiding me away? More lies? Acting as though you're ashamed of me? You truly think that's the answer?"

"It's the only way we can be together. No one will suspect anything while I'm engaged. I'll break things off at the right time, I swear. Milly will be fine. She's a pragmatic kind of girl."

Alice was appalled. Had he *always* been this immature? This selfish? As Jonny reached for her again she held up her hands to hold him at bay.

"If you're prepared to announce your engagement to another girl, you can't love *me*," she said – and as though the words spoken aloud had broken a spell, a door in Alice's mind opened wide and she stepped through it into the light. She was free, because now she knew for sure that Jonny didn't love her. He thought he did, and perhaps in his way he even believed it, but he didn't love her properly. Not in the way Alice understood it meant to love and be loved. Not the way Henry had loved his Rose.

"Of course I do!"

"You don't," she said gently. "And I don't love you. Not the way I ought to. Not the way I once did."

Alice was at peace with this knowledge. It no longer had the power to shred her heart. Jonny was just a boy, a sweet and adorable spoilt boy; but what she wanted was the steadfast and abiding love of a man. A man who would stand at her side through the darkest of times, who didn't bend with the wind, and who saw the best and worst of her and still remained true. A man who was her friend, her confidant and her lover.

A man just like Henry.

Jonny was shocked. "You don't mean that, Ally. You *love* me."

"I did, Jonny. I loved you and longed for you ever since that first time you caught my eye across the terrace. I dreamed of you and I ached for you and I thought I'd die when you told me it was over. I did love you – but then things changed. You had eyes only for Milly and I …"

He groaned. "You met the Captain."

She closed her eyes for a moment.

"Yes."

"And you're in love with *him*?"

"He became my friend. There's no more to it than that, but it's changed things. He's changed how I see the world and how I see this situation. It wasn't right that you and I were together – but you can't go ahead and marry Milly, either. That's not fair."

His mouth twisted.

"Fine. So are you really saying that even if I walked into the house right now and finished things with Milly and told my parents that I love you, you *still* wouldn't want to be with me? You'd want to be with him? Because I *will* do it, Ally. If that's what you want me to do. If that's what it takes for you to choose me."

The air grew heavy. The wind held its breath. Far across the lawn the lights of the house, huddled together against the darkness, leaned forward to catch her answer. Even the lanterns seemed to sway a little closer.

Choose, whispered Fortune. *Choose.*

"You could love me again, I know you could," said Jonny. "The Captain isn't right for you. He's older – and he's so cold. You belong with me, Ally. We both know it …"

"Fine," he continued. "To hell with it all. Let's tell my parents."

Alice felt a slow collapse against her sternum. Jonny could be hers. She had the thing she had longed for and prayed for at her fingertips – but now it was within her grasp she knew it was false coin, for it had been offered unwillingly and would have sprung from a place of unhappiness. It was tainted. Jonny had been her first love, but now, as a strange underwater sensation washed over Alice, she felt decades older than him because she knew there was no true choice.

Recalling how she had felt seeing Henry's leonine head dipping so close to the unknown woman's dark curls, misery coiled in Alice's heart. It was the thought of Henry with another woman which caused her to flinch now, and the thought of losing their friendship was utterly unbearable. It was Henry she loved, and it was a true love built on respect and friendship and kindness rather than infatuation and fleeting passions. Why had it taken her until tonight to see it?

Jonny, the scar which had never truly felt a wound, had never really been able to empathise with Alice, or indeed anyone who suffered. He would marry Millicent, inherit his fortune and live the gilded life that had been planned out for him from the cradle. Maybe he'd never had any choice. Maybe he and Alice were both following a destiny decided for them at the start of time and which had been written in the stars above. Or perhaps her love for him was a small part of a far bigger picture? *Who knows?* thought Alice ... well, not her, that was for sure.

She leaned over and kissed Jonny goodbye. It was a tender kiss, filled with all the love and compassion she still felt for this sweet yet troubled young man. There was no anger left or resentment, only a deep hope that one day he too would understand that love wasn't about grand gestures, defying parents or stolen moonlight kisses. It was about honesty, keeping one's word and listening. It was about kindness and trust and strength of character.

"I don't want to be with you, Jonny. It's too late for us."

"But you just asked me to end things with Milly and tell my parents! Why ask that of me if you think we're over?"

Jonny was genuinely confused and, Alice realised, starting to get angry. His ears always went red when he was cross.

"You must end things with Milly if you don't love her. That's only fair," she said. "I wish things could have been different between us, Jonny. I wish we could rewind time to when we first met and live it all again, making different choices and rewriting the past. That way we might have married and had children and grown old together. But I think our moment has passed. We're not meant to be. That isn't lack of love. It's just how things are."

"The Captain isn't for you," he said flatly.

"Maybe not," said Alice, "but it's not about him, Jonny. It's about us, and we're not meant to be. I know that now."

His chin had a stubborn tilt. "You're wrong. Our time will come, Ally. Even if it's when I'm old and grey, I'll still love you and I'll win you over, I swear it on this land and on this tide and by these stars. You'll be my wife one day, Alice Pendeen. You'll see."

She didn't argue, knowing he was too upset – and the hiss of the waves breaking on the rocks below sounded a little like agreement. Nature was making a pact, Alice thought with a shiver of precognition. The fishermen and the old Cornish folk in Polwenna still talked of ancient magic, and out in the garden, beneath the old cypress trees and near the watchful sea, she could almost believe in it herself. The hairs stirred on her arms and suddenly she longed to return to the lights and chatter of the party.

She turned from him and adjusted her mask.

"Be happy, Jonny, and be good to Milly. Whatever you decide to do."

"He's not for you, the Captain," Jonny said desperately. "No matter what you think."

Alice thought of Madame Sienna with all her talk of love and soulmates and midsummer kisses. The hairs on the nape of her neck rippled.

"Maybe not," she said slowly. "But I need to find that out for myself."

Alice walked away from him then and for the final time. Ending their love story was the right choice, and part of her heart would always belong to Jonny St Milton. He would always be her first love – but could Henry Tremaine be her last?

This was, Alice realised with a ripple of excitement, a very different proposition.

CHAPTER 26

THE PRESENT

When Alice looked up she was surprised to discover that she was surrounded by an audience. As well as Holly, there were Perry Tregarrick, Big and Little Roger Pollard, Harry Charles, Reverends Neil and Jules, and Jen Wheeler, who had gathered in the aisle and were listening avidly.

"Don't stop now!" begged Jules.

"This is brilliant. You *did* it, Alice. You won him back and then decided you didn't want him any more," cried Holly.

"Respect!" nodded Little Rog. "She showed him, didn't she, Pa?"

"That's right, my boy, that's right!" said his father. "And when the poor sod was gagging for you! Pardon the expression, Alice!"

"Girl power, as we said in the nineties," said Jen approvingly. She liked anything that suggested crushing the oppressive patriarchy, as her downtrodden husband could attest. "You were the Geri of your day! A total triumph!"

Alice smiled. She supposed Jonny had been, as Big Rog so eloquently put it, *gagging*, but at the time she hadn't felt at all triumphant, just sad and weary. It was a lifetime ago, but she could still feel the bone-deep exhaustion which had come after she had shed that heavy load, followed by the wild fluttering of her heart as she had scanned the exotically dressed guests for a glimpse of a sheepskin-collared flying jacket. Even now, the memory of the lurch of dread that had followed each false sighting made her feel seasick.

"Maybe I should have worn a union jack dress," she said to Jen.

"I love the sound of your outfit. You're so good with costumes, Alice," said Jules warmly.

"Elsie helped," Alice said.

"And Lady Yelland. She sounds fun," added Neil.

"Oh, she was a character," nodded Alice. Ironic how after not thinking of her old employer for decades she could recall her now with startling clarity – and with annoyance, too, when some days she lost her purse five times in a row ... The throaty smoker's laugh, bird-bright eyes and face a river delta of age, were as vivid as if she had only seen the elderly lady yesterday. Funny too that now Alice was at least a decade older than Lady Yelland had been at the time. She'd seemed ancient to Alice and Elsie, and they too couldn't have imagined ever being so old. Old age was never happening to them ...

Alice sighed. Elsie had been right, in fact, for she had never made it to old age, which was a huge tragedy. Age was a gift, albeit one with dodgy wrapping, and Alice felt blessed by it. She felt exactly the same inside as ever, although she supposed everybody always did. Like her, they too must feel sad that so many they'd journeyed alongside were long gone. Only one member of her story was still at her side – and who knew for how much longer? She closed her eyes, gripped suddenly by the anticipation of loss to come, that heaviest of taxes on life's joys.

"Alice? Are you all right? Shall I call Dan to help you home?"

Jules was regarding her with concern, and Alice realised she had wandered back into the summerlands of memory. This was another side-effect of old age that nobody warned you about, the sudden drift into the past followed by the shock of returning to the present.

"Sorry, my love, I was miles away," she said with a small shake of her head. The curls were permed now, and thin and white rather than a glossy nut-brown. Oh, how Alice missed the girl she had been! What wouldn't she give to be back on that terrace with the best yet to come?

"Back at the party?" teased Holly. "Waiting to see what Jonny did next?"

"Were you a bit like CeeLo Green in that song?" added Little Rog, starting to hum and sway. His tinsel halo looked set to knock an eye out, and Alice leaned back in alarm.

"What song?" asked his father, pulling off his cap and scratching his head.

"You know, Pa! The one where the singer sees his ex with somebody else and thinks 'eff you'!"

"I'm not sure *that's* a word the Angel Gabriel would say," sniffed Jen. "And in a church. Soap and water for your son's mouth, Roger."

"I don't say the real word! I said eff," said Little Rog, affronted. "Eff! Not f—"

"That's *not* all right, my boy," his father cried, clapping a paw over his son's mouth. "Sorry, Alice!"

That was another thing about getting old, though Alice with mild amusement. Folk thought you were easily offended or hadn't heard Anglo-Saxon before. Whenever she had helped Sam land his catch Alice had heard every word under the sun and even been known to utter a few herself.

"I think my granfer was at that party as a waiter," said Harry Charles proudly. "He was a church warden, just like me. God-fearing Tommy, they called him."

Alice vaguely recalled spotting Tommy Charles necking champagne. Well known for being naughty, he'd been so rolling drunk that evening so long ago that her mum had been forced to hide him in the scullery – but Tommy had wandered out again and gone on to eat his own bodyweight in smoked salmon. He had been thrown out on his ear and banned from working at Polwenna House. Alice decided not to dob him in to his grandson a lifetime on, and undo all Tommy's hard work on reinventing his reputation!

"Most of the villagers were there to help out, if they hadn't been invited as guests. I recall Reverend Sharpe was as guest. Although he looked down his nose at such blatant excess he came along for the free food!" she laughed, remembering how she'd seen him heaping his plate with tasty morsels from the buffet as she'd been searching for Henry.

"Och, I've met the likes of him," shuddered Reverend Neil.

"Never mind all that. I need to know how you finally won Jonny back," said Holly. She turned to Alice and her face was so filled with yearning that Alice's heart ached. "I really need a happy ending, and I know there has to be one, otherwise you wouldn't have told me this story. You thought you loved the Captain, but you got it wrong, didn't you? Jonny broke off the engagement and you lived happily ever after."

Alice feared she might have made a mistake in telling this story. Holly wanted to hear that all would be well and that love conquered all. That was true to some extent, but the road that led to happiness was not always a straightforward one and Alice's was no more filled with dead ends, U-turns and road blocks than anyone else's. Oh dear. She had done her new young friend a disservice if she'd led her to think otherwise.

"Not quite," she said nervously.

"Don't keep us in suspense!" begged Neil. "I think I know what happened next, but this is like a box set and I need tae binge!"

Alice swept her eyes over her friends and neighbours. Most of them knew her story, and she wanted to share this final part with Holly alone. It was the key to everything – and, Alice hoped, to setting Holly free. She glanced at Jules, who she knew would understand.

"Okay, team!" announced the vicar. "We have about half an hour before I'm officially kicking you all out of St Wenn's and into the pub for mulled wine. You've all done quite enough, and anything that isn't done now can be left until later. Alice, you're invited, too, and anyone else."

Alice made a show of looking at her watch, declaring that she needed to be home to finish wrapping her gifts rather than starting a mulled-wine marathon in The Ship. Excuses made and the rest of her audience shooed away, she asked Holly to accompany her home:

"I feel a little wobbly, and it'd be lovely to have your company. I can finish the story on the way down."

Holly said she was more than happy, and once she had helped Alice to her feet (stiffening up was such a bore) the two linked arms and crossed the time-worn flagstones. As Alice exchanged the warmth of the church for the cold evening air and began the gentle walk downhill, she suspected she wouldn't return for Midnight Mass. She tired so easily these days, and the thought of an early night before the family Christmas bunfight was very appealing.

It was properly dark now, the world sagging beneath the sudden heaviness of midwinter nightfall, but the drizzle had stopped and a brisk wind was blowing away the clouds from a moon which was doing backstroke in the sky. Without the cover of cloud there was ice in the air, and Alice burned with cold, burrowing deeper into her coat. The party at Polwenna House and balmy weather of that beautiful summer night belonged to another world.

"It was Christmas Eve when your story started," remarked Holly as they passed through the lych-gate and stepped onto Church Lane. "It's funny, Alice, but I feel as though I know everyone now. It's as if they're my friends and I can picture how it used to be here. I don't suppose much changes in Polwenna Bay."

Below, the myriad lighted windows framed Christmas lights and trees, flinging jewels into the dark water of the harbour. Alice picked out Cobbles, small windows all lit up for Christmas, and glanced across at Seaspray, which was pouring warm light into the wintry darkness as well. It made her think of how Henry had thrown light into her darkness on that long past Christmas Eve. Where had the years gone? Holly was right; Polwenna Bay never changed much, and Sam and Barry and her dear parents would still recognise it if they appeared now. But as Alice was no longer the wild young woman who had dreamed of couture and slipped out to get dressed in the net store and meet her secret lover, they probably wouldn't recognise *her*.

"They do say you arrive in Polwenna Bay a stranger and leave as a friend," said Alice thoughtfully. "I think the place finds people. It draws them in and it heals them. People the world over hold Polwenna close to their hearts."

Holly glanced at her. "Will it heal me?"

"I think that's up to you. There's always a choice, Holly. You can let life happen to you, or you can make a decision to grasp it with both hands, give it a shake and move on."

"Is that your way of telling me I need to get over Jamie?"

"I'd never presume to tell anyone what to do. It's more a case of life being what *you* choose to focus on. I'd focused so much on Jonny and what I thought I wanted that I'd failed to see the bigger picture. I'd turned myself inside out to try and win him back when he didn't really deserve the effort. Or," she added almost to herself, "perhaps it was just a matter of timing. Maybe that's all life is. We meet the right people at the wrong time, or we choose wrongly and think that's it … the point is, my love, we can always choose again."

"But you *did* choose Jonny, didn't you?" Holly was confused. "You got your man! There's hope for me."

They were only a little further down the lane, but already Alice was tired. She leaned against a low wall and stared out to sea. Somewhere in that restless water was her brother, taken too young and his longing for adventure unquenched. Unlike him, this young woman had the precious gift of a future held in her hands. She had no understanding that it was as fragile as a Ming vase. One slip, one false step, and it could shatter.

Alice couldn't let that happen. If her story could help then she would have made sense of it all. The tears she'd wept on that cold Christmas Eve would not have been in vain.

"Let me tell you what happened next, Holly," she said. "Let me show you how there's always hope – even if it's just not always where you expect to find it."

CHAPTER 27

1954

There was no sign of Henry in the garden. Disappointed, Alice hurried along the terrace and into the house, weaving through the guests and frantic to catch sight of him. She couldn't believe how stupid she had been, so set on pursuing what she'd believed was what she wanted rather than seeing the treasure that had been there all along. Was it too late to tell Henry how she felt about him? She would be devastated if this was the case, but she would understand too, for she had never once indicated she felt more for him than friendship. Why would he not take her at her word and, no matter what he might have felt for her, look elsewhere?

In her haste Alice tripped on her skirt and would have fallen if hands hadn't steadied her. How she wished Elsie had plumped for more practical costumes! What Alice wouldn't give to be Robin Hood or a highwayman, and able to move freely through the throng. The hoops stitched into the skirt made movement awkward and the plumed hat was so striking it was impossible to pass through the ballroom without being noticed. When a masked Egyptian took her hand and pulled her into a dance Alice had no choice but to allow herself to be twirled across the shiny floor.

"You are absolutely *divine*," said the Egyptian, wafting brandy-laced breath down into her face while one sweaty palm was clamped in the small of her back. "Might find myself a Cornish girl if they're all as pretty as you!"

Alice shot him a bland smile and tried not to recoil. Hoping Hugo and Elsie weren't somewhere in the throng of dancers, she allowed herself to follow this man in the waltz, but all the time they danced she was scanning the room for Henry. There was no sign of him or his beautiful companion, and her heart sank. Had they slipped away somewhere more private?

A cold wash of misery broke over Alice and she told herself sternly it was far more likely that Henry had grown tired of making polite chit-chat to the other guests – never his forte – and had ventured elsewhere. Maybe he was in the old stables, admiring one of Mr St Milton's cars, running his hand over the gleaming chassis of the latest acquisition and talking with his host about the Polvethen hill-climb. That would be far more to Henry's taste than the ballroom, for he belonged to the elements and the outdoors. He loved to walk and sail and ride, and he found, he'd said, small talk and social politics stupefying.

The music changed and now the band was playing swing. The atmosphere shifted, becoming both bittersweet and cheerful as guests recalled the dances and lost faces of the war years. Henry once said Glen Miller was guaranteed to get toes tapping even when hearts were well and truly lodged in boots.

Imagining what Henry had endured during the war, and knowing that he too could have been killed, the violence of her longing for him shook Alice so greatly she excused herself and fled from her Egyptian admirer.

Spotting Jonny in the throng, with Milly and watched by his beaming parents, she allowed herself to feel a brief pang for the beautiful dream she'd shared with him. She would never love like that again, thought Alice, so completely and so intensely. That had been a young girl's love. She would love as a woman one day. and that love would be open-eyed and honest. It would be based on far more than stolen kisses and the racing of her heart. It would be a union built on friendship and equality and understanding – as well as on passion and the undeniable pull of attraction.

It was *that* love she felt for Henry Tremaine. Her feelings for him had ambushed her, creeping up on her and sweeping her away when she least expected it. Henry *saw* her and he knew her. He had been at her side through the darkest times and had never asked anything from her but friendship. Yet beneath the manners and the reserve, Alice had always sensed there was more. And now it was too late. She'd failed to recognise true treasure, but other women would not be as foolish …

"Would you like to dance, Alice?"

She looked up and as though she had manifested him through thought alone, a dashing airman stood beside her with his gloved hand outstretched.

"How do you know it's me?" she asked.

"I'd know you anywhere, Alice Pendeen. Disguised or not. I knew you the moment I first saw you, remember?"

His blue eyes, meeting hers, were now as dark as his mask and equally mysterious. Alice looked away. Her mouth had dried because she'd known him too, even if she hadn't understood who he was and what he would come to mean to her.

Why else would she have allowed a stranger to drive her home and carry her to the front door? Let him see her grief and the workings of her heart?

"You look utterly ravishing, by the way," Henry added.

"Thank you," said Alice. Blushing under her mask, she placed her hand in his. "You look very dashing, Biggles."

He laughed. "My brothers and I loved those books as boys, and I knew we had Pa's old flying gear stashed away somewhere. Ma dug it out last night. I wasn't going to bother with a costume but Elizabeth said I'd be letting Connie down if I didn't do *something*. Ma wasn't having that!"

Connie must be the beautiful goddess. She was clearly somebody he knew well, for he had said her name with such ease and warmth. Alice felt devastated. Who was she? An old family friend? An old flame? A new one? Alice had to know. She was dredging up the courage to ask when the music changed again and Henry tugged her into the dancing.

"In the Mood!" he cried. "Come on, Alice!"

"I don't know how to swing," she protested.

"I do. Just follow me," Henry said. "Don't think, Alice. Just dance."

So Alice did as he asked and let the beat of the music sweep her away and with it all thoughts of Greek goddesses and broken hearts. To her surprise, she soon discovered that it didn't really matter at all if she knew the steps or not, for all she had to do was follow his lead and the rest seemed to flow. She soon lost herself in the feeling of his hands circling her waist as he lifted her up and swung her through the air. As Henry spun her around her skirts billowed and Alice laughed for pure joy, feeling as though she was flying. She watched the ballroom revolve around her and the masked faces spin and blur until all she could see was the blue of his eyes and the white of his smile. Dancing with Henry was magical and wonderful, and she never wanted to stop. While she danced she couldn't think about anything else but this moment. Grief and sadness and broken hearts were forgotten, for nothing else existed.

Song after song flew by, until eventually when one finished Henry said, "I'll fetch us some drinks and we can step outside for some fresh air and catch our breath. It's very hot in here."

The doors of the ballroom opened onto the terrace, overlooking the gardens and the black sea beyond. Henry fetched two glasses of champagne and once they were safely through the crowds and alone at the farthest end, he passed one to Alice.

"Steady," he warned as she took a large gulp of the deliciously cold drink. "That'll go straight to your head after the heat in the ballroom. Take a few breaths."

Alice rested the glass on the lichen-furred balustrade and breathed in cool air laden with the scent of mown grass and the coconut sweetness of the clifftop gorse. The lanterns cast a flickering light across the worn paving stones, and the fairy lights strung in the trees swayed gently – but it wasn't the champagne or the whirling around on the dance floor that made her feel giddy. It was being alone with Henry.

"Midnight Fireworks in ten minutes!" she heard somebody on the lawn cry, and there was a cheer followed by the popping of a champagne cork and laughter.

Alice looked out at the moon-glazed sea and star-speckled sky, and was suddenly filled with a deep melancholy. It was not because Jonny would be soon officially engaged, but because this magical night was very nearly over. She was so happy to have danced with Henry and to be here with him but coming close to this happiness meant sadness too once the evening had ended. Alice could hardly bear it. This night would never come again. There would never be another like it, and she knew that when she was old and grey she would close her eyes and recall it, would hear the band playing, smell the jasmine which scrambled up the granite walls and remember how it had felt to be held by Henry Tremaine. This magical night and the enchanted moments on the dance floor were already as much a part of her past as her precious friendship with Henry was, if he was in love with the mysterious Connie.

It was no use. Alice had to know the state of play. She pulled off her mask.

"Who's Connie?"

Henry had been sipping champagne and for a moment couldn't reply. His brows were raised and the eyes behind the mask amused.

"Is she the lady I saw you with? Dressed as a Greek goddess?" Alice continued. She was committed now and she pressed on, her face burning because he couldn't fail to know why she was asking. While the question hung between them she picked up her glass and pretended to be fascinated by the beads of condensation which slipped down the stem like tears.

"When did you see us?" he asked.

"Earlier on. You were sitting together in the garden."

"And you didn't come and say hello? I'm disappointed, Alice. I thought we were friends."

"We are, but I didn't know what to think and I didn't want to …"

He regarded her thoughtfully. "What?"

She shrugged. "Interrupt."

"Ah. You thought there was something between us? Were you jealous?"

Alice's flush deepened. "Of course not."

"Are you sure?"

She raised her chin.

"Of course I'm sure."

"That's a shame," said Henry. "For a moment I thought you might care. You see, Alice, in my experience people only get jealous when they have feelings."

He was right, of course. She had been horribly jealous, and it must be obvious. Then her eyes widened. Why would he want her to care or have feelings for him? Was this some game? How dare he question her feelings? What about his for this Connie?

"Do you love her?" she asked and her voice sounded all tight and strange.

Henry peeled off his mask. "Yes. Yes, I do."

Alice felt as though the fairy lights, the stars and the moon had all been extinguished.

"She's beautiful and I hope you'll be very happy," she said flatly.

Summoning all the dignity she could muster, Alice tried to turn on her heel but Henry caught her elbow and spun her around to face him.

"Oh Alice, you goose! It's not like that. Connie's my sister-in-law. She and my nieces are all we have left of Eddie. Of course I love her. I love them all dearly."

Her eyes widened. Henry had once mentioned his nieces, who lived in London, and she knew that their mother had recently remarried. Mired in her own problems, Alice realised she hadn't listened closely enough to recall the name of Eddie Tremaine's widow.

"She's here to say goodbye. Con's leaving for America with her new husband, so she and the girls are having a last Cornish holiday before they sail." Henry looked wistful. "I'm glad for Con, of course. Her new husband's a good man, but it feels like losing Ed all over again. My mother's devastated – not that she'd ever say a word."

"Oh," said Alice weakly. It was as though the world had

tilted. Now that she saw everything from a different perspective it all looked totally different. She had seen a farewell, one seasoned with love, reminisces and sadness, not a moonlight tryst. "I thought …"

"I know what you thought," said Henry gently, "and for a moment I thought you might feel the way I always do when you speak about Jonny."

"How is that?" she hardly dared ask.

"As though the world is suddenly darker and colder. As if it's ending."

This was *exactly* how Alice had felt moments earlier! She was utterly astonished to think Henry had been jealous of Jonny.

"Do you still love him?" Henry asked. He was still holding her arm tightly as though she was all that tethered him to the earth.

The intensity in his question made Alice's heart race.

"No," she said.

"But you *did* love him." It wasn't a question.

"I *thought* I did, but now I wonder if it was real. The feelings I had then are a shadow compared to how I feel now."

She heard his sharp intake of breath.

"Now?"

"Right now," Alice whispered. "With you."

A muscle clenched in his jaw. It was the closest Henry ever came to showing his emotions, and she recognised he was fighting to keep them in check.

"Alice, do I stand a chance? I've waited, *hoped,* that your feelings might change towards me. I'm not sure I can live in limbo much more."

Alice couldn't speak. The stars were spinning.

"I'm in love with you Alice," Henry said. "I feel as though I've known you all my life, and I want to spend the rest of it with you. If you don't feel the same way, or if the idea of loving an old man like me disgusts you, just tell me and I promise I'll never trouble you again."

She shook her head. "You're not an old man and you could never disgust me."

"So could you love me?"

His whispered breath was soft against her cheek. Henry smelt of sandalwood and engine oil, the familiar scents that always conjured the sensation of being held and comforted.

Dear Henry. Her friend. Her ally. The soulmate Madame Sienna had foreseen. The man who melted the marrow in her bones.

"I do love you, Henry," she said. "It crept up on me unawares, but I love you and so very much that I wonder there was ever a time when I didn't."

A wide smile lit his face, wiping years and care from the austere countenance and filling his eyes with jades and sapphires. His joy was a sunblaze, and Alice smiled back, filled with wonder. How was it that she had been granted so much? How was it that she was so lucky?

"And I love you, Alice Pendeen. I have since the first time I saw you. It felt as though I'd known you before. Another life, maybe. I've always known you."

Alice closed her eyes in wonder as Henry's kiss banished all the months of sadness. What she had felt for Jonny dissolved like sea fret in sunlight, like a half-remembered dream and just as insubstantial, for this was a man's kiss and one filled with strength and passion. It was utterly compelling. Henry's mouth on hers was both a question and an answer, one Alice knew she had been asking too, and searching to solve for her whole life. His kiss held the promise of the future they would share and of a love that would sustain them for a lifetime.

They parted, staring at one another with delight while the music played and chatter floated in the breeze like a language from another world. They didn't speak. There was no need for words. Beneath the stars and to the murmur of distant waves, Henry Tremaine held Alice Pendeen against his heart, where she would stay for the rest of his life. High above them fireworks sprayed the darkness and jewelled the sea while applause and cheers rang out.

As Alice kissed Henry again the church clock struck twelve. Midsummer slipped into autumn's waiting arms – and far away, her wagon pitched beneath the star-splashed sky, a wise fortune teller gazed into the dancing flames of a camp fire and smiled.

CHAPTER 28

THE PRESENT

"You kissed *Henry* at midsummer?"

The question wrenched Alice from the sultry heat of that long-ago summer evening back to the mid-December darkness. She blinked, momentarily disorientated, as Henry, fireworks and the party faded, and she felt rather shocked to no longer be clasped in her lover's arms but leaning heavily on a young woman.

"I certainly did," Alice sighed, feeling rather warm from the glow of that unforgettable moment. What a kiss it had been! What a *night* it had been! She'd leave that part of the story out, though. Some things should remain private …

"*Henry* was the midsummer kiss? Not Jonny?"

Alice laughed. "He was indeed. I was almost as surprised as you."

"I bet. So, what happened next? Was Jonny angry? Gutted? Did he come after you and beg?"

"Nothing like that," said Alice.

The truth was that Jonny had been far too busy celebrating his engagement to notice Alice and Henry slipping away from the party, wrapped in one another's arms. She'd heard the cries of excitement, the cheers and the popping of corks as she walked with Henry towards Seaspray – and for Jonny, who had settled for less than true love, she felt only a twist of sadness. Alice knew he would regret this choice one day, but he was weaker than her and had chosen what appeared to him to be the best path. But what Alice needed was strength in her life. She needed a man who would never let her down.

"I know!" cried Holly. You made him so jealous that he eventually stood up to his mother. Then he won you back and you lived happily ever after?"

This was the stuff of Hallmark movies. But real life was, Alice now understood, far less formulaic and a lot more painful. People messed up. They hurt one another. They made mistakes that they regretted terribly and which took a lifetime to rectify. Some lived a lifetime mourning the road untravelled, and yearning for the life they should have led.

"Jonny married Milly and made his parents happy, my love. He inherited his money and made a big success of the business too. His life fell into place just as the St Miltons had expected."

Holly stared at Alice, puzzled as pieces of the jigsaw puzzle fell into place to reveal a picture she hadn't anticipated.

"I'm confused. You loved Jonny so much and he loved you."

"Sometimes that isn't enough," Alice said gently. "Sometimes these things are a matter of timing as much as they are of love."

"But Alice! Your whole reason for going to that party was to win Jonny back. He was meant to be the midsummer kiss the gypsy predicted. Why *Henry* all of a sudden?"

Why indeed, thought Alice? There wasn't time now, or

even the words, to describe how completely her love for Henry had taken her unawares. Nor could she attempt to explain how loving one man hadn't negated her feelings for the other. When you were young life was so black and white. Age, and Henry's wisdom, had taught Alice that nothing was clear-cut. Not just being able to discern who was good and who was bad, and certainly not what love meant; everything was a thousand swirling shades of grey. It was only now that Alice finally understood that love was as equally about seasons of life as it was passion. She and Jonny weren't meant to be when she was seventeen because it hadn't been their time. The stars hadn't written that destiny for them because there another course had been set.

"Oh, I loved him. I thought I'd have died for that love," she said quietly. "I loved him with the intensity of first love which is magical and all-consuming, but without realising it I'd come to understand that love alone isn't enough. There needs to be more."

"But what's more important than love?"

"Passion fades, my love, but friendship and trust last forever. A strong marriage is built on those just as much as it is upon love. Never underestimate the importance of kindness and loyalty. Henry had proven himself to be a friend, and he had been there for me through some of the hardest times of my life. I knew he'd never let me down."

"So did you marry Henry?"

"I did," Alice said. "We were married for over fifty years."

She looked out across the village. High on the clifftop, a steep climb that was too much for her nowadays, the lights of Seaspray soothed the darkness. It had been her home for a lifetime, a home she had shared with the man she loved and with whom she had built a family. That life was also in the past, for Henry was long gone. Their eldest grandson lived there now, but like the man who had carried her over the threshold as a young bride, and who had offered his heart with such openness, the house would always be a part of her. Alice would always love Seaspray just as she would always love Henry Tremaine. Neither the house nor the man featured in her daily life now as they once had, but they were no less important and no less cherished.

Alice knew this wasn't the neat ending her new young friend had been expecting or hoping for. Holly had wanted the happy ever after so she could apply it to her own situation and live in hope. There had been a happy ending, of course – but it hadn't unfolded in the manner this young woman had clearly expected. Holly had wanted the fairy tale. She had needed Jonny and Alice to fall into one another's arms at the party, past grievances all forgotten and forgiven, and their future glittering and filled with wonder. It was a Hollywood climax – but this wasn't *quite* the way life worked …

Holly looked crestfallen. "I thought you two would have got together and lived happily ever after. I thought that was why you were telling me this story, Alice. I thought you were saying that there was hope for me."

"But there *is* hope for you! That's *exactly* what I want you to take away from this story, my dear. When life seems darkest, that's often when the most amazing things are about to take place. Hope is always there. It's just that we need to see beyond what we *think* we want and what we *believe* is best in order to receive so much more than we could ever imagine. And now you know that there was a Christmas Eve when I'd thought my life was over and my heart broken for ever – but that old cliché about the night being darkest before the dawn is true."

"And Henry Tremaine was the light in your darkness?"

"Oh, yes," sighed Alice wistfully, longing for that young girl and the handsome young man to step out of the shadows so that Holly could see how happy they were. Henry had carried her along this very cobbled street on Christmas Eve, holding her close to his heart and bringing her safely home in every way.

"Loving Henry took me totally by surprise, but he was perfect for me in every way, even if it took me a while to understand that. I'd been staring at Jonny for far too long, you see, and he'd dazzled me like sunshine dancing on the sea. Jonny could do that to a girl, Holly. He shimmered and glittered and he was beautiful – and he was always changing. Henry was the bedrock beneath the village – and beneath the water. Unremarkable at first until you understand it's the foundation for everything."

Holly fell silent and, both deep in thought, they continued on their way to Alice's house. Although it was a cold night the streets were as busy as they had been at the height of the summer season, and the shop windows blazed with fairy lights. The pub was filled to bursting, and every now and then the door opened to admit more revellers, sending the sound of singing and chatter into the night. These were shanties her father and brother would have known well, and Alice felt sure that somewhere Sam and her dad would be leaning on a bar, tankards and voices raised as they celebrated the arrival of Christmas. Polwenna was a timeless place, and even with the embroidery of the years, so little had changed here. She felt unexpectedly emotional and squeezed Holly's arm.

"There *is* a happy ending," she said. "I promise."

"You had a happy marriage and a family," guessed Holly.

"I did. I was blessed," agreed Alice.

Yet there was more, and as they wove their way through the narrow lanes, waving at neighbours calling out Christmas wishes and being smiled at by excited holidaymakers bundled up in new hats and scarves, Alice sought the words to explain this. Her ending was indeed the happy after – but would Holly see it that way? Alice wasn't sure she would have done at the age of thirty. She would have probably been horrified. Oh dear, maybe this retelling of her own life hadn't done Holly any favours after all?

"So there's hope for me yet. I might meet a Henry of my own," mused Holly. Then she shook her head. "I'm not sure I want to, Alice. I can't imagine ever loving anyone the way I love Jamie or being brave enough to risk getting hurt again."

"You won 't love anyone the way you've loved your fiancé. That isn't how love works. If – when – you meet somebody really special, your love for him will be another entity entirely. It doesn't mean you never loved your Jamie any more than my love for Henry meant I hadn't loved Jonny. Fate has its own design, Holly – and one we can only see much later on."

"I'm not sure I believe in Fate or destiny. I don't even read my horoscope."

"In my experience Fate doesn't care whether you believe in it or not. There's a path to follow, and follow it we do," said Alice.

"So Henry was the soulmate the gypsy predicted?"

Alice allowed her mind to tumble back through the years. She could still feel the wash of deep bliss which consumed her when Henry's lips brushed her mouth in a tender kiss which spoke of promises yet to be made and the lifetime of love which lay ahead of them. He had pressed his lips into her hair, whispering softly again about how he had loved her from the very moment they had first met, and Alice had shivered deliciously at the passion in those words, knowing that an ocean of desire was pressed against the floodgates of restraint.

Yes, loving Henry had been unexpected and unsought, yet as soon as their lips had met Alice felt her bones melt with relief. Being held by him was peaceful. It was a sense of finally arriving home after a long and arduous journey, a sensation akin to sinking into a deep feather bed, the sweet relief of mooring safely in the harbour while the storm broke beyond the weed-draped wall and waves hammered their watery fists on the closed lock gates.

That kiss had taken place a lifetime ago, but Alice could still hear the creak of the flying jacket as his arms drew her against him, and scent the tang of the leather and notes of engine oil and sandalwood which seemed to fill the air. Opening her eyes again, Alice was certain that for the briefest shiver of a moments she'd slipped through time and been in his arms once more. Although Henry had left her behind a long time ago, his love remained. He was in the smile of their son, and he lived on in his grandchildren; Henry was part of them all. A hundred years from now, when his face was lost to memory, he would remain in a gesture, a ghost of a smile or the fall of wheaten fringe over blue eyes. These things would echo through the years and whisper that Alice Pendeen had loved Henry Tremaine and he had loved her too. How lucky she had been.

How lucky she still was.

A tear slipped down her cheek and she dashed it away with the back of her hand.

"He really *was* my soulmate," she told Holly. "Madame Sienna was right."

"I didn't mean to make you talk about things that are painful."

"It's a happy tear, Holly. I've been blessed with love in my life, and that often walks hand in hand with sadness as people leave us to continue their journeys elsewhere. Sam and my parents. Elsie and Hugo. Lady Yelland. Elizabeth Tremaine. Dear Henry. All long gone now – but always with me in my heart."

Alice had come to understand that the ones we love are never far away, and this notion was comforting to her now rather than being a reason to yearn for what had been lost and could never come again. The older one grew the more the past and present collided, reality becoming little more than a subtle dislocation of the world that existed in her memory. Age granted you a broader perspective; just as when climbing up the hill to Seaspray and gazing down at Polwenna from that vantage point, you were able to see much more of the whole picture. Alice felt utterly sure that one day Holly would feel this way too; she would look back on this Christmas Eve and know she had come to Polwenna Bay for a reason.

Everything happened for a reason. Even things that sometimes seemed impossible to explain: the loss of a lover, the death of a beloved brother, the shattering of a dream … Looking back, it had become clear to Alice that there was a pattern and a purpose, even if these weren't the ones she would have asked for. She supposed these were what Reverend Jules called 'mysterious ways'. How lucky was she to have lived long enough to reflect on them and to pass on what little wisdom she might have gained.

"So what happened to Jonny?" asked Holly as they passed the Codfather, doors flung open to the evening to fill the air with the smell of chips, before reaching the gate of Harbour Watch, Alice's home.

"He and Milly had a son. He inherited a great deal of money, and they eventually turned Polwenna House into a successful hotel," said Alice. She held the gate for Holly and rummaged in her bag for her door keys. Why did they always go to the bottom? "He did very well, and in a strange quirk of fate his granddaughter's married to my grandson. A happy ending several generations later, perhaps."

The keys were nowhere to be found, so Alice rapped the brass door knocker hard, and several times for good measure.

"I was hoping he realised he'd made the biggest mistake of his life and did everything he could to win you back," said Holly sadly.

The door swung open. Honeyed light spilled out into the darkness and framed the man in the hallway in a comforting oblong of warmth, chasing away the shadows creeping across the path like ghosts of the past. He peered into the night, glasses askew with his thick hair flattened on one side, tell-tale signs that he'd nodded off by the fire even though he would deny this. Alice's heart melted to see him, as it always did. As it always had. He was old and, like her, scarred by life's battles. His tall frame was stooped and frail. His eyes had dimmed but his hair remained thick, and still flopped over his eyes as it had a lifetime ago, even if it was snow-white now. Alice barely registered this, or indeed the lines and the wrinkles superimposed on the face she had known for so long. She didn't see a grumpy curmudgeon (as his grandchildren called him) but the raven-haired youth she had loved so dearly, just as in his eyes she was forever the beautiful seventeen-year-old Alice Pendeen.

"I was starting to worry you'd run away with that good-looking curate!" he huffed, but there was no real impatience in his words and an ocean of love swelled beneath.

"You know it takes me a while to walk home these days," said Alice. "Holly here was kind enough to lend an arm and listen to me ramble on about the past."

Spotting Holly behind Alice, the elderly man greeted her with an outstretched hand and a warm smile.

"Thanks for helping my wife home, m'dear, but don't believe a word of what she'll have told you about me. I was never as bad as she likes to make out."

"True. You were ten times worse," said Alice tartly.

Holly's eyes were wide. She turned to Alice.

"Jonny?"

Alice's soul sang to know that Holly was able to recognise in this old man the beautiful boy he'd once been – the boy who had been young and afraid and headstrong and sometimes weak, but never bad. Jonny had made mistakes, as all young men do, and young women too, and he had spent a lifetime longing to atone for them. Winning Alice back had taken him six decades – and a lot of grovelling.

"Oh dear," Jonny sighed. "She's been telling you all about me, hasn't she?"

Holly blushed. "A little."

"That means a lot. I think you need to come in for some mulled wine and hear my side of the story."

"I'd love that," said Holly. She'd lost her pinched look and was smiling up at Jonny. He was good at putting people at their ease – especially pretty young women, thought Alice indulgently. Talk about still being twenty in his head!

As her husband took their coats and ushered them into the sitting room, Alice hoped that hearing their story and seeing the patchwork eiderdown which had created their life together would ease the young woman's sadness and give her hope that a brighter future lay ahead. Alice didn't know whether this Jamie character would have a change of heart and realise what he'd thrown away, or whether Holly would eventually think she'd had a lucky escape. Whatever the outcome, Alice hoped that Holly now understood that life was richer and more nuanced than she had thought. New friends and opportunities were often found where they were least expected, in a dark lane on long past Christmas Eve – or on a summer's morning a few short years earlier, when she had opened her front door to discover on the doorstep a puffed-out elderly gentleman armed with flowers and a smile that could still melt her heart.

Once settled in front of the log fire with a glass of mulled wine, Holly looked from Alice to Jonny wonderingly:

"So you guys got married after all?"

"In the end," Jonny said. "And after a long time. I wasn't going to let Ally go again. I'd made that mistake once before."

He took Alice's hand and squeezed it. In that touch Alice knew he was admitting yet again that he'd messed up before, just as her answering pressure told him that it was all in the past. Whatever time they had left would be spent together now.

"All those wasted years apart," said Holly sadly.

"Ah, but they weren't wasted. We both lived full and rich lives, and we don't regret those. Far from it," Alice told her firmly. "Jonny and Milly travelled and built a successful family business. Henry and I were happy at Seaspray. So *very* happy. I loved him, my dear, and loving Jonny doesn't lessen that. We had a wonderful marriage, and a wonderful family. I wanted to tell you my story so you could see that when life seems darkest something new is about to emerge. Something that could be wonderful and take you in a new direction."

Holly swirled her drink. "I think I understand. No more moping in the holiday cottage and stewing about what Jamie might be up to. I need to enjoy whatever this holiday, strange as it is, offers me. It could lead me somewhere new, couldn't it?"

"Yes," said Jonny firmly. "And one day you may find yourself back at the start, who knows? Or not. It doesn't matter, because it's the journey that makes us who we are."

"The people we meet and love and lose along the way are all part of it, you see," Alice added, "because they make us who we are even if they hurt us or do us wrong. And there is a bigger picture. You just need to be old like us to see it."

"Who are you calling old?" Jonny asked, outraged. "Now, who's for a top-up? Or will it make us all too tiddly for Midnight Mass? Although I do seem to recall a time when turning up half-cut and having a scrap was the thing to do …"

Holly and Alice held out their glasses and laughed.

There could be more than one love in your life, Alice reflected as she watched her husband shuffle into the kitchen to fetch more drinks. She understood this now, and knew it didn't mean that there was any less love accorded to those who came first or last. Love didn't work like that. Love wasn't finite, and the more you gave the more you had. Alice St Milton was in no doubt of it. Maybe learning that had been the greatest lesson of all for her.

She rested her hand on Holly's arm. "So, will you join us all for Christmas lunch tomorrow? There's more than enough to go round, and you might find it fun."

Holly hesitated. She was, Alice knew, hesitating on the edge of the precipice of deciding whether to leap from the security of the past into the unknown void that was the future. Comfort or chance? The familiar safety of misery, or the risk of new happiness? Alice held her breath, sensing this was one of those rare and profound moments when life turned on a sixpence. A moment like allowing a stranger to help you home or stealing away from a midsummer party with the man you loved. Alice hoped Holly would be brave enough to leap into the unknown and find new adventures.

Fate was poised. The stars waited to align.

Then Holly smiled:

"I'd love to, thanks."

And Alice smiled back, certain that somewhere an unseen door creaked ajar leaving Holly Green's future wide open – just as wide open and wonderful as her own had been all those Christmas Eves ago.

EPILOGUE

THE PRESENT

Christmas Day dawned as bright and crisp as any greetings card artist could wish. After a cloudless and star-splashed night, perfect for Santa's deliveries and for worshippers walking home from church, frost was sprinkled on the ground and icing the boughs of trees. But icy mornings, although pretty, made walking treacherous for old folk, and to Alice and Jonny's frustration they were forced to exchange a festive walk to Polwenna Manor for a drive there in the Tremaine Marine four-by-four.

Although the manor itself belonged to Perry Tregarrick, its coach house, which hosted a boutique restaurant, was home to Alice's grandson Symon, his wife Ella, who was also Jonny's granddaughter, and their lively twins. Perry inhabited a wing of the old Jacobean house, which didn't look as if it had been touched since the days of Hugo's great-grandparents, but as the car drew closer and the house slipped into view, set in the overgrown parkland like a precious jewel on a velvet cushion, to Alice's eyes it seemed just as imposing as it had when she was a girl. How strange to think that it was *her* family that lived there now! The Pendeens had come some way from Cobbles Cottage.

The old barn which had once held the Christmas Eve dance had tumbled down long ago, and was now no more than a jumble of ivy-draped stones. When Jake drove past its brambled footprint Alice couldn't resist digging Jonny in the ribs and reminding him of his past transgression. Her chat with Holly the day before had resurrected the past hurt, and it was surprising just how indignant Alice still felt on the behalf of her seventeen-year-old self.

"I know, I know," Jonny muttered. "I was a bloody idiot letting you go that Christmas Eve. But was it my fault Henry Tremaine didn't waste a second moving in on you? I think he always had it planned."

"Hardly," said Alice, touched and amused by the flash of jealousy. "He only drove me home."

"And lucky for me he did," Jake pointed out while the happily married couple squabbled on the back seat.

"And for me," added his girlfriend, Summer Penhalligan, placing her hand on Jake's knee and gazing adoringly up at him. "I can't imagine life without you."

Summer, Barry's great-granddaughter, shared his kind heart and generous nature, qualities quite overlooked by seventeen-year-old girls but treasured highly once you grew older and knew their worth. Hard to believe that it was over a decade that Barry had been gone; Alice still missed him and often thought of him with great fondness, for although he had been an unwelcome suitor he had become a dear friend. When Alice had lost Henry, Barry had been swift to help with the practical things like drains and the pointing, insisting that saving her from the Pollards was the least he could do for Sam's little sister! Funny to think that if Sam had lived and married Betty Penhalligan, Barry would have become her brother-in-law. There might be even more family gathered at the table today, a cluster of freckled redheads with big smiles and even bigger hearts.

Alice sighed. There were so many *what ifs* and *maybes*. Life was a strange kettle of fish, with so many missed chances and sliding doors, to mix her metaphors. It was probably best that you never truly knew what could have been if you had acted differently. If Sam had never taken the boat that day. If Henry hadn't taken to pipe-smoking. If her son's wife hadn't died young. On and on the scenarios stretched, and Alice knew that only madness lay that way; there was enough to fret about as it was, never mind wasting energy on what might have come, or not come, to pass.

"And lucky for your grandchildren," Summer was saying now to Jonny.

"And for Sy!" grinned Jake, as he manoeuvred the car to park it. "If it wasn't for Ella I can't imagine my little bro would have got his act together sufficiently to run this place. He'd still be scowling at anyone who tried to organise his kitchen and storming out on them."

"He wouldn't *dare* do that to Ella," said Jonny. "She's like her grandmother. Utterly terrifying. Never, *ever* cross Ella."

Summer laughed. "She's perfect for Sy – oh, here they are. Look at the twins. How cute! I love their Santa hats."

"I guess my not messing up that Christmas Eve would have meant no Teddy and Ella and no twins. I can never regret my son and my grandchildren," Jonny said quietly to Alice, while Summer and Jake were greeted with huge excitement by the children – which was nothing at all to do with the presents being fished out of the boot …

Alice kissed her husband's lined cheek, savouring these last peaceful moments before the celebrations began in earnest.

"It wasn't messing up, love. It was how things were meant to be. You know that."

"I do," he said. "But that doesn't mean I'm proud of what I did, Ally. I'll always regret hurting you."

"You've more than made up for it."

Alice meant this. Finding love so late in her life had come as a surprise, and she treasured it. Jonny was her dear friend and her first love. He would always be special, and to have a second chance at love at her age had been a blessing. Madame Sienna had said she would have two great loves in her life, and she had been right.

She'd been right about it all.

Jonny and Alice linked hands just as they had all those years ago, knowing they were in almost the exact spot where he'd told her it was over. Their hands were wrinkled now, youthful smoothness just a memory, their skin now tissue-paper thin. Seven decades had passed in the blink of an eye. How was that even possible when Alice still felt seventeen? It was something science would never be able to explain, that mystery of how your essence, the very you-ness that rendered a person unique, remained eternally young while its casing withered away.

Then the car door was being opened and the time to dwell on such existential matters was over in a heartbeat as Alice and Jonny were plunged into the chaos of a family Christmas. Symon helped Alice climb down out of the car, while Ella attended to Jonny, bossing him about by making him use his loathed walking frame to navigate the icy path.

"It makes me look old!" Jonny complained.

"You *are* old, Grandpa! Suck it up or break a hip," Ella barked.

Alice clutched Symon's arm for dear life. She had no such qualms about looking elderly, but she wondered when she had become so feeble. It must have happened by degrees; an ache here, a twinge there until suddenly you were more wobbly than Big Roger Pollard after a drinking session. As her stick slithered on the frozen path she smiled to recall how she and Sam had scraped ice slides outside the Cobbles only to earn a big telling off from her dad when he'd almost disappeared off one into the harbour. She was glad time's sandpaper had worn away the painful edges of her memories of her brother.

It was a relief to reach the restaurant in one piece. The low-beamed room, once home to thoroughbreds and carriages, was now filled with a huge table and decorated to the nines. Ivy was wound around the beams and threaded with white fairy lights, fat beeswax candles were placed in sconces and set amid arrangements of greenery and berries, while hand-tied scarlet bows had been attached to the chair backs. A huge Christmas tree, tastefully adorned with white and green baubles, dominated the far end of the room, where it stood guard over a huge pile of presents, all wrapped perfectly to co-ordinate with the colour scheme. This was Ella's handiwork, of course, and Alice smiled to see such evidence of Millicent Jago's neat and precise qualities being passed down to her granddaughter – and also her difficult nature, according to Symon, although Alice was under no illusions that a red-headed creative chef was easy to live with, either! The two were perfect for one another, and without Ella possessing Milly's 'strength of character' as Alice preferred to put it, she was sure her grandson would still be wasting his talent on pub grub. She supposed it was another gift of old age that you were able to look back with some fondness on even those you hadn't much liked.

The restaurant wasn't large. As it was filled to bursting

point with people, the event was almost overwhelming for Alice. Voices, shrill with excitement and raised to compete with the bubble of pans and the Christmas music, grew louder with every passing second. Children ran about shrieking, somewhere a cork was being popped and the family dogs were zooming about beneath the jumble of tables in the hunt for scraps. Alice spotted Harry Charles cross-legged beneath the tree, tucking into a huge tin of Quality Street which he was sharing with the delighted twins, and felt amused to discover that the Pollards, who had gate-crashed, were already on the sherry. Amid the chaos nobody seemed to notice these interlopers, and even if they had no one would mind; this was Polwenna Bay, where everyone was family, and strangers were friends ready to be made.

Talking of strangers, would Holly come to the lunch? Alice really hoped so. There would be nothing worse for her than being alone on her birthday with only a broken heart for company. Holly would brood, and that was no good. Alice was convinced the life and laughter of a Tremaine family Christmas was just what was needed to lift her spirits and take her mind off her broken dreams.

Alice's granddaughter, Mo, burst into the room, with Ashley, her husband, in tow, and trailing dogs and children while complaining loudly about not being able to drink any champagne.

"You're not up the duff again are you?" asked Nick, Alice's youngest grandson, in disbelief. He turned to his girlfriend. "Whatever chair she sits on, you are *not* to go near it."

"Ha bloody ha," said Mo. "Of course I am. When am I not these days, thanks to Ashley? He isn't drinking," she added sharply as Symon approached the couple with a tray of sherries. "Isn't that right, darling? Seems only fair to keep me company since this is all your fault."

"My fault? You're the one who wants six children! I'm shattered just *thinking* about three more," said her husband, trying hard to unpeel a toddler from his leg with one hand while holding a bottle of Prosecco behind his back with the other. "And for your information, Nick, there is no one chair or bed or barn where I'm safe from your sister. Take pity on a broken man, angel. Just one drink."

Mo tossed her red curls, an impatient gesture that always reminded Alice of Sam. Another bittersweet echo.

"What a fuss you make, Ashley. Do you see Dandy moaning?"

"As thrilled as I am to be compared to your prize stallion, he doesn't have to purée carrots for his foals or do night feeds. I think the very least I deserve as a stud fee is one glass of bubbly!"

As they teased one another, more of Alice's memories fell thick and fast as snow. Sam's temper. May's smile. Henry's sharp wit. All these qualities were in Mo, too – and feeling almost giddy with the speed of her thoughts, Alice sat down heavily at the table.

"I'm fine," she said to Jonny when he voiced concern. "Don't fuss. I'm just hot."

But nobody listened; they all fussed anyway until Henry bought her some iced water and made sure she was comfortable by opening a window. Alice thanked him several times before realising she was actually speaking to Jake. Oh Lord. The faces of the past seemed to overlap those of the present so much these days that sometimes it was hard to remember quite where she was or who she was with. They'd think she was going gaga – but who needed portals or standing stones to travel in time when they had family around them? It was impossible to anchor herself on occasions like these.

"It's busy and loud in here, Granny," Jake said, brushing

away her embarrassment. "Just rest for a moment. You're probably exhausted after Midnight Mass."

"I didn't go," confessed Alice. "Jonny and I were far too tired. We had an early night."

Jake seldom attended the service; he was always up early for the marina, baling out boats or tightening lines, and sometimes closing the harbour's storm gates. Henry's boatyard vision had expanded so greatly that his grandson was busy all year round and seldom took a day off. Even in winter, hardy yachty types would choose to moor up in Polwenna's marina. For the past few nights masts had been lit up in jaunty primary colours which spilled onto the dark water and quivered as the boats gently rode their moorings.

"That's a shame. You should have asked me. I'd have driven you up – and carried you the last bit, too, if I'd had to," Jake said. "Maybe I need to carry on the family tradition? I don't think Dad will."

Alice smiled. Kind and thoughtful and true, Jake really was Henry's grandson, and the most like him.

"Leave all that to Danny and Jules. You and Summer need to make your own celebrations and traditions, love. As for your father, I imagine he's also making new traditions now he's living in The Priory."

Her thoughts drifted again. The Priory, once home to dear Lady Yelland, and where she and Elsie had devised their master plan, had changed hands so many times in its long history that the old house was probably as confused about its occupants as she was. Her son, Jimmy, was just the latest custodian and busy putting his mark on the place with his new partner. Alice wouldn't have believed this possible all those years ago and often had to pinch herself. What would her mum and dad have made of their grandson living in such a grand place? Would they have said he had ideas above his station? Or would they have been proud?

"Not quite the Priory that we all had in mind for Jimmy – but it's done him good," said Jonny, who was pleased his sixty-something stepson had finally settled down.

Alice nodded. "I'm not feeling guilty I missed the service. It's always packed, but I would've liked to have known if the girl I was speaking to yesterday went. I'd invited her for Christmas lunch. Holly's had a tough time."

"Holly, did you say?" asked Symon, passing by with a plate of canapés held high above his head in order to evade the reach of a teenage boy who was complaining he was "*Starving! Fact!'* "She's in the kitchen with Perry, helping to plate up the starters."

Alice stared at him. "She is?"

Sy nodded and then, when he lowered his tray, the teenager eyed it beadily.

"You look like a seagull, Morgan. Take two, *but no more* or I'll set Ella on you. Fact!"

Returning his attention to Alice, Symon continued to fill her in.

"Yes, Holly Green – great name – was at Midnight Mass. I wandered down with Perry, and he spotted her at once and said we ought to sit with her. He introduced us and said she'd been there with you earlier. She said it was her birthday today and she looked pretty bleak about it. Well, you know Perry, Granny. He can't bear to see anyone in distress, so he invited her back for some birthday cake."

Alice was touched. "That was kind."

"It was," agreed Symon. "But in our cunning plan there was one flaw; we didn't have a birthday cake. So after a few drinks I had a great idea and used the Christmas cake. Ella nearly went into orbit when she saw I'd stuck candles into it and hacked a chunk out. She said it was meant for Christmas Day."

"You *were* eating it on Christmas Day. Fact," said Morgan through a mouthful of mini-Yorkshire pudding.

"True, mate, but don't say that to Ella," warned Symon. "Anyway, once I'd calmed her down she was fine about it – but let's not push our luck."

"So Holly came back here last night with you and Perry?"

Alice wanted to get this straight. Painfully shy, Perry was not known for bringing girls back to the Manor. He found it hard enough to talk to them, yet if he saw someone in pain, Alice suspected the need to help would overcome any awkwardness. Hugo had been kind too, she recalled. It was often an underrated virtue – but, she felt, the most important of them all.

"She certainly did. We all had a glass of wine and then I bailed out. I think she and P were talking until the small hours and then she crashed on the Reception sofa, but you'd have to ask them for details because they could have carried on drinking. Or something." Symon raised an eyebrow and grinned. His meaning was clear.

"Oh," said Alice. What it was to be young!

"I did notice that although Santa's carrots and mince pies hadn't gone, the sherry bottle Ella had put out for him was empty," Symon continued. "Drinking and eating continued into the small hours."

"Maybe Santa ate the cake?" suggested Jake hastily in case any of the children were listening in.

"Or hid it from grown-ups?" said Summer.

"Or drank the sherry?" laughed Sy.

"He'll have a headache if he does that in every house he visits," pointed out Jonny.

Morgan almost spat out his second canapé.

"Santa doesn't—"

He yelped as Jonny elbowed him in the ribs:

"Shush! There are children in the room!"

Morgan rubbed his ribcage and glowered.

"I was going to say that Santa doesn't drink. Fact. He can't, can he? Not if he's driving a sleigh."

A bicker then began about whether or not it was illegal to drink-drive if holding reindeer reins. Alice only half-listened; she was lost in thoughts of roads not taken and new directions chosen. Had Holly Green taken one of those without even knowing? When she was old and grey would she look back on a distant Christmas Eve and know that this was the moment when everything had changed? When the gift of recognising love had been passed on to her? And if so, would she too meet a broken-hearted young woman and feel compelled to pass on her story, and with it some of the knowledge she had gleaned of life?

Alice couldn't know for sure, but as Symon headed back into the kitchen and the heavy door swung open she glimpsed Holly and Perry, heads close together as they placed wisps of smoked salmon onto crostini while chatting away with ease, and she sensed one circle reaching completion as a new one began spooling away. This new friendship might be the start of something wonderful. It might be no more substantial than sea fret. It might be the first tentative step on a new road away from what had been before, or the first which led away for ever. Alice knew better than anyone that there was no way of telling.

Even so, she felt sure that no matter what shape it took, Holly's future would be rich and wonderful. How could it be anything else when it had begun, just as her own had, out of the blue and thanks to the kindness of a stranger? With a glimmer of hope when life seemed darkest? This overwhelming darkness was the very time when the stars were ready to shine their brightest, and Alice knew that somewhere amongst them was the very brightest star of all, the handsome Captain who had always made the stars shine for her.

Sending Henry a thank you from the most secret part of her heart, where she kept his cherished memory safe, Alice turned her attention to the present. Now it was time to focus on dear Jonny, who so loved her and the noisy, happy family that had somehow grown from the very best of them all. Despite all the mistakes made along the way, and the sadness that had often tempered joy, Alice knew that showing Holly how to recognise and embrace love had been Henry Tremaine's gift to her. All the good things in her life had sprung from that knowledge, and Alice could never, ever thank him enough, because to love and to be loved was the greatest gift of all.

So when Perry said something which made Holly laugh joyously, Alice raised her champagne glass in a silent toast to her beloved Henry, knowing she had passed his precious gift on *exactly* as he would have wanted.

The End

and

The Beginning...

AUTHOR'S NOTE

I really hope you have enjoyed reading THE GIFT

Alice and Henry's love story is the first novel in my new POLWENNA PAST series, where I travel back in to revisit characters and places that are familiar to, and cherished by, the readers of my Cornish set POLWENNA BAY series. If you haven't visited POLWENNA BAY before now, you might enjoy a visit. The books read as standalone novels, but also build on one another to add depth, enjoyment and a sense of belonging for their readers. It's also fun to spot familiar names and faces – as Holly discovers in THE GIFT!

* * *

OTHER TITLES BY RUTH SABERTON

INCLUDING RUTH'S PEN NAME TITLES

♥ **Polwenna Bay** – open the first page a stranger, turn the last as a friend ♥

Runaway Summer
A Time For Living
Winter Wishes
Treasure Of The Heart
Recipe For Love
Rhythm Of The Tide
Catching Hearts
Christmas By Candlelight *
Journey's End

POLWENNA NOVELLAS

Cornwall For Christmas *
Polwenna Day Trips

THE ROSECRADDICK CHRONICLES

THE GIFT was a joy to write because it brings together all my favourite novel ingredients – a beautiful Cornish setting, forbidden love, conflict and a dual time narrative. If you enjoyed these aspects of the novel, you may enjoy my Rosecraddick Chronicles, three books which take place between 1914 and the present and are set in Cornwall.

The Letter
The Locket
Oyster Shore
The Lost Angel (a companion novella)*

PENCALLYN - CORNWALL AT WAR

Set between WW2 and the present, the Pencallyn novels explore the 'friendly invasion' of American GIs to Cornwall and the impact, emotionally and socially, on the local people as well as the aftermath seventy years on. Secrets, forbidden love and betrayal leave a legacy that will last decades...

The Promise
The Last Card (a companion novella) *

OTHER NOVELS SET IN CORNWALL

The Island Legacy
Hobb's Cottage (a novella)

ROMANTIC COMEDIES

Katy Carter Wants A Hero
Ellie Andrews has Second Thoughts
Amber Scott is Starting Over
Dead Romantic
Escape For The Summer
Escape For Christmas *

CHRISTMAS BOOKS

The Season For Second Chances
Christmas on the Creek
Plus all books marked *

Pen Name Books

Writing as Jessica Fox
THE ONE THAT GOT AWAY
EASTERN PROMISE
HARD TO GET
UNLUCKY IN LOVE
ALWAYS THE BRIDE

WRITING AS HOLLY CAVENDISH

LOOKING FOR FIREWORKS

Writing as Georgie Carter

THE PERFECT CHRISTMAS *

REVIEWS

I really hope you have enjoyed reading this book. If you did, please pop a review on Amazon or Goodreads. It makes all the difference for a writer and helps other readers to discover and enjoy my books.

ABOUT THE AUTHOR

Ruth Saberton is the bestselling author of *The Letter, Katy Carter Wants a Hero* and *Escape for the Summer*. She also writes upmarket commercial fiction under the pen names Jessica Fox, Georgie Carter and Holly Cavendish.

Born in London, Ruth now lives in beautiful Cornwall. She has travelled to many places, but nothing compares to the rugged beauty of the Cornish coast which never fails to provide her with inspiration for her writing. For the latest on Ruth and her writing you can also follow her on social media.

Web: www.ruthsaberton.com

Printed in Great Britain
by Amazon

54734062R00192